# TWO SHAKESPEAREAN SEQUENCES

# TWO SHAKESPEAREAN SEQUENCES

*Henry VI* to *Richard II*
and
*Pericles* to *Timon of Athens*

F. W. BROWNLOW

– WHAT IS POETRY? – THE FEELING OF A FORMER WORLD
AND FUTURE. *Byron*

University of Pittsburgh Press

*Published in Great Britain 1977 by*
THE MACMILLAN PRESS LTD

*Published in the U.S.A. 1977 by the*
UNIVERSITY OF PITTSBURGH PRESS,
*Pittsburgh, Pa. 15260*

*Printed in Great Britain*


*Library of Congress Cataloging in Publication Data*

Brownlow, Frank Walsh, 1934–
   Two Shakespearean sequences.

      Includes bibliographical references and index.
1.   Shakespeare,   William,   1564–1616—Criticism
and interpretation.   2.   Shakespeare, William, 1564–
1616.   Histories.   3.   Shakespeare, William, 1564–
1616.   Chronology. I.   Title.
PR2976.B76   822.3′3   77–7671
ISBN 0–8229–1127–2

# Contents

# Acknowledgements

Everyone writing about Shakespeare is under an enormous and un-assessable debt to the community of scholars, critics and readers, past and present, each of whom has contributed his portion to the common treasury of Shakespearean traditions. In my own case I also feel obliged to acknowledge certain more specific if not quite tangible debts, especially to former teachers, colleagues and students. My teacher Kenneth Muir has influenced my reading of Shakespeare in ways for which I shall always be grateful, not least by sending me off, as a graduate student, to study the life and work of the brilliant and satirical Jacobean archbishop, Samuel Harsnett. I owe a similar debt to R. T. Davies who first guided me through fifteenth-century poetry, and gave me a sense of the continuity of the mediaeval and Elizabethan worlds. Philip Edwards's evocation, in his *Shakespeare and the Confines of Art*, of the archaic strangeness of the history plays, encouraged me to attempt some explanation of the strain of mediaeval Catholic feeling in them, so much at odds with their predominant atmosphere of rowdy, secular brutality. I must also thank Professor Edwards for his generous criticism of some chapters of this present book.

I would also like to thank the students of the Shakespeare seminar at Mount Holyoke College, South Hadley, Massachusetts, 1970–3, for their part in the discussion of several of the plays here considered; I am especially mindful of the work of Miss Susan Carleton, Miss Nanette Clinch, Miss Susan Schwarz and Miss Roye Werner.

Above all I must thank my wife, Jeanne Brownlow, for her patience, criticism and help at every stage of the writing of this book.

*Ripon, 1976*                                                                                    F.W.B.

# Note on Quotations

Quotations from Shakespeare's plays and poems follow the text of *The Complete Plays and Poems of William Shakespeare*, ed. W. A. Neilson and C. J. Hill (Cambridge, Mass., 1942). The line-numbering of this edition follows that of the *Globe* edition. In the case of *The Two Noble Kinsmen*, quotations and references are from the text prepared by Clifford Leech for *The Signet Classic Shakespeare* (New York and London, 1966).

All quotations, except for those from literature written before 1500, are modernised.

# Introduction

Although Hamlet is doubtful of many things, he knows exactly what he expects of the drama. Its purpose, he says:

> both at the first and now, was and is, to hold, as 'twere, the mirror up to nature; to show virtue her own feature, scorn her own image, and the very age and body of the time his form and pressure. (III. ii. 23)

It is not surprising that a well-educated sixteenth-century prince should expect topical interest and a moral attitude in literature; but, as the slightly difficult wording of Hamlet's last phrase shows, he is not only saying in an elaborate way that plays ought to be about life, praising the good and exposing the bad. His idea that 'the age and body of the time' has a 'form and pressure' is analogous to Aristotle's conception of a play's plot as its 'soul'.[1] The times, like a play, have an outward form answering to an inward, shaping principle; and this suggests something else very interesting: that history is a process of comprehensible, and therefore significant, change.

Thus a poetic dramatist is an authority showing in his work things perhaps not otherwise knowable and, like a scientist, owing his knowledge not to occult faculties but to observation and imitation. This idea epitomises Renaissance humanism, and it suits Hamlet, himself the epitome of a Renaissance ideal. Its rationality and empiricism are in keeping with Hamlet's other views, with his taste for a natural style of acting, and with his description of the players as 'the abstracts and brief chronicles of the time'. Not many critics, however, associate such thinking with Shakespeare himself, who is generally believed to have been a more modest, less conscious artist.

Shakespeare is more tentative than the fictional prince (who has his own reasons for believing that he understands the drift of the times). In Sonnet 59, speaking about change in a voice more nearly his own, Shakespeare asks if it is true that there is 'nothing new'. If it is, then writers fool themselves: 'Labouring for invention,' they 'bear amiss/The second burden of a former child.' It is always possible that change is an illusion, but Shakespeare's witty metaphor

turns the thought into an absurdity: events can no more repeat themselves than the same child can be born twice. Like the prince, the
poet shows himself to have an empirical, experimenting mind. He
wishes that he could put the idea of change to a test; if he could see
an image of his friend 'in some antique book' five hundred years old,
he would be able to see what the old world made of his friend's
beauty, and he would know:

> Whe'er we are mended, or whe'er better they,
> Or whether revolution be the same.

These two references to time and change are themselves examples
of what Hamlet is talking about, signs of the poet's awareness of
ideas and of his ability to use them. We can easily miss the presence
of ideas in Shakespeare because his characters do not often read
the audience lectures or talk the topical stuff of the day. Like
Mozart, Shakespeare was too complete an artist to thrust unassimi-
lated material upon his audience. He converts ideas and allusions to
the forms of his medium, as a few more examples will show.

Overtly topical allusions are rare in Shakespeare, and when they
occur they make their effect, like good witticisms, by suggestion and
implication. In *Twelfth Night*, a play about love, longing and ambition, the comparison of Malvolio's smiling face to the new map of
the Indies (III. ii. 83) besides referring to the voyages of discovery
reflects an attitude to the New World which bears on the themes of
the play: Malvolio is a caricature of man on the make. In *Hamlet* a
macabre, punning reference to the Imperial Diet held at Worms in
1521, made in connection with Hamlet's equivocations about the
whereabouts of Polonius' body, brings into the play an echo of the
Reformation and the controversies about the sacrament:

> — Now, Hamlet, where's Polonius?
> — At supper.
> — At supper! Where?
> — Not where he eats, but where he is eaten. A certain convocation
>   of politic worms are e'en at him. Your worm is your only
>   emperor for diet. (IV. iii. 17–22)

Like *Lear*, *Hamlet* is full of religious anxiety which is not explicitly
stated but, through these allusions and others like them, related to
significant public events. Such references have a conversational tone;
they are charged with nervous, intellectual energy, and they are the
kind of thing that Shakespeare might have produced in company:
they are riddling and need interpreting by a co-operative and sympa-

thetic audience. More important, they are exemplars in little of themes writ large in the design of their respective plays.

Under a censorship as autocratic and as sensitive as the Tudors', a dramatist had to be circumspect in the way he touched upon current events and ideas. Any kind of topical reference could be dangerous, and religion and politics were forbidden subjects—unless the authorities commissioned a play, or an author wanted to congratulate the government. Yet we know that Elizabethan plays are full of covert, figurative allusions to events great and small, allusions so handled that, unless a play caused a riot or otherwise drew attention, author and actors were safe from prosecution. Hamlet's commissioning of *The Murder of Gonzago* shows how dangerous matter could be safely treated. This old play, performed before Claudius, acquires an unequivocal meaning for those who suspect him of murder; but the figurative form of the allusion secures Hamlet and his actors from open reprisal. For the uninformed, the king's response and Hamlet's excitement are equally mystifying. The modern reader of Elizabethan literature is often in the position of Claudius' ignorant courtiers, and it is a puzzle for him, used as he is to the conventions of a free press, to know how the Elizabethan audience recognised the presence of forbidden themes. The obvious answer is that they must have been alert to figurative meaning, and that authors must have had ways of signalling its presence. Hamlet no doubt intends to supply such a signal in the 'speech of some dozen or sixteen lines' which he requests the First Player to insert into *The Murder of Gonzago*.

No real play, one might think, would be used to prove the reigning monarch a murderer, but *The Murder of Gonzago* has a Shakespearean precedent. It is well known that the Essex conspirators paid for a performance of *Richard II* immediately before making their attempt at deposing Elizabeth, and that no less a person than the Queen recognised an allusion to herself in the character of the king. Yet the relationship between the play, the rebellion and the Queen is not a simple one. The treatment of the king is so sympathetic, especially after his fall, that one cannot imagine the play inflaming a usurper; and the real Queen and the player king seem very different. When questioned by the authorities, the actors cleared themselves, as Hamlet's players might have done, saying that the play was an old one. Nevertheless the deposition scene was never printed in Elizabeth's time.

The key to the allusiveness of *Richard II* probably lies in the opening scenes. The play is about an important political change: one kind of king falls, and another takes his place. Underlying that change, causing and explaining it, is another brought about by

Richard's murder of his uncle, Gloucester. This event, the subject of the opening scenes, is never explained politically, and Richard's real attitude to it never comes out. But the murder is described, in eloquent language, as a sacrilege; it is the first cause of the King's fall, and it prefigures the sacrilege of deposition and murder committed against himself. Richard's fall, therefore, and the ruin of England are bound up with his own act of violence against royalty. Elizabethans alert for figurative allusion would see the parallel because Elizabeth I had also committed (through a servant whom she later disowned, as Richard disowns Mowbray) an act of sacrilegious violence when she ordered the beheading of her kinswoman, the Queen of Scots. We can be reasonably sure that when Queen Elizabeth said 'I am Richard II, know ye not that?' she was remembering Mary's death and understanding very well that it licensed the rebellion against herself.[2]

Richard's offence is essential to the play's action, turning it from a sad story to a tragedy; placed in the context of contemporary events, it becomes dangerously topical. Whether this was accidental or intentional is now irrelevant because the important fact is that Shakespeare so handled his historical material that drama and events coincided. In fact *Richard II* was a prophetic play, prefiguring not only Elizabeth's situation on the eve of the Essex rebellion, but Charles I's when he was tried for breaking his own laws, and James II's when men determined to eradicate sacred kingship drove him from the throne. This history play, therefore, is as much a mirror of the present as any other form of drama. *King John*, often associated with *Richard II*, is another instance. Not only is the final speech an example of 'Armada idiom',[3] the whole play deals figuratively with the national crisis that the coming of the Armada resolved.

By such means as these Shakespeare shows 'the very age and body of the time his form and pressure.' He pays his tribute of pride and affection to the past, but the organising principles of his histories reflect, inevitably, the present. In the long run it may be true that such contemporary significations are detachable from Elizabethan drama in the way that the historical level of meaning may be detached from an allegory: to appreciate the integrity of *Richard II* one may not *have* to know that the King's guilt takes in a figurative allusion to Elizabeth. It is certainly true that the play and the history are mutually illuminating. The real question for the modern reader concerned with 'approaches' to Shakespeare will probably be whether, without a feeling for the plays' contemporary significance, one can have a proper grasp of their meaning. Experience suggests that because all great literature is bound up in an imaginative relationship to its times, interpretation not related to a sense of history can go astray. Yet one ought no to be doctrinaire about criticism, a form of writing that depends as much on the writer's perceptiveness as on his method. Nothing, a priori, is irrelevant to one's reading, but it is important that interpretation and criticism should grow out of the work itself.

* * *

The object in taking a 'Hamletian' approach to Shakespeare is not of course to hunt for topical allusions. It is rather to see that a play's unity and significance reflect the poet's mastery, in some part at least, of the form, meaning and direction of his times. Unity and significance, whether of the individual work of the whole *œuvre*, are commonplace ideas of criticism, but they come to us from the comparatively recent Romantic past, not from Shakespeare. Whereas Hamlet suggests that drama changes in response to realities external to it and the writer, we tend to see change in a writer's work as a more subjective, inward process. Similarly, although in Sonnet 59 Shakespeare seems to think that 'revolution', if it is real, comes about because the poet's brain '[labours] for invention', we tend to attribute the process to largely unconscious causes, treating literature as if it were to all intents and purposes autonomous.

We owe these biases to the legacy of intense subjectivism we inherit from the Romantics, who seized upon the belief that the works of a creative artist reveal the essential story of their creator's inner life and show its true form as a work of art with a beginning, a middle and an end. So we find Coleridge performing upon Shakespeare the two operations necessary for transforming him into an artist of the Romantic kind: he identifies the author with his creations, and he divides the author's creative life, as if it were the microcosm of an historical era, into periods.[4] The most succinct version of the Romantic approach to Shakespeare however, and probably its most famous, is Keats's epigram delivered in a letter to his brother George in February 1819: 'Shakespeare led a life of Allegory; his works are the comment on it.'

As this epigram so beautifully illustrates, Romantic criticism is based more on faith than on fact, and the essential article of its creed is belief in the integrity and beauty of the individual life, worked out in its own terms, and manifested in art. According to Hamlet's definition, art and its times are mutually illuminating; but according to Keats's the mutually illuminating pair are art and the artist's inner life. One can know something about history, but one can have little if any certain knowledge about anyone's inner life. Consequently a great deal of criticism since the Romantics has been unverifiable biography.

In contemporary criticism of several major writers and artists one still finds Romantic doctrine of the relationship between art and life applied with no apparent sense of its fallacies, but this is not so with the criticism of Shakespeare. Biographical interpretation of his work has always met opposition for quite practical reasons. Little is known about Shakespeare, and the biographical interpretations as a result have differed so widely that an attack on the method was inevitable. Yet even though the original Romantic exuberance has gone, the basic beliefs remain. Dowden's windy Hegelianism has entered the limbo of the unreadable but his famous division of the author's life into four periods remains as an apparently self-evident division of Shakespeare's work.[5] Other biographical assumptions lead a ghostly existence behind the lines, as it were, of contemporary criticism. In recent discussions of the religious element in Shakespeare it is sometimes assumed that the poet's beliefs are ideologically important because it is thought that proof of, say, his Christianity might determine the way his plays are read. Biographical considerations also underlie the continuing debate over *King Lear*. It would be interesting no doubt to know whether Shakespeare took a gloomy or an optimistic view of the world; but all we really know is that he wrote a play which has the property of stimulating conflicting responses, not only from different readers but, if we tell the truth, from the same reader at different times.

The most vigorous elements of Romanticism to survive in contemporary criticism, however, are belief in the wholeness of Shakespeare's *œuvre* and in its organic, historical development. Like all familiar and useful beliefs, these seem eminently reasonable. Yet Shakespeare's *œuvre* as we have it is a fragment, whatever its hypothetical wholeness. We know the titles of two missing plays (*Love's Labours Won* and *Cardenio*), and there were almost certainly others that have vanished without trace, especially from his first years as a writer. The integrity of the extant plays is also questionable. The text of *Pericles* is a pirated chaos. The possibility of collaboration is still a live issue, particularly in connection with *Henry VIII* and *The Two Noble Kinsmen*. *Macbeth* has non-Shakespearean material in it and, as variants between the Folio and Quarto texts of other plays show, textual integrity is an idea that hardly applies to Elizabethan drama.[6] All these well-known but seldom emphasised facts make one wary of criticism which takes the unity of Shakespeare's works too much for granted.

There is similar reason for scepticism about the idea of organic development. Its application depends upon a knowledge of the chronological order of the plays; but Shakespearean chronology is not an exact science. The order of completion and performance may not always be the same as the order of conception and drafting. The order of many individual plays is doubtful and, as arguments in favour of an earlier dating of the first plays show,[7] the old consensus that Shakespeare began to write about 1591–2 was based on unverifiable assumptions. Undocumented assumptions affect the general view of the end of Shakespeare's career too.

Every writer assumes that Shakespeare spent his last years in Stratford, retired from writing and acting alike. The retirement story goes back, like other traditions, to Nicholas Rowe, Shakespeare's first biographer;[8] but the finished version of it is another Romantic invention according to which Shakespeare, knowing that his work was complete, wrote *The Tempest* both as a poetic *summa* and as an allegorical farewell to poetry and the stage. Yet *The Tempest* is not Shakespeare's last play, and it is not necessarily a personal allegory. Life does not arrange itself so neatly. Authors neither die nor retire because their mission is finished.

As a matter of fact Shakespeare's activities in London are documented to within a year of his death. In 1613, the year of *The Two Noble Kinsmen*, he bought a house in London, and in 1615 he was engaged in a Chancery suit over the same property. It is generally thought that he bought the house as an investment, but that belief is based on the prior assumption that he had retired in 1611. It is just as likely that he bought the house for the same reason that, earlier in his career, he had acquired lodgings in Shoreditch and on the south bank of the river: to be near his theatre.

If one disregards Romantic presuppositions about *The Tempest*, then it appears that Shakespeare's active life continued after 1611 and that his semi-retirement (for it never seems to have been more than that) probably began a few years earlier. The facts leading to this conclusion are soon summarised. In the early years of the seventeenth century Shakespeare was lodging in London with a Huguenot tire-maker called Mountjoy; in 1606 the tire-maker's wife died and the man took to an irregular life which led to quarrels and business troubles. This will have given Shakespeare a good reason for leaving his lodgings. Then, in early 1608, the plague broke out, closing the theatres and driving people out of the city. Finally, it was after 1607–8 that Shakespeare's output of plays settled down to one a year.

In 1608, when his 'last plays' began, Shakespeare was forty-four, and he had achieved what every sensible man desires: financial independence and the freedom, within limits, to do what he wanted. This included writing more plays; but there is no reason to believe that Shakespeare consciously thought of them as his last, or that the muse, knowing better than he, was about to leave him. Presumably he wrote his last plays, as he wrote his first, because he had something to say and because circumstances and his own genius prompted him to say it in dramatic form. 'Last' and 'first' are merely descriptive words. When he wrote his first plays he did the best he could under less than ideal conditions, and there are things in them that he never surpassed. When he wrote his last plays the conditions were ideal, a circumstance reflected in the technical virtuosity of the plays' construction and composition. The end, when it came, was no doubt unexpected.

\*     \*     \*

The form criticism takes should reflect an approach that is true to the nature of the material studied. Like music, drama is an art experienced in time, and a consecutive, expository form of criticism seems to serve it best, keeping the critic's attention focused on specific works and discouraging him from tendentious generalisations. One play leads to another, however, for author, spectator and critic alike. This progression is as much a part of one's own subjective experience as it is a part of the drama itself; it provides criticism with its *mythos*, and neither its nature nor its significance is self-evident. There are customary ways of arranging the progression of an author's work, grouping plays by genre, for instance, by chronological succession, or by period according to a theory of the author's career. Because they are familiar, such arrangements acquire an appearance of objectivity. In Shakespeare's case however little is known about his literary career and opinions, and one needs to be more than usually wary of arrangements that, however familiar, are really based upon unsubstantiated assumptions. The *mythos* of criticism can easily turn into a myth.

A natural approach to Shakespeare, therefore, will be empirical, working outward from specific plays grouped in an order based on facts and a minimum of reasonable assumptions. This book deals with two groups of plays, one from the beginning, the other from the end of Shakespeare's career. Both sequences differ a little from more familiar groupings. The first consists of the early histories, taken in chronological succession from *I Henry VI* to *King John* and *Richard II*. The two later plays are included because they conclude the working-out of a form and an idea that begins in *Henry VI*. The plays of the first sequence, then, are grouped partly by genre, partly by chronological succession. In them we see Shakespeare following out a single ambitious design to the point where, in *Richard II*, he succeeds in depicting his first, typically Shakespearean tragic hero. The second sequence, beginning with *Pericles* as the prologue-play to the later comedies, is more entirely chronological. Within it we trace Shakespeare's career beyond *The Tempest*, and we see him, as inventive as ever, working until almost the very end of his life.

The juxtaposition of the two sequences forms a diptych drawing

attention not only to more familiar signs of change and development
in Shakespeare's work, but to some unchanging features in it as well.
A thematic parallel emerges for instance between the politics of
*Cymbeline* and *King John*; and there is a technical parallel in the
self-parodying stylistic comedy of *Richard II* and *The Winter's Tale*.
The imaginative parallels, however, are the most interesting. By
tracing Shakespeare's progress through *The Tempest* to *Henry VIII*
and *The Two Noble Kinsmen* we can see his mind turning again to
the tragic conflict between capacity and imagination of which
Richard II, in prison, is so eloquent an expression. Timon's burial
by the sea is another resolution of that conflict. As noble as it is
pathetic, it is also a mute comment on the hubris that led to it.

Of the various consequences of this book's method, the placing of
*Timon of Athens* last in the order of Shakespeare's plays is probably
the most controversial. While we shall never certainly know when
the play was written, its unfinished condition suggests that it was
last. As I hope to have been able to show, the play fits so well in the
sequence of Shakesepare's late work that, if it did not exist, one
could with a fair show of accuracy have predicted something of its
quality. Needless to say, the hypothesis that *Timon of Athens* is
Shakespeare's last work has no bearing, as far as I am aware, on
the poet's state of mind when he wrote it. Like his other plays, *Timon*
makes good sense if one reads it having in mind Hamlet's idea of
the relationship between the drama and the times. Applied without
dogmatism or rigidity, Hamlet's idea encourages one to see an
element of commitment and criticism in Shakespeare's work and to
recognise its intellectual bite. *Timon of Athens* objectifies a sane and
clear analysis of the consequences of some ideas, newly current in
Shakespeareare's time, about the basis and purpose of life. Its form
is spare and, like its characterisation, tends towards the diagrammatic
and abstract. These are the marks of Shakespeare's very late work;
but the play's ideas, as the reader will see, have a long Shakespearean
history, making their first appearance in the early history plays.

# The Way to Dover Cliff:

## *Henry VI* to *Richard II*

# Possession, Property and the Crown

# 1. The First Part of King Henry the Sixth

The series of histories comprising the three parts of *Henry VI* and *The Life and Death of Richard III* begins with the death of Henry V and deals with the loss of his French conquests and the coming of civil war during his son Henry VI's reign; it ends with Henry Tudor's invasion, his defeat of Richard III, and the inauguration of a new order under the family of Tudor. The plays cover sixty-three complicated years from 1422 to 1485, and the general theory under which the dramatist arranged his materials was familiar because it provided a well-publicised case for the Tudors' legitimacy. Edward Hall, whose *The Union of the Two Noble and Illustre Families of Lancaster and York* was in itself and through Holinshed's *Chronicles* Shakespeare's chief source, announces the theory in his opening sentences:

> What mischief hath insurged in realms by intestine division, what depopulation hath ensued in countries by civil dissension, what detestable murder hath been committed in cities by separate factions ... this noble realm of England can apparently declare and make demonstration.
> ... But the old divided controversy between the fore-named families of Lancaster and York, by the union of matrimony celebrate and consummate between the high and mighty prince King Henry the Seventh and the Lady Elizabeth his most worthy queen, the one being indubitate heir of the house of Lancaster, and the other of York, was suspended and appalled in the person of their most noble, puissant and mighty heir King Henry the Eight.[1]

Hall's narrative unfolds the causes of dissension and the whole unhappy sequel of war and usurpation as a prelude to the Tudors' glory. He was their advocate, a humanist believing in the moral value of history, in the persuasive power of language (as his rumbling Latinisms, his elaborate, sometimes sprawling periods show), and a Protestant. He writes with a believer's enthusiasm. He took his

facts and his interpretations of them from a variety of sources, but
he brought the whole to a high finish, with a beginning, a middle
and a splendid ending.

Richard II, so the story goes, for despotic rule, wilfulness and
extravagance was deposed by his cousin Henry of Lancaster; and
this usurpation, however justifiable politically, entailed an aftermath
of ramifying disorders upon the usurper, his successors and subjects.
These disorders appear immediately in the rebellions of Henry IV's
reign, and though there seems to be a relief in the reign of his son
Henry V, the strife resumes upon his early death and the succession
of his infant son. Henry VI's infancy and, later on, his incapacity
leave the kingdom with no effective defence against ambitious noblemen. France is lost. In exchange England receives in Margaret of
Anjou termagant disorder personified. Civil war follows, with every
kind of allegiance broken in a rampage of murder and feud. York,
as Edward IV, usurps Lancaster. Then York, as Richard of
Gloucester, usurps York. Richard III is the anti-King, deformed, a
multiple homicide, fratricide and infanticide, a rough boar (his
heraldic crest) rooting up the state. Finally, even as evil is revealed
as absolute, a thing in itself, Providence sends Henry Tudor to defeat
the tyrant and inaugurate the Tudors' peace.

This exciting plot is a variant of the grand Christian melodrama
that Shakespeare drew on, consciously or unconsciously, for the plots
of most of his tragedies and tragi-comedies. The story begins with
an offence against sacred obligation; its middle deals with its unhappy consequences, and the end either brings about or anticipates
a restoration of happiness. The tale's original is the Christian story
of the world's progress from creation to apocalypse; or perhaps one
should say that the Christian story is the authoritative version in our
culture of a tale which, in some versions, precedes it. The difference
between the Christian version and others, whether foreshadowings,
analogues or derivatives, is that the former (to those who believe it)
is fact, the latter are fictions. Whatever may be the attitude of the
ignorant or superstitious towards fictions, they are not matters of
belief, but means of expression, ways of putting experience into a
narrative form.

The purpose of the Christian narrative is action, not expression;
its plot is meant to glorify God and save souls. Its events happen in
the real world, its *personæ* are persons, its hero is simultaneously
God and man. One of its characters, however, never appears in
proper person; this is the antagonist. He is a fallen angel, a demon,
a kind of infectious moral disease, and his prophesied incarnation as
the Antichrist is one of the cloudier doctrines of Christian eschato-
logy. The unreality of the antagonist is also a feature of the story's

imitations, where he is usually a symbol of something dreadful or unpopular over which the hero can triumph. The imitations have their own special problems too, especially with the hero and the people he delivers. Who is to be cast in the redeemer's role, and how is he to act? There is an obvious difference between the pre-Christian hero, a beefy strong man who kills dragons and drives off marauders, and the post-Christian hero who leads his people through a last, apocalyptic battle to a new paradise. Probably neither the hero nor the people will be able to bear the weight of glory imputed to them. Christ's purpose is the saving of individual souls, not of empires, nations, professions, trades or any other kind of social organisation. The only society he recognises is the Church. Treating a nation or a race as types of the Church Militant, like treating its enemies as Antichrist, is a dangerous superstition, a form of idolatry. (One can monitor the idolising of the secular state and its doings in the imagery of seventeenth- and eighteenth-century English poetry.)

The Tudors' application of the Christian theme to recent English history is the first major case, in England, of political propaganda, requiring at some point in its invention and transmission a conspiracy to lie (unless of course Henry VII really thought he was a man sent from God which, from what we know of his character, is very unlikely). Modern historians are right to call the Tudors' version of the events that brought them the crown the 'Tudor myth', a myth being by definition a lie. Such a propagandist tale was bound to cause difficulties for a dramatist aiming at neither melodrama nor propaganda, but at the imitation of life and character. On the one hand the myth is a ready-made way of organising a confused mass of material; on the other hand it falsifies the material by treating people as walking allegories and events as types of the absolute.

We find it hard to read the history plays with this sense of a difference between the human material and the organising myth. This is because the 'Tudor myth' has had a remarkable hold on the English imagination, outlasting many other historical traditions. Some school textbooks still date the beginning of modern England by the 'watershed' of 1485, and almost all Shakespeare's readers assume that he and his readers agreed with government propaganda. But this is unlikely on general grounds. Even if people's knowledge of written history derived from officially sanctioned chronicles, there were *some* less orthodox views in circulation, and there was always the tendency of men everywhere to think for themselves, even if only *to* themselves. In this connection the appearance is very interesting, in James I's reign, of two works rehabilitating Richard III. *The Encomium of Richard III*, 'an oppressed and defamed king', by

Sir William Cornwallis, a member of Prince Henry's household, was
addressed to John Donne. *The History of the Life and Reign of
Richard III* was by Sir George Buc, a Master of the Revels, a man
who, as censor of plays, had more incentive than most for brooding
on the difference between truth and fiction. He is also a good
example of the persistence of loyalty across generations; for his
great-grandfather, Sir John Buc, was Comptroller of the Household
to King Richard III. Sir John fought at Bosworth and was beheaded
at Leicester after the battle. His wife was Margaret, daughter of
Henry Saville. Saville and Buc were Yorkshire families, although
Buc went south under the Howards' protection after the Yorkist
débâcle.[2]

The use of national history to express national pride, whatever
the political myth of the moment, is a very different thing from its
use as propaganda for the régime, and as a matter of fact Shakespeare's histories though enthusiastically English are remarkably diffi-
dent on the subject of the Tudors. For one thing he kept off the
subject, ending his histories in 1485; like Sir William Cornwallis
and Sir George Buc he kept dangerous matter such as the subject
of his *Henry VIII* until the reign of James I. For another, he kept his
counsel. In the opening of Edward Hall's work the marriage of
Henry Tudor and Elizabeth of York prompts a cascade of analogues
of which the first is 'the union of the Godhead to the manhood'.[3]
Parody could do no better. Shakespeare nowhere approaches that
sort of thing; he pays the dynasty's founders no lavish compliments,
and whenever his history plays were given a topical interpretation
it seems to have been a subversive one.[4]

There is one example in *Henry VI* of a gratuitous compliment to
Henry VII:

> *K. Hen. VI.*   Come hither, England's hope. If secret powers
> Suggest but truth to my divining thoughts,
> This pretty lad will prove our country's bliss.
> His looks are full of peaceful majesty,
> His head by nature fram'd to wear a crown,
> His hand to wield a sceptre, and himself
> Likely in time to bless a regal throne.
>
>                    (*III. Hen. VI*, IV. vi. 68–74)

Henry VI's prophecy about young Henry Richmond is in Hall, but
in the play it comes strangely at a time when Henry VI and his own
son are enjoying a spell of prosperity. The lines are poor, even silly,
and Dr Johnson, always sensitive to a false note, has a dry comment
on the passage:

He was afterwards Henry VII. A man who put an end to the civil war of the two houses, but not otherwise remarkable for virtue. Shakespeare knew his trade. Henry VII was grandfather to Queen Elizabeth. . . .[5]

If the lines are Shakespeare's, they are evidence that thoughts of Henry VII did not heat his imagination. The histories, especially the earlier ones, have a number of such dead patches. Sometimes Shakespeare enlivened a dull part of his subject by 'sending it up', treating it in a burlesque manner; but sometimes, comic treatment being out of the question, he negligently cobbled together the necessary lines and left it at that.[6]

As soon as Shakespeare began to turn the Tudor story into drama, acting it out as a sequence of causes and effects embodied in characters and their motives, the shortcomings of the myth began to appear. Because the history, story or myth of English affairs from 1400 to 1485 was a ready-made fiction with heroes, villains, debates and dialectical battles, it must have translated quite easily into theatrical form; after all, allegorical moralities and typological mysteries had been the most popular theatrical genres until well into Shakespeare's lifetime. But as Thomas Nash's famous description of *I Henry VI* in performance tells us, the audience was more interested in character and life than in the mythical framework supporting them.[7] The experience of the long series of plays, for author and audience, was bound to be a kind of enacted criticism of a style of drama as well as of the story it told.

\*     \*     \*

Whoever plotted the three parts of *Henry VI*, whether Shakespeare or a committee, the series was conceived as a whole. The idea probable grew out of a practical wish on the actors' parts to develop their repertory in a way to keep an audience's interest. The epilogue to *Henry V*, written some ten years after *Henry VI*, implies that the later set of histories was an addition to a cycle still in the repertory. C. B. Young's statement that with Benson's production at Stratford in 1906, 'the whole *Henry VI* trilogy was acted together for the first time in recorded history',[8] may be literally true, but is probably untrue in the only sense that matters; for the epilogue to *Henry V* proves that the whole eight-play set was performed in Shakespeare's time, whether the fact was recorded or not. The planning of the first trilogy, therefore, arose out of the audience's habit of theatre-going, which encouraged the dramatist to look for a large theme, one ready to hand and capable of animating a series of plays. The original idea in fact was probably to mount a secular, up-to-date version of the mystery cycles.

The overall theme of *Henry VI* is the weakening of government and the rising tide of civil disorder. The first, visible cause of this large event is the youth, then the incapacity, of Henry VI, but it makes its effects through a group of subsidiary causes that recur as motifs of all three plays: dissension among quarrelling noblemen; the ambition of Richard, Duke of York, which continues in his sons; breaches of loyalty between kindred; and (not much noticed hitherto) the disorderly rule of women. These motifs are all worked into *I Henry VI*, sometimes quite awkwardly.

The centre of interest in that play is dissension at home and the loss of France. It opens with Henry V's funeral procession, its stately ritual interrupted by a quarrel between Gloucester and Beaufort, by messengers telling of battles lost in France through misrule at home and cowardice in the field. During the Gloucester-Beaufort quarrel, the cardinal tells the duke, 'Thy wife is proud; she holdeth thee in awe' (I. i. 39). Since this is the only mention of the duchess in the play it looks like an irrelevant detail; but since the duchess's attempt to domineer over her husband and the kingdom are an important theme of *II Henry VI*, the two lines might be an example of authorial foresight. Once one is aware of the theme of female domination one sees that, like the quarrelling kinsmen and nobles, the mention of Eleanor starts a theme; and the single element that holds these separate themes in a unity, as a *cantus firmus* holds the voices in vocal polyphony, is the stage presence of the dead hero-king, Henry V.

Whatever the inadequacies of *I Henry VI* as a finished work of art, it shows from the first scene onwards a grasp of dramatic form. An example of this, more confidently treated than other parts of the play, is the episode in the Temple garden. Although bad feeling between Somerset (a Beaufort and Lancastrian) and York causes Talbot's defeat and death in Act IV, dynastic faction is not the plays' main theme until Gloucester's death in *II Henry VI*. Nonetheless the civil wars are the main subject of the trilogy; faction and the loss of France are the prelude to them, and the repeated symbol of the wars, from beginning to end, is the contrast of the red rose to the white. So Shakespeare invents a trivial quarrel upon an undisclosed point of law between young noblemen in a rose garden where, at Richard Plantagenet's invitation, they take sides by choosing roses, deciding the quarrel by numbers, not by right:

> Since you are tongue-tied and so loath to speak,
> In dumb significants proclaim your thoughts. (II. iv. 25–6)

For the rest of the scene, Shakespeare plays upon the portentous significance of these 'dumb significants', the white rose meaning among other things anger, death and fear, the red rose standing for confidence, wounds and modesty. Some of the lines have a strong, prophetic irony, like Vernon's:

> Stay, lords and gentlemen, and pluck no more
> Till you conclude that he upon whose side
> The fewest roses are cropp'd from the tree
> Shall yield the other in the right opinion.    (ll. 39–42)

Should we realise that in a sense lives are being plucked, the young Shakespeare, as usual, does not leave us to form our own conclusion:

>             This brawl today,
> Grown to this faction in the Temple-garden,
> Shall send between the red rose and the white
> A thousand souls to death and deadly night.    (ll. 124–7)

Rather poor lines, much too theatrically doom-laden in the close; but they touch on a paradoxical suggestion running all through the plays. By using the word 'brawl' for a quarrel which, as we have seen it, has had so much fire and grace in it, Warwick arouses in us a foreboding pity that so much spirit, passion and valour should go to destruction. The rose-symbolism contributes to this feeling because it usually suggests memories of girls and love-gardens, not a prospect of war. It is as if Chaucer's squire had suddenly turned into a hoodlum.

This scene and its successor in which the dying Mortimer bequeaths his right in the crown to Richard Plantagenet, soon to be Duke of York, proves that *Henry VI* was planned from the start as a tragic whole. As the roses have turned into symbols of violence, so royalty has become a curse. Being heir to the throne has ruined Mortimer, keeping him, 'all [his] flow'ring youth' (II. v. 56) in 'a loathsome dungeon'. Mortimer's appeal to York's ambition, his injunction to him to be wary and politic, his own self-pity (however justified), all lay the ground for *III Henry VI*, introducing the 'sense of injur'd merit' which underlies the Yorkist cause. Young York is a a flower, too, a rose, 'sweet stem from York's great stock' (l. 41). Mortimer's 'fainting kiss' (l. 40) is a quick visual emblem of the transmission of the blight from one generation to the next. This theme of some disease ruining all the accumulated wealth and promise of life brings out the true Shakespearean elegiac tone:

> In prison hast thou spent a pilgrimage
> And like a hermit overpass'd thy days.    (ll. 116–17)

The theme and the imagery are Shakespeare's, and they are a sign of a shift away from conventional views of the story; it is being treated as a tragedy, not as a prelude to glory.

In general the formal design-work in *I Henry VI* is by no means so subtle; although theatrically effective, it does not have the imaginative warmth of the York–Mortimer scenes. For instance, the first two parts of the trilogy are somewhat arbitrarily linked. *I Henry VI* really ends with Talbot's death, the trial and condemnation of Joan of Arc, and the subsequent peace proposals, but Shakespeare prepares for *II Henry VI* by including Suffolk's guilty wooing of Margaret of Anjou in Act v. Another kind of schematic planning explains otherwise puzzling scenes. After the recapture of Orleans (ii. ii), a messenger invites Talbot to visit the Countess of Auvergne. He goes, but the Countess has prepared a trap for him. Talbot however is ready for her. He blows his horn, his men make a rescue and the Countess apologises:

> For I am sorry that with reverence
> I did not entertain thee as thou art.   (ii. iii. 71–2)

Because of its lack of connection with anything else and its near buffoonery, this scene is a puzzle. If however one recognises the baleful influence of women as a running motif in *Henry VI*, then the scene makes sense; it is important that old Talbot, loyal to the King, to his companions and his soldiers, should be shown rising superior to the dangers signified by the Countess's invitation. Charles the Dauphin and the Earl of Suffolk both fail this test.

Although this is the meaning of the scene, it is not explicit. There is no chorus or 'presenter' to interpret it. We are left to reach our own conclusions from such things as the Countess's confession of irreverence or Talbot's explanation of his true identity (ii. iii. 50–6, 63–6); and when we realise that the scene is an *exemplum* of manly valour controlling female temptations, we do so because the Joan of Arc episodes have shown that this is one of the play's themes, and also because we are so familiar with the idea that we need only a hint to recognise it. Such allegorical use of dramatic action was familiar to Shakespeare from the religious and moral drama of his youth. It is used so constantly in *Henry VI*, where it is the source of both plays' weaknesses and strengths, that it is probably the schematic principle according to which Shakespeare first designed the plot of the whole series.

This probably explains the slowness of post-Elizabethan readers to see any form or art at all in the plays' construction. The average reader takes up a history play as he would a history book

or an historical novel, assuming that the priciple of construction
is the sequence of events and that the events chosen are, quite
simply, the ones that are most important or provide most entertainment.

Read in expectation of character, incident and poetry, *Henry VI*
can be a disappointment, and many a reader has turned to another
play having come to the conclusion that these early histories are just
'one thing after another'. This makes it all the more interesting that
when scholars began to explain the dramatist's art its method became so obvious, once the chief principles had been grasped, as to
be crude. Evidently the wrong thing had been looked for, as if
people had gone to Byrd's Masses looking for good tunes. But what
reading concealed, performance revealed. When Gloucester and
Beaufort quarrel before the Tower and an affray breaks out between
their servants, 'blue coats' and 'tawny coats', who can miss the
simple visual symbolism of faction? In Act III, scene i, the servants'
quarrel erupts into the parliament; and when in answer to the
King's pleadings Gloucester and Beaufort agree to a peace, we are
told that the truce is hypocritical. Exeter, ending the scene as
chorus, is explicit:

> This late dissension grown betwixt the peers
> Burns under feigned ashes of forg'd love,
> And will at last break out into a flame.     (III. i. 189–91)

In the next scene Joan takes Rouen by stratagem, and her signal is
thus described in the stage direction: '*Enter* LA PUCELLE *on the top,
thrusting out a torch burning.*' To the modern reader, disappointed
that these events are mainly narrated, not explained, it comes as a
happy discovery that Joan's torch is a version of the same destructive
fire of misrule and disorder named by Exeter.[9] With her diabolic
agents and unchastity, Joan embodies ruinous, burning lust and
rebellion, and in the theatre these correspondences are revealed in
one swift, visually significant action.

The play's action unfolds in a sequence of such 'shows' of which
the significance is continually being pointed out. This is why these
plays, even the first of them, are so effective on the stage. The dramatist brings his action *to* the audience with every spectacular technique of staging available to him. The symbolic 'show and tell'
method depends, however, upon the audience's recognition of the
themes, and it is surprising how much, especially in *I Henry VI*, is
taken for granted. Motives remain a mystery, and so do the actual
issues of the debates and battles. Gloucester, Beaufort and the
factions in the rose garden are mindless, quarrelling automata; and

where it is necessary that a motive be explained, as in Burgundy's desertion of England, the effect is unsubtle.

Yet even this incident is a striking example of the dramatist's confidence in his ability to use the stage. Burgundy has only nine lines in which to explain his conversion to the French cause; and since there is nothing in Joan's arguments that could come as a surprise to him, one concludes that he has either been an ass all along or has suddenly become one. Perhaps the scene drew groans and catcalls from its first audiences; Burgundy's first two lines, spoken aside, are certainly an invitation to some kind of derisive comment:

> Either she hath bewitch'd me with her words,
> Or nature makes me suddenly relent.   (III. iii. 58–9)

His second speech is also partly spoken aside, and the language is so absurd ('. . . these haughty words of hers/Have batter'd me like roaring cannon-shot') that we can be sure the audience is expected to laugh. Joan's comment on Burgundy's change of mind is ambiguous as well as spoken aside: 'Done like a Frenchman!' For a moment one wonders which is more French, his patriotism or his imbecility, but Joan clears the doubt in another aside: 'Turn, and turn again.' One can hear in the mind's ear the roar that greeted that remark.

Shakespeare is so confident of the audience's grasp of Joan's character and of the role of the French that he can take Joan right out of character in order to use her for a larger effect. He has diverted our attention from the 'problem' of Burgundy's motive, which may have been also a problem of his own technique, by making us laugh at the problem by means of the technique. He has used his very formal, stiff 'show and tell' methods for a burlesque caricature of his own limitations.

*I Henry VI* could be Shakespeare's first play, and in it Shakespeare's mastery of the medium and the audience, his superb confidence, are revealed simply, even barbarically, in sheer theatrical power. Because the meaning of the action, the significance of the shows and symbols, and the qualities of the characters are taken for granted, the play approaches demagoguery, being filled with common prejudices and heartlessnesses, and making its effect through continual playing on attitudes the spectators have brought into the theatre with them. The language hardly ever rises above the decorative and the rhetorical. But when it does, the tone is unmistakable, as in the Mortimer scene, or as in Talbot's

> How are we park'd and bounded in a pale,
> A little herd of England's timorous deer.   (IV. ii. 45–6)

The Burgundy scene shows another, equally Shakespearean quality; it is a foretaste of the virtuoso effects possible for a dramatist who is ready to expose his technique to an audience's lively sense of reality.

# 2. The Second Part of King Henry the Sixth

*II Henry VI* is about the collapse of Henry VI's government and the coming of civil war. The play is set wholly in England, in the comparatively recent past, and the story told is so terrible that the dramatist has to do more than 'show' incidents, anticipating the audience's simple response. There is nothing unexpected about French perfidy, or about the misbehaviour of powerful men during a boy king's minority; but how is the war of English with English to be explained? For a long time after a civil war the reunited country feels that renewed faction is possible, and it has the war's language on the tip of the tongue. Thirty years ago in some parts of Cheshire little boys soon knew whether they were for King or Parliament, and on Oak Apple Day some little cavaliers wore oak leaves to school. That war was three hundred years ago. We can be sure that among the audiences surrounding the stage where *Henry VI* was first performed, many spectators knew which of the roses they would wear for choice. The motives of York and the rage of Clifford will have been personal matters to those people, and the plays must have touched their lives in a way that had no precedent in the secular theatre. Not that Shakespeare wrote from a Yorkist or Lancastrian point of view; like Walter Scott's Jacobite novels, the history plays are remarkably impartial. A nation's past, however, like memories of childhood, can erupt in strange ways, and we know how sensitive Elizabethan government could be about history. Shakespeare and Scott, his great Romantic disciple, realised that works of fiction based on the recent past could have a strong appeal just because they brought out feelings and thoughts customarily, even necessarily, repressed. Both men wrote about civil war and national failure, and both, seeing their subject from a secure position of national unity and success, could delineate failure and suffering with such sympathetic power that their versions of Henry VI, Richard II and Charles Edward Stuart have become part of national mythology.

The official explanation of the civil war was common knowledge. Everyone *knew* that Divine Providence put down the Plantagenets and raised up the Tudors. But even if, in the long run, the actors in such events are puppets of the divine will, down here on middle-earth men want to know how that will takes human effect. What sort of man was York that his legitimate claim to the crown caused a war? What sort of government was Henry VI's that York's claims destroyed it? This is the kind of question from which Shakespeare seems to have started, because he begins in the midst of things with the Lancastrian collapse, not at the historical beginning with Richard II.

Richard II's deposition and its theoretical consequences play little part in these plays, being brought in to rationalise and justify actions having more immediate and practical causes. So, in *I Henry VI*, talk of York's ancestry and his scene with Mortimer *follow* the Temple garden quarrel; and in *II Henry VI* York's explanation to Warwick and Salisbury of his claim comes after the loss of Maine, the emergence of the Queen's party, and the plot against Gloucester. Whatever the official interpretation of the history upon which they are based, the three parts of *Henry VI* do not give the impression of being written to maintain a thesis. There is more of a moral than an historical thesis in their construction, but as the plays develop even this takes second place to the representation of motive and character.

*II Henry VI* begins, like its predecessor, with a spectacular symbolic show. King Henry, the Duke of Gloucester, the Earls of Warwick and Salisbury enter on one side; then, on the other, enter the Queen, Suffolk, York, Somerset and Buckingham. The staging separates the characters into opposing groups, the home party on the one side receiving into England the harbingers of turbulent ambition from the other. The announcement of the royal marriage and its cost affects Humphrey of Gloucester in a way that suggests a sudden stoppage in the current of national life:

> Pardon me, gracious lord;
> Some sudden qualm hath struck me at the heart
> And dimm'd mine eyes, that I can read no further.     (I. i. 53–5)

Later, when he detains the peers to 'unload his grief,/Your grief, the common grief of all the land', Humphrey is the voice of tradition, honour and duty. His language has an energy we recognise as Shakespearean, an effortless generosity in the reduplications and parallelisms that express a mounting but always orderly passion:

> What! did my brother Henry spend his youth,
> His valour, coin, and people, in the wars?

Did he so often lodge in open field,
In winter's cold and summer's parching heat,
To conquer France, his true inheritance?
And did my brother Bedford toil his wits,
To keep by policy what Henry got?
Have you yourselves, Somerset, Buckingham,
Brave York, Salisbury, and victorious Warwick,
Receiv'd deep scars in France and Normandy? . . .
O peers of England, shameful is this league,
Fatal this marriage, cancelling your fame,
Blotting your names from books of memory,
Razing the characters of your renown,
Defacing monuments of conquer'd France,
Undoing all, as all had never been!   (i. i. 78–103)

This speech is a fine example of Shakespeare's oratory, matching art
and passion with an elegance one will not find in contemporary
dramatists. The Cardinal's comment is also Shakespearean:

Nephew, what means this passionate discourse,
This peroration with such circumstance?

Other writers used similar questions—Greene for example, in whose
plays they often serve, clumsily, to keep conversation going. Here
the question draws attention to qualities in the writing that might
otherwise be missed. Shakespeare, always conscious of his technical
adroitness, is teaching his audience to recognise the means he uses
to please them. The habit of annotating his own work stayed with
Shakespeare to the end of his career, a curious little pedantry or
touch of self-consciousness in his style.

    Gloucester's speech is a model of the Shakespearean patriotism
that recurs in later plays. It includes the sense of kindred, pride in a
plainness that suffers hardship without complaint, the recital of
names, each recalling a succession of men as well as a dear landscape, and the apostrophe to 'England' that is familiar from better
known examples. It is also typically Shakespearean that these sim-
plicities should be matters of 'honours' and 'renown', worthy the
most eloquent expression his art can give them. Nevertheless,
although one hears the note of national pride and ambition, this is
still the patriotism of the local, intimate community which civil war
will break up; and the first suggestion of a cause of the wars is made
by the series of Humphrey's verbs, 'cancelling', 'blotting', 'razing',
'defacing', with their implication of revolutionary change, of callous
innovation in contempt of the ordinary legal forms by which

institutions and property are conveyed from one generation to the next. This is also Shakespearean, and it is not surprising that Suffolk, the home cause of the fatal marriage, is 'the new made duke'.

The scene between Gloucester and the peers ends with more emblematic staging. There is a satisfying orderliness about the way the dramatist first detaches Gloucester from the other courtiers and then, after his exit, separates the remainder into factions. The whole technique, staging and characterization, comes from the moralities, as we see by old Salisbury's interpretation of the exit of Buckingham and Somerset: 'Pride went before, ambition follows him.'[1] The two Nevilles, Salisbury and Warwick, left alone with York, are the image of feudal nobility and obligation. As Salisbury puts it, 'While these do labour for their own preferment,/Behoves it us to labour for the realm.' He proposes a league between himself, his son Warwick, and York to which Warwick agrees, 'as he loves the land/And common profit of his country', and to which York agrees because, as he tells the audience in an aside, 'he hath greatest cause.' The Nevilles, like Gloucester, speak the language of 'plain' patriotism; yet they too are men of a faction, albeit a patriotic one. Their exit leaves York finally alone, and if one considers the scene's arrangements allegorically, then an interesting parallel appears between the opening and the conclusion. Gloucester's confrontation of the peers and the court at the beginning treats in the old-fashioned, external, emblematic way the same kind of situation which York's soliloquy at the end treats in a new, inward and expressive way; both men are isolated from their fellows, but whereas Gloucester's isolation is shown, York's is expressed.

Richard of York is a complex personality, a real outsider, psychologically and intellectually. He has the valour, the patriotism, the administrative integrity and the reliability of Gloucester and the Nevilles; but he has also the ambition, the Machiavellian watchfulness and the unwillingness of Beaufort and Suffolk to suffer competition. The source of his trouble is a sense of 'injur'd merit'. He feels it in himself, deprived of the honour due him by birth and made an object of suspicion; he feels it as the head of his family, their rights usurped by Lancaster; and he feels it as an Englishman injured by foreign insult and home-bred faction. All these injuries are real. York is not paranoid. His grievances are as legitimate as his claim to the throne. But in York's case, legitimacy itself is perverted.

Whatever legitimate pride York has as the heir of York, Mortimer and England, it is second to his pride in the difference between him and other men. A deep-rooted sense of injury is something not easily admitted to others, being evidence of a wound and a continuing vulnerability. Yet because it determines much of the sufferer's

thoughts and feelings, it will separate him from others. Secret knowledge of his own motives underlies all York's conversations. He is a
watcher and a manipulator as well as a participant, a doubleness in
the character that Shakespeare reveals chiefly by means of the aside
and the soliloquy. Although York prides himself on his feelings of
secret mastery, he remains an unhappy man because his ambition is
rooted in weakness. The historical Richard of York may have been
a simpler, nobler figure than this, but Shakespeare's York is a tragic
man of the Shakespearean kind.

In the fine soliloquy that ends Act I, scene i, York speaks to the
audience (his only confidants) in passionate, troubled words full of
the egotism of a thoughtful man who is sorry, above all, for himself.
The dismemberment of England and York's feeling of his own dis-
unity are one and the same thing to him, and like other unhappy men
in the histories, he thinks that the sovereign medicine for his wounds
and the nation's would be possession of the crown, the ultimate
symbol of wholeness and singleness of purpose. In the meantime
his bitterness gives him a little touch of the malcontented satirist:

> Nor shall proud Lancaster usurp my right,
> Nor hold the sceptre in his childish fist.

His patient ambition counterpoints Gloucester's watchful care of
the realm with the watchfulness of the spy and thief:

> Then, York, be still a while, till time do serve.
> Watch thou and wake when others be asleep,
> To pry into the secrets of the state.

It is surprising to find so early in literature, let alone in Shakespeare, such a subtle, inward revelation of the mind of a self-pitying
wrongdoer. As long as York is a watcher, we feel the justice of his
complaints more strongly than the criminality of his intention, and
this holds all through the first two acts and up to the plan to murder
Gloucester. York at least dreams of unity and happiness, but the
court party (Margaret, Suffolk and Beaufort) have no end but to
satisfy desire and ambition.

The first and second acts do not maintain the poetic and psychological force of this opening scene, although the dispersed and
digressive scenes that follow show the same kind of thematic and
emblematic planning as *I Henry VI*. The Duchess of Gloucester's
dabbling in witchcraft, her tempting of her husband, continue the
themes of diabolism and 'the monstrous regiment of women' begun
with Joan of Arc; but both themes emerge with much greater effect

when Margaret of Anjou's crimes begin in Act III. Gloucester, like Talbot, is immune to female lures. His impartiality at his wife's trial, like his detection of the fake miracle at St Albans (II. i. 68–164), shows the quality of his justice. In the scene with the petitioners (I. iii) Margaret and Suffolk show their contempt for the people and the realm. In the following court scene, we see Henry VI's exasperating incompetence exemplified in the choice of a regent for France. There is more emblemism when a quarrel between Beaufort and Gloucester is preceded by a scene of falconry in which the birds' behaviour typifies the nobles' emulation (II. i. 1–57).

One could analyse the significance of each scene in some detail, but the significances are not particularly remote, the planning not really rising above the schematic. The real interest of this part of the play is the treatment of York. By a series of subtly placed references and incidents, Shakespeare does much to draw sympathy for him without sentimentalising him. In the affair of the armourer's man (I. iii. 1–42, 180–226, II. iii. 59–108) he is the victim of an accusation which, while true as to his intention, is not yet true in fact; and the outcome of the trial-by-ordeal deprives him of the regency of France to which experience and ability entitle him. Here he is the victim of Suffolk's malice, since everything he says about Somerset's incompetence is true. Henry's own incompetence corresponds so closely to York's earlier portrayal of him that sympathy is bound to veer towards York. When, in yet another garden scene, after a 'simpler supper', he unfolds his ambition to Salisbury and Warwick, who salute him as King, one feels that a 'patriot' party is being formed whose case, *so far as it is made public*, is a good one.

The qualification is important because the atmosphere of the Nevilles' supper with York contrasts in the reader's or spectator's mind with the knowledge of York's other conspiracies. By having York present and active when the Duchess of Gloucester is arrested (I. iv), Shakespeare has shown him to be in some way a party to Suffolk's anti-Gloucester plottings. This kind of private side-taking has a different tone from the privacy of the garden scene with the Nevilles, and Shakespeare represents very neatly the equivocal quality of York's behaviour by means of the affair of the armourer's man. The man accuses his master of speaking treason on York's behalf, and the real issue is not the master's guilt, which is of little importance, but York's. Although the armourer loses his trial by combat because he is incapably drunk and although his man is a lying coward, a kind of indirect but exact justice has been done, a result that reflects York's dubious character and position. But the moral confusion of these scenes contrasts strongly with Gloucester's unequivocal dealings at St Albans.

There are also in these early scenes tiny but telling touches, like Margaret's description of York as 'grumbling York' (I. iii. 73) and Gloucester's later assessment of him (III. i. 158) as 'dogged York, that reaches at the moon.' These phrases remind the audience of its inner knowledge of York, and show that others, without hearing soliloquies, have taken his measure. Altogether the handling of York in these two acts shows an architectonic ability that is very impressive. The forms are still a little stiff, but they convey the thought of an acute and observant moralist.

*        *        *

With Act III, long-impending violence breaks out. The dramatist seizes his play's action in scenes of an intensity hardly to be matched elsewhere in his work. As the plot to destroy Gloucester moves to its climax, the centre of psychological interest shifts from York to the King. Surrounded by evil counsellors bent upon mastering or destroying him the King rises, in trying to protect his uncle, to a moral authority that never really leaves him until his own murder in *III Henry VI*. He even has a moment of regal and manly authority when he banishes Suffolk.

Shakespeare seems to have discovered Henry as the plays grew in poetic scope. In *I Henry VI* he is a dim presence, a bookish innocent who arbitrates the rose quarrel by plucking a red rose for himself, and whose modest control over his own interests is quite overcome by Suffolk's description of Margaret. This is another example of the showing that passes for telling in *I Henry VI*; as a reason for Henry's later subjection to Margaret it does not fit with his chaste, pious character. In *II Henry VI*, Acts I and II, even his piety is so simple-minded that the only possible response to it is either amusement or irritation. In *II Henry VI*, Act III, however, a new Henry appears:

> My Lords, at once; the care you have of us
> To mow down thorns that would annoy our foot
> Is worthy praise; but, shall I speak my conscience,
> Our kinsman Gloucester is as innocent
> From meaning treason to our royal person
> As is the sucking lamb or harmless dove.   (III. i. 66)

We are surprised to find that Henry can speak firmly, courteously and intelligently. His biblical imagery of the lamb and the dove introduces a strain of metaphor that will provide expressive commentary upon Gloucester's fate and the horrors that follow, and it is a sign of new authority in Henry's religious feeling.

Gloucester and Henry are chorus as well as actors in their play.

Gloucester foresees his death, interpreting it as the prologue to a 'plotted tragedy', an allegory acted by vices inhabiting the treacherous courtiers' bodies:

> I know their complot is to have my life,
> And if my death might make this island happy
> And prove the period of their tyranny,
> I would expend it with all willingness;
> But mine is made the prologue to their play;
> For thousands more, that yet suspect no peril,
> Will not conclude their plotted tragedy.
> Beaufort's red sparkling eyes blab his heart's malice,
> And Suffolk's cloudy brow his stormy hate;
> Sharp Buckingham unburdens with his tongue
> The envious load that lies upon his heart;
> And dogged York, that reaches at the moon,
> Whose overweening arm I have pluck'd back,
> By false accuse doth level at my life.   (III. i. 147–60)

Henry, after Gloucester's removal, expresses the scene's 'beastliness' in a long, extended simile:

> And as the butcher takes away the calf
> And binds the wretch and beats it when it strays,
> Bearing it to the bloody slaughter-house,
> Even so remorseless have they borne him hence;
> And as the dam runs lowing up and down,
> Looking the way her harmless young one went,
> And can do nought but wail her darling's loss,
> Even so myself bewails good Gloucester's case.   (III. i. 210–17)

Although Henry leaves the parliament in tears, the conspirators sufficiently fear his passion and the signs of nascent strength in him that they decide to kill Gloucester at once. The King is 'too full of foolish pity'. The irony is that pity, apparently so weak, should be seen by the conspirators for what it is, a potentiality which must be forestalled. In the ethos of Shakespeare's play, pity is more fundamental to humanity than love or reason; it is the emotion through which conscience speaks to men. Repeatedly in his work Shakespeare treats pity as the spring of justice and good actions, and his favourite metaphor for its occasion is the bond between parent and child, for its potentiality the child itself. Under the influence of pity Henry, the childlike king, sees his endangered uncle as a child. Of the conspirators, Margaret and York will both live to be overcome by pity for their children and to have their pity mocked. Denial of pity is a brutality that Shakespeare expresses as the 'butchery' of child-murder, and in starting the motif here in *II Henry VI*, he is judging the 'plotted tragedy' by the strongest of moral standards. He is also drawing into the play by means of implied reference the Christian conception of the relation of divine justice to the world, of the incarnation of the divine judge as a 'naked newborn babe', and of the grand crime of the Antichrist, typified by the Slaughter of the Innocents. At his own murder in Act IV, Suffolk neither asks for nor receives pity from his captors, and this is fitting enough because he has been pitiless himself.

The conspirators' inhumanity is precisely, not just emotionally unnatural. The note of blasphemy is heard in the Queen's addresses to them: 'Thrice-noble Suffolk', 'sweet Somerset', 'good York'. When York becomes a party to the murder plot and shakes hands with Suffolk and Beaufort, he loses any moral justification his situation and psychology might have provided him so far. The impression of evil at this moment is as strong as in *Othello*, when Iago pledges himself to Othello's purpose (III. iii. 453–79); and, as in the later play, Shakespeare's metaphorical explanation for such behaviour in *II Henry VI* brings in the notion of diabolic possession. This emerges strongly in York's second soliloquy (III. i. 331).

In the imagery of this speech he is now, self-named, a 'labouring spider', a 'starved snake'. The nobles who have 'sent him packing' to Ireland have 'put sharp weapons in a madman's hands'. For York, while he raises an army in Ireland, will raise in England a 'black storm', a 'mad-bred flaw' that will not be calmed until the 'golden circuit' shines like the sun upon his head. The strongest evocation of diabolism is in York's description of his 'minister', Cade:

> In Ireland have I seen this stubborn Cade
> Oppose himself against a troop of kerns,
> And fought so long, till that his thighs with darts
> Were almost like a sharp-quill'd porpentine;
> And, in the end being rescued, I have seen
> Him caper upright like a wild Morisco,
> Shaking the bloody darts as he his bells . . .
> This devil here shall be my substitute.

The image of evil as a 'commotion', a 'tempest' caused by the wild 'minister' of a darker power turns up again after the discovery of Gloucester's death.

In this scene (III. ii) Henry, knowing instinctively that Suffolk and Margaret are responsible for the murder, can bear neither their touch nor their sight. Like his 'foolish pity' a little earlier, this action, which amounts to a public accusation of the guilty pair, threatens their whole design. When Margaret sees in Henry's face the possibility that her influence over him is at an end, she embarks upon a long speech of which the ostensible theme is an appeal for sympathy by a young foreigner whose husband has neglected her. As such the speech is out of place (Henry pays no attention to it), and reads like an attack of hysterics. Its real theme is Margaret's coming to England, how nature (wind, sea and cliff, England's natural defences) hindered her landing, how by an act of magic she bewitched the sea into submission and so made her way into Henry's life and country. This speech seems to be forced out of her by some irresistible compulsion. Intending a lie, she tells a stranger truth than one would ever have imagined; intending to express love of Henry, she expresses nothing but hatred of him and England. She acts like an evil thing baulked in the presence of virtue and forced to reveal itself. The irony of her speech is that no one attends either to her overt feelings or to her true confession.

Following upon Margaret's speech there is 'noise within'. Inexplicably, the Commons know of Gloucester's death and are in revolt:

> The commons, like an angry hive of bees
> That want their leader, scatter up and down
> And care not who they sting in his revenge.   (III. ii. 125–7)

It is absolutely right that at this moment when his country has moved irrevocably into chaos and anarchy, Henry should pray for forgiveness should his suspicions of murder be false. A clumsy writer, wishing to show Henry's piety, would have had him pray for 'guidance', perhaps for 'strength', for anything but, at this point, forgiveness. Coming in the midst of murder and rebellion the prayer shows a scrupulosity that could be a little comical, but it gives the measure of Henry's sanctity and its unworldly strength. Despite distress and fear Henry provides a standard of clear perception and right feeling. His prayer prepares for the showing of Humphrey's body which immediately follows with Warwick as 'presenter'.

Warwick's slow reading of the signs of death concentrates the mind on the horror of the deed and also on the mystery of its cause in some corruption of nature:

> Who finds the heifer dead and bleeding fresh
> And sees fast by a butcher with an axe,
> But will suspect 'twas he that made the slaughter?
> Who finds the partridge in the puttock's nest,

But may imagine how the bird was dead,
Although the kite soar with unbloodied beak? (iii. ii. 188–93)

The intention of this passage is to make a strong rhetorical irony, but its real and poetic force is in its imagery. Warwick and Salisbury suspect that men are beasts, that Suffolk is a vampire ('Pernicious blood-sucker of sleeping men') or a serpent ('with forked tongue,/ That slily glided towards your Majesty'), and that Beaufort is a kite. Such images naturally echo in a wider circuit of meaning than the immediate context. Threatened majesty is an image of the order of things, the serpent a type of the original destroyer. When the Commons demand Suffolk's life, his contempt of them ('rude un-polish'd hinds ... a sort of tinkers') brings to mind Shakespeare's constant suspicion of the shining, decorated surface concealing in-ward corruption. Hence the power in the lines on the kite that 'soars with unbloodied beak'.

The third act ends as Cardinal Beaufort, tormented by visions of his murdered nephew, dies obsessed by fiends. Henry, through whose eyes we have been encouraged to see the horrors of the act, shows his sanctity again in another prayer forestalling over-hasty judgement:

> O thou eternal Mover of the heavens,
> Look with a gentle eye upon this wretch!

To Warwick's blunt interpretation of this second death ('So bad a death argues a monstrous life') he replies:

> Forbear to judge, for we are sinners all.
> Close up his eyes and draw the curtain close;
> And let us all to meditation.

Grammatical analysis of the second line, of its implied metaphor and perfect rhythm, comes second to one's sense of the nobility of mind that conceived the scene of Beaufort's death.[2]

\* \* \*

Henry's call to meditation, had it been heeded, would have arrested the 'plotted tragedy' there and then. For, despite the talk of 'bad revolting stars' in *1 Henry VI* or the large theories of Providential interference to be found in the historians, or even the running motif of diabolic possession in the whole tetralogy, the causes of evil in this play and its successors are in men themselves. There is no demonstrable external agency. Henry is asking for a new beginning; meditation is really a way of taking time to put time right. Part of the tragedy's cause is that what Henry is and what he stands for is not understood, is held in contempt, not just because men do not know him, but because they do not know themselves. His piety, innocence and gentleness are absurd to his nobles and his Queen. For them, self-assertion and some form of ambition are the first source of the knowledge that they have a self. Henry's part in Act III shows how, for this king, the base of the natural order is men's knowledge of kindred in their common lot. The source of evil is the perversion of intelligence and affection according to a false notion of good—an idea that Shakespeare reveals by explicit allegory in *III Henry VI*, with the king as onlooker and interpreter of the symbols.

The young Shakespeare's art and understanding do not always go hand in hand in these plays. His language often falls short of the possibilities he has discovered for himself, so that even in the midst of the tense unfoldings of Act III, the nobles can fall into the mindless bickering typical of *I Henry VI*, and considerable areas of potential interest go largely undeveloped. Margaret's and Suffolk's vicious love, upon which so much depends, is never traced to its cause. We are left with the external fact that, loving each other, they love corruption. Suffolk's death, horribly effective as it is, is melodrama:

> And thou that smil'd'st at good Duke Humphrey's death
> Against the senseless winds shall grin in vain.

Suffolk dies as he has lived, a villain absolute, convinced of the nobility of his will, scorning enemies. Like Burgundy in *I Henry VI*, Suffolk is the centre of a strange, theatrical kind of comedy, from the time of his first meeting with Margaret to the scene of his murder in which he calls one of his captors an 'obscure and lousy swain . . . a jaded groom' and speaks such stuff as:

>              No, rather let my head
> Stoop to the block than these knees bow to any
> Save to the God of heaven and to my king,
> And sooner dance upon a bloody pole
> Than stand uncover'd to the vulgar groom.
> True nobility is exempt from fear.    (IV. i. 124–9)

This frankly absurd strain in the character of Suffolk continues after his death when Margaret totes his head about the stage, speaking to it and caressing it:

> Here may his head lie on my throbbing breast;
> But where's the body that I should embrace?    (IV. iv. 5–6)

The rest of Act IV, however, is taken up with Cade's rebellion, and here Shakespeare's mind and art are in harmony again.

A violent, bloody rebellion of the common people is obviously a case of 'disorder'. Our reaction to this rebellion, though, should be based on the fact that, first, it is York's doing and, second, we are to see in it the exact kind of disorder prophesied by Gloucester in Act III. Our difficulty is that we consider public order a separate matter from the order of our everyday social, family and personal lives. Although these latter are the only kinds of life most of us know, we do not make the connection that Shakespeare took for granted, that public order is rooted in the quality of private lives, and that the same general laws govern both spheres. (Elizabethans, for example, interpreted the fifth commandment to cover relations between subjects and government as well as between children and parents.) Our ideas of order are abstract, schematic and academic, as our interpretive criticism on the subject shows. It is tempting to fashion a mould of Elizabethan 'order' out of the theology, law and history of the age, and then by a suitable process of analysis to reduce the literature to a state sufficiently ductile for its adaptation to the mould. The result is generally more doctrinaire than is necessary.

According to one essay on this play, the Cade mob represents the people of England, forced to take the law into their own hands.[3] Thus the mob is the people of the petitioning scene (I. iii), the St Albans miracle (II. i) and the parliament scenes after Gloucester's death (III. ii), driven to extremities. The scheme makes the crowd neatly allegorical, and its tidiness alone makes it attractive. But these different crowds are not the same people at all; they are quite different groups represented for different purposes. The Cade rebels are, quite specifically, the men of Kent, and Cade is York's instrument. Whatever misrule the nobility in general has been guilty of, the rebels' misrule is all their own, a harbinger of the storm York is shortly to raise. With hindsight we can see that it is a parody of their master's rebellion, and that it has the same causes. Their 'virtue is not regarded' (IV. ii. 11); they mean to 'dress the commonwealth, and turn it'. Best's son, the tanner, 'shall have the skins of our enemies', Dick the butcher is to cut iniquity's throat like a calf's, and Smith the weaver is to spin the thread of men's lives. Cade justifies himself with a crazy story of royal birth, but everyone sees through it to his true purpose, which is that 'My mouth shall be the parliament of England' (IV. vii. 17). His rage would destroy, if it could, every sign of life superior to his own. Learning, law, gentility go down before him, while he 'ennobles' himself. His peremptory self-knighting is on a par with York's self-kinging in the garden.

Like York the rebels have their reasons—the loss of France and the perennial complaint of poor grumblers that 'it was never merry world in England since gentlemen came up'—but these are rationalisations of the spirit of crazy destructiveness that possesses them. The rebels know as well as anyone that Cade is a lying clown. The way they mock their leader, their cause and themselves reveals their deeper allegiance to the rules they flout. Although it seems, from the ease with which Clifford persuades them to give up their fight, that any practised orator can have his way with them, Cade's rebuke is really unjustified: 'Was ever feather so lightly blown to and fro as this multitude?' (iv. viii. 57). By the time of Clifford's speech, the rebellion has run its course, having never been more than a wild holiday from continuing obligations. The rebels are not to be blamed for giving up something they never really had their hearts in:

> Cade.   My father was a Mortimer,—
> Dick.   (*Aside.*) He was an honest man, and a good bricklayer.
> Cade.   My mother was a Plantagenet,—
> Dick.   (*Aside.*) I knew her well; she was a midwife.
>
>                       (iv. ii. 41–5)

They are to be blamed for moral, not political reasons. Clifford and Cade are equally contemptuous of them, and make the same estimate of their motives: as Cade says, 'The name of Henry the Fifth hales them to an hundred mischiefs and makes them leave me desolate' (iv. viii. 58–60).

As for Cade himself, after he hardens his heart against Lord Say's plea for mercy, he becomes a terrible object. He ends exiled from human fellowship, dying like a hunted animal in Alexander Iden's garden, famished and weary after five days hidden from search in the woods. The men of Kent go home to their villages and Henry's words 'O graceless men! they know not what they do', are true in so far as the rebels do not understand the real significance of their deeds; but they know well enough what they do while they are doing it in the streets. In this they are similar to the noble rebels, but unlike the nobles they are funny. Their honest speech shows the rebellion up for what it is, a carnival of ill-will and downright silliness, and the implication is that a sufficiently remote spectator might find the grand rebellion itself a comedy.

\*     \*     \*

There is nothing overtly comic about York's return from Ireland which begins Act v, but as his secret desires and imaginings turn into public actions it seems possible that Shakespeare wants us to see the childishness of York's motives:

> I am far better born than is the King,
> More like a king, more kingly in my thoughts.   (v. i. 28–9)

Upon a promise that Somerset is in the Tower he dismisses his soldiers, but when he finds his old enemy still abroad anger drives him into open mutiny. In that moment of self-assertion he has no sense of the effect his wild language has upon the onlookers. The sudden revelation of a man's inward fantasies can be extremely funny (as in Malvolio's case); but for those who are unprepared the effect is more likely to suggest madness. When Somerset arrests York for capital treason, instructing him to kneel for mercy, York replies from a world all his own:

> Wouldst have me kneel? First let me ask of these
> If they can brook I bow a knee to man.   (v. i. 109–10)

He knows no superior beneath the rank of angel. A comic element in the scene, already indicated by York's comparison of himself to Ajax Telamonius (who went mad and attacked sheep and oxen in mistake for enemies), comes out with Clifford's entry at line 123. Clifford kneels in salute to the King, but York behaves as if Clifford has spoken to him, not Henry:

> I thank thee, Clifford. Say, what news with thee?
> Nay, do not fright us with an angry look.
> We are thy sovereign, Clifford, kneel again;
> For thy mistaking so, we pardon thee.

York is playing his new role, royal 'we' as well, but Clifford answers him from the old world of five minutes ago in which the performance was unthinkable: 'To Bedlam with him! Is the man grown mad?' For a short time the scene hovers between grotesque comedy and tragedy as the court discovers that York, mad or not, has shaped an alternative England to Henry's, and is recognised by the Nevilles. Salisbury's behaviour is more puzzling than Warwick's, his 'brain-sick son', of whom he is the 'mad misleader'. 'O, where is faith? O, where is loyalty?' the King asks, and receives his answer:

> My lord, I have considered with myself
> The title of this most renowned duke,
> And in my conscience do repute his Grace
> The rightful heir to England's royal seat.   (v. ii. 175–8)

Two Englands are contending for mastery, and national schism is a fact. Oaths of allegiance are cancelled, the bonds predicated upon the single state of England are revoked. The war that breaks out is a type of the ultimate, apocalyptic war between opposing principles claiming to be the same thing, and the plight of the soldier is that he cannot know surely against whom or what he is fighting.

*II Henry VI* ends with the battle of St Albans, Shakespeare's most complicated battle scene so far. Since it concludes the play's action, which has been the failure of Henry VI's government, the battle has a satisfying finality to it, allowing us a kind of decisiveness, whether for good or for bad. It is also a foreboding prelude to *III Henry VI*, a foretaste of the total war that is the chief theme of that play.

Outside revolutionary circles, no one is disposed nowadays to find anything satisfactory in war, but in this play the resort to arms is a relief. For one thing it brings a promise of order with it, not only because of the possibility of decisive action but because war, as opposed to privy murder and rebellion, has its law and order. The bragging challenges of the rival noblemen (v. i.) have their proper place in the events leading to battle. Even rage can be decorous. The orderliness of war is especially emphasised in the personal combat of York with old Lord Clifford. Though they are enemies to the death, they take time to praise one another, to state their quarrel and to prepare rationally for the fight. This is really trial by combat in which the sword, in theory, is the agent of justice, and the issue peace to victor and vanquished alike. York's couplet over Clifford's body may be riddling, but it is sadly meant:

> Thus war hath given thee peace, for thou art still.
> Peace with his soul, Heaven, if it be thy will! (v. ii. 29–30)

Immediately, however, young Clifford's entry breaks the judicial, knightly tone, bringing to the stage the battle's confusion where men wound their friends in panic and the Lancastrians are in retreat. His first lines convey the *experience* of battle. Instead of watching a formal combat like spectators at a tournament, we are taken by Clifford's words into the midst of battle and into the feelings of a defeated man:

> Shame and confusion! All is on the rout;
> Fear frames disorder, and disorder wounds
> Where it should guard. (v. ii. 31–3)

Literally this means that in the confusion of defeat undisciplined men are attacking the comrades they should be protecting. As is so often the case in Shakespeare, the literal application of figurative

language to the bald facts of the plot seems a perversion of meaning,
let alone a prosy limitation of it. As young Clifford speaks them, his
words impress us like the diagnosis of a general law, more psychological than political or military, which applies as much to the inner
state of a single man as to the external places where whole armies
are in rout. In that more extended sense fear causes, or sets the stage
for, disorder; and disorder, which is the organism's natural protective response, brings, like its close cousin pain, hurt instead of
healing. Yet its anguish prompts quick and stern measures.

The remainder of young Clifford's speech, the most remarkable in
the play, and among the most remarkable in Shakespeare, invokes
the military discipline of war to cure fear and disorder:

> O war, thou son of hell,
> Whom angry heavens do make their minister,
> Throw in the frozen bosoms of our part
> Hot coals of vengeance! *Let no soldier fly.*
> *He that is truly dedicate to war*
> *Hath no self-love, nor he that loves himself*
> *Hath not essentially but by circumstance*
> *The name of valour.*

Those last lines have been called by a modern reader[4] military
nihilism, a reading that shows how inadequately our contemporary
experience prepares us for the experience of the form of things at
their ending, for the vision of chaos. The battle's confusion has
entered into Clifford's soul, and his speech shows the heroic process
of a consciousness mastering chaos. His address to war as the son of
hell, the minister of an angry Providence, glosses over nothing and
tells plainly enough the terms on which war's victims must surrender
themselves to it. In King Henry's piety Shakespeare shows the
passivity of the martyr, perhaps of the saint; in young Clifford he
shows the passivity of the warrior who wins his peace by self-sacrifice
to the battle and, by explicit statement, to the enigmatic justice it
serves.

Young Clifford's address to the army, 'Let no soldier fly', is heroic
and epic. A reader of English literature might hear as a harmony to
it the speech of the retainers at Maldon or Wiglaf's speech as he
goes to Beowulf's aid in the last fight. Shakespeare comes closer, with
Clifford's speech, to the heroic past, indeed to the heroic in all ages,
than anywhere else in his histories except, perhaps, for one scene in
*King John.* Other heroes, Henry V for instance, talk too much; they
play the orator, persuading men to fight as one might persuade them
to vote or increase their output. Cliffords's words have the spareness

of the true heroic which does not argue, but simply announces the conditions under which men might, in extremity, die well.

And yet ... there is something wrong. Young Clifford is alone on the stage. He has fought out a battle in himself, outrunning events, speaking into emptiness, nerving himself for a last stand before its time has come. He represents the typically Shakespearean tragic theme of a protagonist whose inner time is out of phase with outer time; and this is carefully dramatised, because only *after* young Clifford has proclaimed the terms of the soldier's self-sacrifice does he see his father dead on the ground before him. Such an event—a son's finding his father's dead body on a lost battlefield—might well precede heroic self-dedication; instead, it is its undoing. As young Clifford meets this new shock he is driven back into himself, to dedicate himself once again, this time to pitiless, personal revenge. Consequently he too flies from the battle, his heart 'on future mis-chief set'.

So the order of war turns to disorder, and young Clifford's exit bearing his father's body is followed by Richard of Gloucester's killing of Somerset 'underneath an alehouse' paltry sign'. This sordid incident shows what the character of the wars will be. Henry's half-line comment on the battle, 'Can we out-run the heavens?' anticipates the hopelessness of the kingdom's plight. Although Shakespeare counters these foreboding passages a little by the final scene of the Yorkists' mutual congratulations, in which all is external again, the signs of things to come have been so clearly shown that, despite Warwick's enthusiasm in victory, the audience hears a fearful irony in his words, especially in the last line of all:

And more such days as these to us befall!

# 3. The Third Part of King Henry the Sixth

Like its two predecessors this play begins with a large set piece. The Yorkists, fresh from victory at St Albans, come to the parliament house to assert York's claim to the throne. Their gloating over their defeated enemies brings open savagery into the sequence of plays; they display the blood still unwiped from their swords, and Richard of Gloucester, typically and laconically, produces Somerset's severed head. Warwick's threat that 'The bloody parliament shall this be called', taken with King Henry's later avowal that he will not make 'a shambles of the parliament-house', brings in again the imagery of butchering which will be repeated to the end like a *leit motif*, being used at the last by Margaret addressing her followers at Tewksbury, and by Henry speaking to his murderer:

> So first the harmless sheep doth yield his fleece
> And next his throat unto the butcher's knife.   (v. vi. 8–9)[1]

Yet in this first scene York is reluctant when the moment of usurpation comes. Three times he asks for his followers' support, and Warwick's last words to him before the King's entry are 'Resolve thee, Richard; claim the English crown.' To the end of his life, York is an intriguing mixture of nobility and opportunism. His title is legitimist, and Shakespeare seems to have intended that the character should be aware of a contradiction between a legitimist claim and a title won by conquest. 'Assist me, then, sweet Warwick', says York, ' . . . For hither we have broken in by force.'

With the arrival of the King's party the scene turns into a debate over rival titles, interrupted of course by threats, recriminations and insults. Henry's title rests upon his being the third generation in possession, York's in his being the lineal inheritor by successive descent in the female line from Lionel of Clarence, elder brother of John of Gaunt, father of the house of Lancaster. The crux of the argument is whether Henry IV's title was based upon conquest—a good title, always presuming that the possessor can maintain it—

or whether Richard II's 'unconstrained' resignation of the crown was 'prejudicial' to its succession. To this last the Duke of Exeter, himself of the King's party, gives answer:

No; for he could not so resign his crown
But that the next heir should succeed and reign.   (I. i. 145–6)

The argument, which is surprisingly abstract and legal in the midst of savage threats of war, is taken seriously by the chief parties. Warwick himself assures Henry, 'Prove [your title], and thou shalt be king', and there is no suggestion (though a heavy-handed director could easily stage one) that he, like York a legitimist so far, is not sincere. The cold terms of argument take new life when Henry, his 'right' disproved and his inability to maintain it obvious, begs to be allowed to reign 'in quiet' on condition that he nominate York his heir and disinherit his own son. The compromise, shameful to the Lancastrians, is welcome to York who, having entered into an oath to maintain the agreement, announces, 'Now York and Lancaster are reconciled.'

Much of the scene's irony arises out of the disparity in it between words and reality. This is not because the chief actors are hypocrites —they talk as sincerely as they fight or run away—but because no talk is effective against the fact that York has won a battle and Lancaster has lost it. For the time being York acts—in the political jargon of our own time—with restraint because his royalist conscience has the better of his ambition. It could be argued, however, that a conscience like York's is only weakness. Failing to act decisively, he insults and irritates his opponents by his evasions and at the same time leaves his own supporters unsatisfied. This ensures that there will be more war.

One significance of this skilful scene is that, although it seems just possible that reason and law might control rage and ambition, there is really no effective sanction against them except their own weapon, the sword. Not that there might not be another weapon: the idea persists in Shakespeare's histories, whether as memory or prophecy, that in the long run the peace of the realm is stronger than the sword which violates it. If this is really so, however, it is because, in Malcolm's words, 'the powers above put on their instruments' (*Macbeth*, IV. iii. 238), an interpretation of history that does not alter the fact that the realm's peace is proven more often in the breach than the observance. In this first scene of *III Henry VI*, the realm is a piece of property to be squabbled and bargained over. The circumstance that the laws of succession are supposed to prevent has arisen, and since all the actors on stage are in some way accessory to breaking those laws no amount of legal argument can put things right.

This theme can give the scene a retrospective effect in the reader's mind, reminding him of Cade's cry, 'Henceforward all things shall be in common', and of York himself in his first soliloquy, identifying his discontent with the denial of his 'own', comparing himself to the owner of stolen property and, most sinisterly, making a direct link between the fate of the land, his property and his own person. The treatment of the crown as property, the bond between property and personality, and the significance of the talk of possession, inheritance, right and purchase can go unnoticed by a modern reader who takes it for granted that the problem of property, if there is one, is legal or political, not moral or psychological. In Shakespeare's time the kind of polity under which freehold ownership was the condition of liberty and freedom was only just coming into being, and not without violence. Already in early Tudor literature the exploitation of land is a frequent theme; but then the confiscation and sale of the Church's immense estates brought about a rupture in the nation's way of thinking about its land, people and purpose that even now we find impossible to comprehend fully. Naturally such a change had to be moralised. The violent passage of communal land into private hands had to be made respectable, and Shakespeare's generation saw the mutation of a whole class of opportunists into gentlemen and pillars of the state. This process, continued through the subsequent centuries, brought about a really extraordinary moralising of freehold tenure. By about 1850 the apotheosis of the landlord seems to have been complete. In Elizabethan England, however, it was still possible to see ironies a good deal stronger than the merely urbane or amusing in the contemporary economic spectacle. Although Shakespeare himself speculated in property with the earnings of his career, the heroes and heroines whom he means us to admire are contemptuous of people whose *only* recommendation is that they are 'spacious in the possession of dirt'.

To a certain kind of mind, however, in Shakespeare's time and now, a king must typify the ultimate freeholder. In *III Henry VI*, it is fascinating to see how for the Yorkists the crown is not just a remedy for hurt pride, but the means to every kind of gratification of power and pleasure. 'Do but think', says Richard of Gloucester,

> How sweet a thing it is to wear a crown,
> Within whose circuit is Elysium
> And all that poets feign of bliss and joy.        (ɪ. ii. 29–31)

Behind this stagey rhetoric which imitates the rhythms of Marlowe and Greene there is a reality which Shakespeare shows in its material grossness when he makes Edward IV's first act on winning the crown an attempt to purchase Lady Grey for his mistress, the currency of the transaction being provided by her husband's alienated lands. The sharpest comment upon the Yorkists' lust for the crown, so much at variance with their legitimist claims, occurs however in the famous scene at Towton where King Henry, having been 'chid' from the battle, watches as a son speaks over the body of his father, whom he has killed:

> This man whom hand to hand I slew in fight
> May be possessed with some store of crowns;
> And I, that haply take them from him now,
> May yet ere night yield both my life and them
> To some man else, as this dead man doth me.
> Who's this? O God! it is my father's face ...   (II. v. 56–61)

A very philosophical foot soldier, one might think—but of course the dramatist's intention is to interpret the action symbolically, not to portray either character or incident realistically. The 'crown' and all that it means to the contenders is shown degraded to coinage, pillaged from a corpse by a man who may himself be dead at nightfall, and who will certainly be dead one nightfall or another. The scene is allegorically conceived, and may be primitive to some tastes, but there could be no more complete symbol of the futility of the battle for *the* crown; and the explicitness of the allegory brings the author's own authoritative comment into the play. When the unfortunate man says 'Pardon me, God, I knew not what I did!' the parallel with 'Forgive them Father, for they know not what they do', makes itself in our minds as the author no doubt intended that it should. In blind greed, a man has killed his father; ignorant, he has reneged upon the source of his being just as at the Crucifixion men killed their maker. The point of the parallel is not to identify the dead man with Christ; presumably the father has been as much of a ruffian as his son, and indeed this pageant is followed immediately by the entry of a father who has killed his son. Rather the parallel is in the absolute wrongness of the crimes, scriptural and historical, and in the ignorance of the criminals. The point of comparison is provided by deeds not persons, by actions not characters.

In the scene of York's degradation and murder (I. iv), Shakespeare had already used the same scriptural parallel to make a similar point. Worn out with fight, abandoned by his retreating army, York is pursued and surrounded by the chiefs of the Lancastrian army. They take him, like a 'cony ... in the net' (1. 62), and at Margaret's command they stand him upon a molehill. She tells him of his youngest son's murder and gives him, to wipe his tears, a napkin stained with the boy's blood. Then as a last mockery she crowns him with a paper crown.

Here also we have an image of the illusoriness of the crown York has fought for, as well as a parallel with the Crucifixion. Here too the emphasis is upon deeds rather than characters. To crown York at the point of death with a symbol of his unhappy longings is a terrible psychological cruelty. Northumberland weeps at the spectacle and, chorus-like, his words prompt the reader/spectator to a fitting response of pity and forgiveness:

> Had he been slaughter-man to all my kin,
> I should not for my life but weep with him,
> To see how inly sorrow gripes his soul. (I. iv. 169–71)

Shakespeare does not reproduce the source's explicit comparison of this scene to the Crucifixion.[2] Nonetheless the molehill, the mock crowning and the blood-stained handkerchief associate themselves inevitably with Calvary, the crown of thorns and the sponge soaked with vinegar and gall. If the scene's details are historical—and the presumption is that they are—then specific comparison is superfluous in re-enacting them. The historical characters who originally did these things did them intentionally, knowing that they needed no commentary to be 'understanded of the people'. Both in history and in the theatre York's murder is a parody of the Crucifixion, and in both cases the point is that York's killers, proudly and consciously, identify themselves with the crucifiers.

Evidently, in both the Wakefield and the Towton scenes, Shakespeare was dramatising something he took to be real evil. In the one case the characters are quite conscious of their acts, in the other less so, but the causes and effects are the same: desire of a good which is nothing but *goods*, and the hardening of the heart in its pursuit. Put that way, it sounds cold, formal, moralistic, didactic— everything Shakespeare is supposed not to be. Yet the evil of these wars exists in the source, independent of any intention Shakespeare might or might not have had. It is the given, unalterable fact at the centre of the plays' action, and it calls into being the immense, compassionate force of Shakespeare's verse:

> This cloth thou dipp'dst in blood of my sweet boy,
> And I with tears do wash the blood away.
> Keep thou the napkin and go boast of this;
> And if thou tell'st the heavy story right,

Upon my soul, the hearers will shed tears,
Yea, even my foes will shed fast-falling tears.
And say, 'Alas, it was a piteous deed!'
There, take the crown, and, with the crown, my curse.
                                        (i. iv. 157–64)

No one had written like that in English before.

With the blood-stained napkin and the mingling of the father's tears with the child's blood, Shakespeare brings out a further, pitiful meaning of the rose-symbolism. Unfamiliar today, it derives from a long devotional tradition that was still alive for many of Shakespeare's audience. Its best and, to my knowledge, most concentrated and explicit literary treatment is in a poem of Lydgate's, 'As a Midsummer Rose'. For most of this longish poem, the rose is a sign of the transitoriness of life; but then towards the end it changes into a sign of everlasting life as Lydgate brings in its Christian significance. The hidden 'sentence' of Lydgate's symbolism is that Christ is the one true knight and that the red and white of his wounds (i.e. the blood and water) are the true Christian's heraldry. Lydgate, a sensitive, pacifist monk, wrote during the troubled times that led to the wars of York and Lancaster, and in this poem, in his covert, allegorical way, he is almost certainly referring to contemporary politics. In symbolic language he describes, as an alternative to military chivalry, a suffering, pacifist Christian chivalry. The conception grows out of the patient contemplation of mutability, error and mistaken loyalty:

The remembraunce/of every famous knyght
Ground considerid/is bilt on rihtwisnesse
Race out ech quarel/that is not bilt on riht
Withoute trouthe/what vaileth hih noblesse
Lawrer of martirs/foundid on hoolynesse
Whit was mad red/ther tryumphes to discloose
The whit lillye/was ther chaast clennesse
Ther bloody suffraunce was no somyr roose

It was the roose of the bloody feeld
Roose of Iericho/that greuh in Beedlem
The five Roosys/portrayed in the sheeld
Splayed in the baneer/at Ierusalem
The sonne was clips and dirk in every rem
Whan Crist Ihesu/five wellys lyst uncloose
Toward Paradys/callyd the rede strem
Of whos five woundys/prent in your hert a roose.[3]

The connection between this symbolism and Shakespeare's in *III*
*Henry VI* is unmistakable once one associates the play's analogues
to the Crucifixion with the symbolism of the roses. In the allegorical
scene at Towton, after the entry of the son who has killed his father,
there comes a father who has killed his son, and he too is bent upon
looting the corpse when he discovers its identity. King Henry,
watching these acts, prays:

> O pity, pity, gentle heaven, pity!
> The red rose and the white are on his face . . .   (III. v. 96–7)

In these two marvellous lines, the colours' meanings echo in the
mind with a rich suggestiveness: red blood and fair flesh, signs of
youth and love, of the body's wholeness; red rose and white rose,
signs of the commonwealth's integrity, of singleness in variety; red
and white, the colours of violent death and sacrifice. Henry, standing
to one side, pointing perhaps, like the evangelist in a painting of
the Crucifixion, directs our sympathies, and no one instructed
in Christian practice can fail to supply a scriptural and liturgical
parallel. The scene will awaken the dimmest memories of such things
as the complaint from the Cross, of the Lamentations of Jeremiah:
'Is it nothing to you, all ye that pass by? Behold, and see, if there
be any sorrow like unto my sorrow.'

To return from the pitiful effect to its cause in greed for property
seems anti-climactic but, to quote another scriptural passage that
bears on the ideas Shakespeare deploys in this play, 'What shall it
profit a man if he gain the whole world and lose his own soul?' By
tracing the cause of anarchy to the desire to possess property, Shakespeare was bringing into the secular drama ideas usually associated
with the severest religious teaching. If in this first set of histories the
Yorkists are mistaken (to put it mildly) in thinking that the 'Crown'
which is the supreme symbol of the social order, the things and ideas
that comprise it, is a property to be acquired, worn, defended and
bequeathed, then naturally one looks for an alternative notion. What
is the crown? To say it is the symbol of the stage begs the question,
'What kind of state?'

Henry VI answers this question when in Act III, scene i, after
Towton he is captured by keepers. 'If thou be a king,' asks the first
keeper, 'where is thy crown?' And Henry has an answer:

> My crown is in my heart, not on my head;
> Not deck'd with diamonds and Indian stones,
> Nor to be seen. My crown is called content;
> A crown it is that seldom kings enjoy.   (ll. 62–5)

The keeper does not resist the temptation to mock the King's piety; yet ineffectual though Henry is as the head of a turbulent state, Shakespeare has taken pains to give him a theoretical, if not a practical, authority. In plays as wild as these the meaning of 'content' is worth some thought. That Henry's 'content' is Christian, not just rational and philosophical, is shown in a simple, emblematic way here and later in the Tower by his holding a prayer-book. At Towton, in the famous pastoral soliloquy (II. v. 1–54), Henry explains his 'content', and, in the midst of 'this fell war', exemplifies it. It is a question, first, of understanding one's place in time—'Lord, make me to know mine end, and the measure of my days, what it is' (*Psalms* xxxix. 4)—and, second, of putting one's days in order—'To everything there is a season, and a time to every purpose under heaven' (*Ecclesiastes* iii. 1):

> O God! methinks it were a happy life
> To be no better than a homely swain;
> To sit upon a hill, as I do now,
> To carve out dials quaintly, point by point,
> Thereby to see the minutes how they run,
> How many makes the hour full complete,
> How many hours brings about the day,
> How many days will finish up the year,
> How many years a mortal man may live.
> When this is known, then to divide the times:
> So many hours must I tend my flock,
> So many hours must I take my rest.
> So many hours must I contemplate,
> So many hours must I sport myself;
> So many days my ewes have been with young,
> So many weeks ere the poor fools will ean,
> So many years ere I shall shear the fleece.
> So minutes, hours, days, months, and years,
> Pass'd over to the end they were created,
> Would bring white hairs unto a quiet grave . . .

Work, play, contemplation and rest in their due order make the ideal life, and the harmony of life's varied acts is the outward sign of an inward harmony. The pastoral language (which shows how much there was in Shakespeare, as in Spenser and Milton, of Christian humanism) does not depict the king-as-shepherd watching his flock. Instead it suggests an idea that Shakespeare later made much of, that the lives of king and shepherd are bound together in the same order of which the true crown is the symbol.

The 'crown of content' is no object of anyone's lust for goods. Not only is it the symbol of the well-ordered kingdom that is within, it is also, in this ideal Christian politics, the symbol of the external, social kingdom too, being in both senses of the word the 'state' of our being. Possession of such a crown is a different thing from ownership. If nature is thought of as a given, providentially ordered and sustained system of being, and if men are a part of it, then who can own anything at all in freehold, whether material goods or his own soul? This question is answered in a practical way by the old conventional form of Christian wills, including the form of Shakespeare's own, in which before any bequests of property are made, the soul is bequeathed to God who has redeemed it and the body is bequeathed to the earth of which it is made.[4] The question of title, its nature and legitimacy, goes to the root of social and psychological order, especially in a culture in which personal integrity is called 'self-possession' and thereby related to the holding of property. 'Self-possession' is by now a dead metaphor, but it was once very much alive. In the three hundred years following Shakespeare's time, the tenure of property seems to have offered the nearest thing to a working definition of 'sacrament' available in so radically secular a civilisation; ownership, that is, was 'an outward and visible sign of an inward and spiritual grace', and England was dominated by the values of successful Yorks, their moral and psychological doubts resolved by title deeds.

In these early histories the Lancastrian usurpation (itself much embroiled with questions of property, as readers of *Richard II* will anticipate) has caused a general psychological disturbance that shows itself in a rage, an attempt to re-establish order by violence; and being a rage, it kills where it should cure or, in Clifford's words already quoted,

> Fear frames disorder, and disorder wounds
> Where it should guard.

So, by his middle twenties, Shakespeare had found one of his characteristic themes, the nature of the thing men call the crown; a study of usurpation is his first attempt upon the mystery of evil, the cause 'that makes these hard hearts'. Shakespeare's cause turns out to be rather different from the angry Providence of common belief. To a man living in a Christian society, Divine Providence is naturally the ultimate cause of events; but the immediate causes of events in these histories are in men themselves. Providence may punish, but it does so through men's own, consenting wills. Consequently there is always, especially in *III Henry VI*, a sense of freedom. Men choose to be what they are. They can, if they wish, be otherwise; and always, even at their worst, they have the freedom of knowledge. Evil, in short, is natural. Men are not the helpless victims either of circumstance or the supernatural. Shakespeare, like Bacon and the great Anglican divines, is anti-occultist, believing in the primacy of reason and the freedom of the will.

Therefore it seems to me quite wrong to describe these plays as 'doom-laden'. We should not mistake for predestination the retrospective ordering of events into a plot. Even the metaphor of diabolic interference is only a metaphor. There are (except for *I Henry VI*, v. iii) no demons, furies or destinies. 'Madness' may be *like* diabolic possession, but is not identical with it. The characters are free of everything except the sickness that they can cure, and the pity and the horror of *III Henry VI* arise from acts which are a conscious and continuous violence against men's better natures.

Shakespeare repeatedly makes a point of this. 'Bloody Clifford', when he shuts his ears to the plea, 'Murder not this innocent child', is no happy killer, not even a stage monster. Bent upon revenging his father's death, he sees himself as a victim:

> The sight of any of the house of York
> Is as a fury to torment my soul;
> And till I root out their accursed line
> And leave not one alive, I live in hell.   (i. iii. 30–3)

Clifford's first reply to Rutland shows that the spirit in him is still alive: 'In vain thou speak'st, poor boy; my father's blood/Hath stopp'd the passage where thy words should enter' (ll. 21–2). Right up to the murder it seems possible that Clifford might relent. When Rutland's 'Thou hast no cause' draws from him the cry, 'No cause! Thy father slew my father; therefore die', the violent orderliness of his illogicality shows how much Clifford's cruelty is the effect of the conscious will. Not surprisingly, when he is dying in the Yorkist victory at Towton and his fierce will is broken, his last words are of light, order, mercy and pity:

> Here burns my candle out; ay, here it dies,
> Which, whiles it lasted, gave King Henry light. . . .
> And, Henry, hadst thou sway'd as kings should do,
> Or as thy father and his father did,
> Giving no ground unto the house of York,
> They never then had sprung like summer flies;
> I and ten thousand in this luckless realm
> Had left no mourning widows for our death;

> And thou this day hadst kept thy chair in peace. . . .
> Bootless are plaints, and cureless are my wounds.
> No way to fly, nor strength to hold out flight.
> The foe is merciless, and will not pity,
> For at their hands I have deserv'd no pity.   (II. vi. 1–26)

Even Margaret, 'she-wolf of France', who shares in the pitiless killing of Gloucester and the tormenting of York, is brought by misfortune and solicitude for her son and her husband to understand events more clearly. When she speaks to her soldiers before Tewkesbury she has the authority of a chorus:

>                Henry, your sovereign,
> Is prisoner to the foe; his state usurp'd,
> His realm a slaughter-house, his subjects slain,
> His statutes cancell'd, and his treasure spent;
> And yonder is the wolf that makes this spoil.   (v. iv. 76–80)

Tewkesbury, the last battle, is the worst. Edward IV promises that the Lancastrian Prince of Wales will not be killed, but when the Prince, instead of submitting, twits the Yorkist brothers ('Lascivious Edward, and thou perjur'd George,/and thou mis-shapen Dick'), all three of them stab him. For all its horror, Rutland's murder was the revenge of a tormented man; this is sudden, savage violence that breaks Margaret's heart:

> Butchers and villains! bloody cannibals!
> How sweet a plant have you untimely cropp'd!
> You have no children, butchers! if you had,
> The thought of them would have stirr'd up remorse.   (v. v. 61–4)

York's sons are gangsters, habitual criminals. Even so Edward, the best of the three, restrains Richard as he moves to stab Margaret too: 'Hold, Richard, hold; for we have done too much.' Something of mind and conscience still live in Edward if not in Richard, whose departure for London 'to make a bloody supper in the Tower' gives point to Margaret's cry, 'Bloody cannibals!' At the end, as Edward's curious remark 'He's sudden if a thing comes in his head' suggests, Richard like other great criminals is virtually mad, a person of diminished moral responsibility: but his first soliloquy (III. ii. 124–95) shows even Richard as a man whose evil originates in suffering and whose crimes, like his father's rebellion, are caused by his longing for the tranquillity promised by the crown. Until that soliloquy Richard has been shown as an ironic soldier; nothing prepares us for the sudden passion of this long speech that suggests possibilities in the character that Shakespeare, rapidly making Richard into an absolute villain, chose not to follow—perhaps because the result might have been too much a repetition of his father's character, more probably because it would have produced a Richard who could not be fitted into the planned scheme of the histories.

Edward's wooing of Lady Grey sets Richard off, angering the politician in him who aims at the throne, as well as the hunchback foresworn by love 'in [his] mother's womb'. His confession—

> Why, I can smile, and murder whiles I smile. . . .
> I can add colours to the chameleon,
> Change shapes with Proteus for advantages,
> And set the murderous Machiavel to school

—is a preliminary version of the stage monster of *Richard III*; but his understanding of his motives and his knowledge of the ultimate futility of his ambition reveal a character genuinely, if criminally, human:

> Why, then, I do but dream on sovereignty,
> Like one that stands upon a promontory
> And spies a far-off shore where he would tread,
> Wishing his foot were equal with his eye,
> And chides the sea that sunders him from thence,
> Saying, he'll lade it dry to have his way.
> So do I wish the crown, being so far off;
> And so I chide the means that keeps me from it;
> And so I say, I'll cut the causes off,
> Flattering me with impossibilities.
> My eye's too quick, my heart o'erweens too much,
> Unless my hand and strength could equal them.
>                                         (III. ii. 134–45)

The man standing on a promontory opposing his will to the infinity of the sea will recur in Shakespeare, as will the vain intention of matching the hand's strength to the heart's bottomless pride. These metaphors also reveal the cause of pride as well as its character. They express a refusal to accept the conditions of life, and a rebellion against nature; they put nature in the role of tyrant and the rebel in the role of the suffering victim:

> And I,—like one lost in a thorny wood,
> That rends the thorns and is rent with the thorns,

> Seeking a way and straying from the way,
> Not knowing how to find the open air
> But toiling desperately to find it out,—
> Torment myself to catch the English crown;
> And from that torment I will free myself
> Or hew my way out with a bloody axe.   (ll. 174–81)

To hew one's way out, we notice, is not the same as to free oneself. The old, moving figure of a man lost in a wood, a normal expression of lost direction and bewilderment, is also an expression of claustrophobia and suffocation, a recurrent Shakespearean image for discontented ambition. Ambition is so often 'choking' in Shakespeare's plays that after a time one hardly notices it any more than one notices the breathing of fresh air as an image of its opposite. This toiling, self-tormented cripple, lost, forsworn by love, whose heaven it is to dream upon a crown, is potentially a far more interesting study than the hero of *Richard III*. This is not because he is more 'human' in any vaguely sentimental sense, but because like all the characters of *III Henry VI*, he has the freedom of self-knowledge and choice.

The note of pain is in Richard's voice to the end of the play. As he murders Henry, he deludes himself with the notion that he is the agent of some dark justice: 'For this, amongst the rest, was I ordained' (v. vi. 58), and he takes up again the theme of his separateness and isolation:

> Then, since the heavens have shap'd my body so,
> Let hell make crook'd my mind to answer it.
> I have no brother, I am like no brother;
> And this word 'love', which greybeards call divine,
> Be resident in men like one another
> And not in me. I am myself alone.   (ll. 78–83)

Richard feels superior to others, but at the same time he also feels badly done to, and this weird combination of contradictory feelings, like his determinism and his egoism, are signs that Richard is a 'modern' character, one of the first in a long line. The historians allowed no free will to their Richard because otherwise the story made no psychological sense. The dramatist's Richard deprives himself of freedom by his own choice. The 'heavens' which he claims have ordained him to evil are a figment of his own solipsist imagination, the projection of his own will, put out at interest and returning with increase. His cry, 'I have no brother', is an almost comical violence against fact, and its near-repetition, 'I am like no brother', even as it seems to be an attempt to turn repetition into something like reason, is, like Clifford's 'Thy father slew my father', a case of the passionate will at war with the mind, coercing reality into the shape of its own rage. If Richard of Gloucester is anything in *III Henry VI*, he is a brother and has brothers. In this detail the play is what it has been throughout, a dramatisation of violence against the facts of life, against what the Elizabethans meant by Nature with a capital N. The death of the pitiful King is the attempted murder of pity itself by one who, in claiming to have neither pity, love nor fear, makes himself an outlaw to the human family, and the object of *our* pity as well as our horror. Moreover, he knows it: 'I am myself alone.'

The recurrent natural imagery that so many critics have noticed in these plays has its essential place in the poetic argument. Such details as the smallest worm that turns, being trodden on, the doves that peck in safeguard of their brood (II. ii. 17–18), or that peck the falcon's piercing talons (I. iv. 41), the harmless sheep yielding its throat to the butcher (v. vi. 8–9) and the trembling lamb environed with wolves (I. i. 242) are more than *exempla* or expressions of feeling, being images of the thing itself that is at stake. More powerful than these, however, because it expresses the cause of the play's suffering, is the iterated image of the angry sea. A figure for chaos unruled and unrulable, the sea brings into Shakespeare and into our literature the idea of an infinity inimical to human life, whose spaces are not only in the external universe but in the soul. The battle of Towton 'sways ... like a mighty sea', and at Wakefield the Lancastrian forces are 'over-matching waves'; but Richard, looking in imagination from his promontory and chiding the sea that sunders him from the far-off shore, is himself that intervenient sea, an 'envious gulf' that swallows up life, or with his brothers he is, as Margaret says, one of the sea's dangers:

> And what is Edward but a ruthless sea?
> What Clarence but a quicksand of deceit?
> And Richard but a ragged fatal rock?   (v. iv. 25–7)

In fact, remembering Richard's 'bloody supper' in the Tower, we can look forward to *King Lear* and Albany's prophecy that, 'It will come,/Humanity must perforce prey on itself,/Like monsters of the deep' (*King Lear*, IV. ii. 48–50).

If my reading of these plays is at all true, then the disorder that threatens in Shakespeare's histories, although mediated by historical events, is a profounder anarchy than anything political. There is an impendent war in nature that threatens inundation of everything, visible and invisible. The Wars of the Roses take shape as pre-figurings of total war—political and external; psychological and in-ternal; and, because of the religious and symbolic frame of reference, metaphysical and cosmic. There could hardly be a more eloquent image of the struggle between order, wholeness, fullness and strength on one hand, and an unshaped, irresistible dynamism on the other than York's portrayal of the battle of Wakefield:

> With this we charg'd again; but, out, alas!
> We budg'd again; as I have seen a swan
> With bootless labour swim against the tide
> And spend her strength with over-matching waves.
>
> (I. iv. 18–21)

This image inevitably reminds a literary-minded reader of Yeats's swan afloat on a darkening flood, and the reference connects the wars that were for each poet archetypal: Troy and the Roses, both fought for a delusive prize. In Shakespeare, however, there is no glorifi-cation of violence. Rather the scale of his conception and his treat-ment of the wars' detail bring him closer to Wilfred Owen than to any other modern poet. As Owen said of his own work, 'The poetry is in the pity.'

*    *    *

These early plays have many faults, among them too much emblem-atic spectacle and too many 'choric' speeches conveying information the dramatist has not learned to embody in deeds and character. The language is often surprisingly pedantic, with too much scriptural and classical allusion and a tendency not to leave well alone, but to develop ideas by elaborate rhetoric into prettiness and show. (Yeats diagnosed a similar fault in Byron's style, praising the energetic syn-tax but observing how often the energy tailed off into what he called a 'mind-created' substitution for the original force.[5] Henry's 'The red rose and the white are on his face' is fine, but the three-line commentary on its meaning that follows is as unnecessary as it is obvious and only pretty. The young Shakespeare does this too often; but, as always with genius, weakness is strength unshaped. The plays' faults derive from abundance, energy and confidence.

Their most striking quality is the steady growth in them of in-tellectual and poetic strength. We are in the presence of a mind to which language and gesture are the immediate means of under-standing. The theatre is not so much his medium of expression into which he translates his material, as the means through which he finds its true nature. His plays are experimental in the true sense of the word and, in their general atmosphere, sceptical. This is especially so of the histories, in which so much of the material is given, more or less fixed. Enactment on stage tests material and theory alike, and the great theme of the Shakespearean drama emerges as the dramatisation of truth and falsehood, the attempt to distinguish between what seems to be, what is said to be and what is.

There could hardly be anything more interesting to the reader of Shakespeare than to watch him, at the outset of his career, undertaking to change into the forms of his art the material of Tudor history which may, after all, be one of the biggest lies in English history. Of Shakespeare's political sympathies we know nothing directly. No doubt when he began the histories he had little knowledge of the past beyond what he had heard in talk and read in the authorities that we would call 'standard'. We know however that quite early on he began to consult less accessible sources,[6] and we also know that when he came to deal with the climax of the Tudors' version of the past, putting the monster-king Richard III on the stage, he turned the character into an actor and a master of illusion. Presumably, he decided there was no other way to do it.

# PART TWO

# The State, the Soul
# and Legitimacy

# 4. The Tragedy of Richard III

As our reading of *Henry VI* has shown, the imaginative drift of the plays, if we consider them as works of art, is towards a tragic view of the history they narrate. As a set of publicly performed plays, however, they had to end happily with the coming of the Tudor saviour. In a similar way the second tetralogy, which seems aesthetically to require a dark, inconclusive ending, turns into a happy triumph with the death of Falstaff and the transformation of the Prince. In both sets of plays conflicts that Shakespeare had traced to causes in the nature of character and society are resolved by something tantamount to divine intervention, and the result, however flattering to national self-esteem or effective in the theatre, leaves a good many questions unanswered. The problem is not that such interventions never occur but that, if they do, a dramatist writing for a fundamentally secular theatre will be hard pressed to represent them convincingly. In both *Richard III* and *Henry V*, goodness and national self-interest coincide and triumph but only after a good deal of moral simplification.

*Richard III* especially is a brilliant triumph of theatricality over nature. The title role has been a star part for actors so long, and the play in consequence so frequently performed, that there must always have been many spectators, perhaps a majority of its audiences, who did not know it was the last of a series. Such spectators cannot have thought the play a history in quite the same way that *Richard II* is a history. Unlike the other histories, it contains almost nothing of normal, workaday historical fact (even its one battle has a procession of midnight ghosts for prelude), and its king is more a study of malign artistry than of politics. With all the other histories one feels in some way the limiting force of historical fact on the writer's invention; but *Richard III* seems unlimited by fact or probability. The result is less a history than a melodramatic fantasy, taking historical events and persons as the hooks on which to hang its fiction.

In some ways the play returns to the methods of *I Henry VI*. The fundamental idea, in this case Richard's villainy, is taken for granted, as were the diabolism of Joan of Arc and the quarrelling of the

nobles in the earlier work. Similarly the dramatist uses theatrical
rhetoric to persuade his audience of the effectiveness of his a priori
fictions. Queen Margaret is kept in England, slily lurking about the
confines (IV. iv. 3), so that she may join the other mourning women
in proving by their lamentations and curses the truth of the play's
horrors. Meanwhile the dramatist either evades essential questions
of motive or, meeting them head on, takes our breath away by
showing us the impossible taking place before our eyes. The Duke
of Buckingham's assistance in Richard's usurpation is in the sources
and the play, but Shakespeare gives no hint of his motive. Buckingham changes from an apparently well-meaning man into a cons-
pirator in five evasive lines at the end of Act II, scene ii, where we
learn that he and Richard are already in league: 'For, by the way,
I'll sort occasion,/As index to the story we late talk'd of,/To part
the Queen's proud kindred from the Prince.' One could have spared
some of the women's wailings to know why 'princely Buckingham'
(I. iii. 280, II. i. 29) chose despite Margaret's warning (I. iii. 289) to
ally himself to the 'bunch-back'd toad' (I. iii. 246). Evidently Richard
was not a toad to Buckingham, or Buckingham was less princely
than he seemed to Margaret and Edward, but either way the
question of Buckingham's motive could not have been convincingly
settled without some damage to the play's premise: that Richard
is wholly villainous.

Where the motive is essential to the fiction Shakespeare can over-
ride it with Olympian impudence. It is a matter of fact that Richard
of Gloucester married Anne Neville, daughter of Warwick the King-
maker, slain by the Yorkists at Barnet. She was the widow of Prince
Edward of Wales and daughter-in-law to Henry VI, both of whom,
according to the sources, Gloucester killed with his own hand.
Shakespeare chose not merely to mention Anne's peculiar marriage
to her husband's and father-in-law's murderer, but to invent a two-
hundred-line scene in which Richard woos her in the presence of
Henry's bleeding corpse. This is one of those scenes where, if the
audience has not already recognised Shakespeare's confidence in his
mastery of the theatre, the writer himself draws attention to it. He
does this by having Richard describe the first part of his conversation
with Anne as 'this keen encounter of our wits' (I. ii. 115) and by
ending the scene with Richard's famous rhetorical question:

> Was ever woman in this humour woo'd?
> Was ever woman in this humour won?

The implied answer—'Never, outside of a theatre'—puts us right
where Shakespeare wants us, in the palm of his hand, and casts us

in the role of his accomplices. He delighted in theatrical conjuring tricks to the end of his career. This one has its parallel in two rhetorical rules as old as the art of lying: never expose the weakness of your case by defending the indefensible, and a bold argument on weak grounds is better than a weak argument on strong ones.

In the case of Buckingham's behaviour, if our attention were once drawn to the lack of motive we would consider it a weakness in a play about political events. As it is, our deductive powers are sufficiently occupied by the narrative. By the time we have understood that a conspiracy is afoot and that Buckingham is part of it, there is a new scene (II. iii) upon the stage showing anxious citizens commenting upon the course of events; and like all such scenes in Shakespeare, it makes no sense unless its audience pays the closest attention. We therefore come to take Buckingham's role in the usurpation quite for granted; either we knew the story all along and felt no need to question the narrative, or being, like all audiences, fundamentally modest, and having succeeded in deducing the story from the stage evidence given us, we see no reason to be difficult if more knowing heads about us go unscratched. In fact, like people bemused by a procession of rabbits from a conjurer's hat, we have seen what we were meant to see, have not asked to see what we were not meant to see, and are on the whole happy and satisfied.

Nonetheless, as the sage said, 'Politics ain't bean-bag', and a critical spectator would seize on the omission of Buckingham's motive as a flaw in the play's case against Richard. Where love, marriage and women are the theme, however, ancient prejudice allows that reason, even decency, need have no place in the story. So Shakespeare shows at the outset Richard's triumph over a woman's weakness, and we accept the monster's mastery as proven, settling ourselves comfortably to four more acts of it. The trick works because of another Shakespearean invention, namely Richard's characterisation as a sardonic actor of his own scenarios. By making this idea the basis of the play, Shakespeare was able to stage the wholly villainous character he found in his sources, setting himself the challenge of finding a mastery of his own to match his villain's. To do this he had to drop for the time being the Richard whose inward being surfaced in the speeches of *III Henry VI*, resuming him only at the end after his visitations by the ghosts before Bosworth: 'I shall despair. There is no creature loves me' (v. iii. 200). Until then the actor-king's confidence fails only when men refuse to perform in his inventions, when Buckingham hesitates over the murder of the princes or when, with Richmond's landing, the control of events begins to pass from him. Yet even in this latter part of the play, when he begins to be troubled by insecurity, Richard can persuade the Queen-Mother whose boys he has killed to agree to his marriage with her daughter; and when she yields to his arguments he can dismiss her from his mind with, 'Relenting fool, and shallow, changing woman!' (IV. iv. 431). True, we hear briefly from Anne that his sleep is disturbed by 'timorous dreams' (IV. i. 85), but any such inner life is kept hidden from the King's own knowledge.

Two ideas underlie the making of Richard into an actor: the ancient notion of the devil as the ape of God, father of lies, and practical joker; and the modern one of the Machiavellian politician, cool, interesting and ruthless, shaping events to his own ends. In both cases the author of an evil is considered to be separate from the community of his victims, who suffer it. The devil of course is simply not human by definition. The Machiavellian is supposed to operate on the assumption that the will only is real, and that bonds of sympathetic feeling in any of their forms are just sentimental fictions for the strong to exploit. As theories of evil both those notions are attractive because of their simplicity. They reduce the complexity of events to a single cause and at the same time they flatter mankind's self-esteem. If the cause of evil is diabolic, it is other than human and so no part of our responsibility; at the same time it is evidence that attention, of a kind, is being paid to us. If however the cause of evil is said to be the Machiavellian will, then it also offers us the titillating possibility of being involved with something beyond the ordinarily human which, while it frightens, also delights by suggesting to us that mastery can be had, for a price. Further, since both notions trace suffering to a symbolic or figurative cause (what after all do such words as 'devil' or 'will' mean?), they hide the truth even as they seem to reveal it. They are a perfect form of the conspiratorial theory of history and potentially they can explain anything. In this connection it is interesting that Richard the diabolic Machiavellian has his greatest triumphs in those incidents which are the most unlikely, the wooing of Anne, the tricking of Clarence and the persuading of Queen Elizabeth. But why bother with devils and Machiavels unless events are inexplicable without them?

The Tudor story of Richard III is largely fabrication, and herein lies the reason for the play's separateness from its predecessors. The dramatist had to make incredible villainies credible. In *Henry VI* dissension and its attendant crimes are traced to family pride and dynastic ambition. The plays show the perversion of natural feelings, and in doing so agree with the classic understanding of evil, that it is perverted good. In *Richard III*, though, we are supposed to see the very principle of criminality and tyranny born as a child of the Plantagenets. It is one thing to speak of dissension figuratively as 'breeding', but we know we can't breed a family for evil as we breed prize bulls. The infliction of Richard upon England, if taken as fact, can only be a case of interference by some Providential agency in the natural historical process; and whether Shakespeare believed in the possibility of such interference or not, as dramatic material it is at odds with the interest in character and natural causes he had already shown in *Henry VI*.

In *III Henry VI* the natural and the extra-natural Richard exist side by side, but the poetic strength is all on the side of the natural man. He is a dangerous criminal type but like Macbeth he is recognisably human. The extra-natural Richard on the other hand is the only possible author of the outrageous villainies fathered upon him by tradition and the dramatist; and in *Richard III* Shakespeare, forced by his material, dramatises its prodigious fictions at the moment of their invention by an actor of irrepressible, exuberant genius. The implication, as we catch our breath, is that if we will believe this, we will believe anything. And so we will—inside a theatre. But the spectator who realises that between the first soliloquy and the coming of retribution in Act IV Richard speaks hardly a word that is not part of a lie will doubt the reality of the man supposed to be animating the actor. Richard's 'I am I' has a certain truth to it in its circularity. He is that and nothing more, a fiction begetting fictions.

Among the histories *Richard III* is the least historical play, not so much because of its falsification and disordering of events (in which *King John* is a rival to it), but because of its open-eyed falsification of nature. That Shakespeare's Richard should have been so long believed in as a portrait of a man is a sign of people's appetite for prodigies and marvels. As Paul Murray Kendall says of Gairdner's *History of Richard III*, 'What is astounding . . . is not so much that Gairdner supposes the sensational protagonist of *Richard III* to be a portrait of the real Richard, but that he supposes it to be, in any way, the portrait of a human being.'[1] In considering the lifelikeness of Shakespeare's Richard it is best to resist the temptation to draw historical parallels and find large, wide-ranging relevances. *Richard III* is Shakespeare's solution to an artistic problem set by the sources and the circumstances of its writing. Whether the solution is satisfactory or not is a question that will always be debatable; but although there is no knowing what kind of play Shakespeare would have written about Stalin, Hitler, Gilles de Rais, the original Count Dracula or any other candidate for monstrosity, ancient or modern, it seems to me that *Richard III* is implicitly (whether intentionally or unintentionally) an exposure of the falseness of the Tudor myth. Put to the test of the dramaturgy that developed in *Henry VI*, the Tudor version of Richard III's character could survive only by being made into a completely theatrical fiction. At Bosworth Field Henry of Richmond killed the best actor in England.

The knowledge derived from the ordinary experience of daily human life is a touchstone that will always expose the falsehoods on which ideological, propagandist literature is based. But although it may be a pack of lies such literature can have, in fact for many people always does have, a considerable aesthetic and emotional appeal. Consequently the touchstone is seldom applied. In the case of *Richard III*, if we allow ourselves the luxury of a wholly aesthetic judgement, we will praise the play very highly. As sustained theatrical bravura it could hardly be surpassed. Richard's inventiveness is equal to his boasts. Nothing he does, and almost nothing he is, is without some precedent in *Henry VI*; but if, for the sake of our pleasure in the play, we admit the belief that a diabolic agency underlying all those tragic events is now being revealed in proper person, then the way the dramatist admits us, through Richard's soliloquies and trickeries, into the secrets of an inhuman destructiveness is as thrilling as the hypothesis requires. If some absolute principle has power, however limited, over human affairs, then here it is in all its inhumanity: scheming, inventive, shameless and swift in action, enraged and helpless when the limit to its activity is drawn. As soon as one refers the play to a world outside the theatre the illusion is no more compelling than a Punch and Judy show. Those choric women lamenting the whole sequence of events as types and prefigurings of the last horror of Crookback's rule are shown for the rhetorical props they are, and we see Richard himself as just an actor with a hump on his shoulder, a limp, an arm dangling withered at his side, delighting the crowd with his mops and mows. Few critics have chosen to think of the play away from the theatre, but Dr Johnson is one of them:

> This is one of the most celebrated of our author's performances; yet I know not whether it has not happened to him as to others, to be praised most when praise is not most deserved. That this play has scenes noble in themselves, and very well contrived to strike in the exhibition, cannot be denied. But some parts are trifling, others shocking, and some improbable.[2]

Within the theatre Dr Johnson's objections will not arise unless one is determined, like a man keeping his hand on his wallet in a crowd, not to be taken advantage of. John Dover Wilson has gone so far as to say that if such objections arise at all, this is because of our modern one-track-mindedness, which confuses morals and aesthetics and imposes its rigid categories upon the 'myriad-minded-

ness' of our ancestors.[3] He thinks the critical difficulty arises because
Richard is monstrous and enjoyable at the same time and remarks
that there was nothing novel for an Elizabethan audience 'in con-
demning on moral grounds a character thoroughly enjoyable on
aesthetic ones'. This difficulty, which has given rise to the writing
of thousands of pages justifying our enjoyment of Falstaff, Macbeth,
Iago and indeed just about every notable rascal in literature, is not
really to the point of the difficulty with Richard III. The trouble
there, although it involves a conflict in one's mind between aesthetic
and moral pleasure, does not arise out of Richard's character, but
out of the play's action, which is the immediate cause of Richard's
character. *Richard III* is a history, not a moral interlude or a mystery
play. Its characters are not allegories or symbolic types (such as
Herod or the Vice), but imitations of men and women who lived. Its
subject is a series of events in the history of a real country. That
being so, if the action can only be 'justified' at the expense of the
characters' humanity, then something is seriously wrong; and when
we observe that the play's psychology and interpretation of the
meaning of events are regressions from the promise of *III Henry VI*
to the power-theatrics of *I Henry VI*, then we have further reason
to question its success, the way it has held our attention, aroused our
wonder and delight.

In *Richard III* art triumphs at the expense of humane truth. Never
again did Shakespeare fit history into so simplistic a moral scheme.
Meanwhile he took such opportunities of pursuing his characteristic
themes as the materials allowed, producing as he did so analyses of
character and politics which, if applied generally to the play's subject, would have led to a revaluation of Richard's character and
motives.

\*        \*        \*

Thought and conscience enter the play in the scene of Clarence's
dream and murder (i. iv), and are indeed confined to the scene as
Clarence is confined to the Tower. A pragmatic director would
probably cut the scene heavily. Clarence was a minor character in
*III Henry VI*, which dealt briefly with his double perjury (he broke
faith with his brother Edward, then with Warwick and Margaret)
and showed him taking part in the stabbing of Prince Edward at
Tewkesbury. An audience seeing *Richard III* alone can have very
little notion of Clarence's identity, and even one that had watched
the other play would find Richard's 'simple plain' Clarence a surprising character. It seems that in the situation of Clarence Shakespeare saw a chance to bring into the play matter of a kind excluded
from its main plot, and his 'invention' of Clarence for that purpose
anticipates such wholesale inventions as Falconbridge and Falstaff.

One sympathises with the director and his puzzled audience, but in Clarence, the man in prison awaiting death, we have a continuation of the best of *Henry VI* and a glimmering of the play that Shakespeare, had he been free of the Chronicles and reasons of state, might have written about the last Plantagenet and the coming of the Tudors.

In his dream, Clarence has 'broken from the Tower' in company with his brother Richard, and they are 'embark'd to cross to Burgundy'; but we soon feel that his escape is fom England and the past as well as from the Tower. As he and his brother 'walk upon the hatches', they look 'toward England,/And [cite] up a thousand heavy times/During the wars of York and Lancaster/That [have] befall'n [them].' The dream rehearses real escapes that the brothers have had, looks forward to a last escape and, with a feeling of weariness and finality, looks back over the 'thousand heavy times' of the long wars. The absence of political feeling is remarkable in view of what we know from Richard of the brothers' relationship. Although he 'tempts' his brother to walk the hatches, Richard is sharing his experience as well as his memories of old and now-remote battles. In a way Clarence's dream is an answer to Richard's words in *III Henry VI*, 'I have no brother'; but then Richard stumbles and strikes Clarence 'that thought to stay him, overboard/ Into the tumbling billows of the main.' A sad succession of confused events could not be more limpidly, pitifully suggested. Now Clarence, fallen into the stormy sea, experiences in his dream the truth implied by Richard when he dreamed of sovereignty 'Like one that stands upon a promontory', and described himself as 'One lost in a thorny wood ... Not knowing how to find the open air.' Undersea, Clarence is in a suffocating place of treasures unattainable and always lost, a world of life-in-death:

> Methoughts I saw a thousand fearful wrecks,
> A thousand men that fishes gnaw'd upon,
> Wedges of gold, great anchors, heaps of pearl,
> Inestimable stones, unvalued jewels,
> All scatt'red in the bottom of the sea.
> Some lay in dead men's skulls; and, in the holes
> Where eyes did once inhabit, there were crept,
> As 'twere in scorn of eyes, reflecting gems,
> That woo'd the slimy bottom of the deep
> And mock'd the dead bones that lay scatt'red by.

The ancient idea of the sea as another world, the mirror image of our own where, in Marvell's line, 'each kind/Does straight its own resemblance find', enters here to give Clarence in poetic form a vision of the reality of his own and his brother's ambitions. No overt moral enters the lines because their truth is deeper than moral: the undersea world has a ghastly beauty, perfectly caught in the image of jewels 'where eyes did once inhabit'. The image, which recurs in Shakespeare, plays on the paradox that 'In the midst of life we are in death.' Here are a beauty, stillness, security, and changelessness that 'mock the dead bones'; but, like Spenser's Bower of Bliss and House of Busirane, these jewelled eyes also mock the living. The whole vision intimates a living death:

> And often did I strive
> To yield the ghost; but still the envious flood
> Stopp'd in my soul and would not let it forth
> To find the empty, vast, and wand'ring air,
> But smother'd it within my panting bulk,
> Who almost burst to belch it in the sea.

Clarence's first dream vision, which ends here, is a lyrical epitome of the strongest themes of *II* and *III Henry VI*: loss of life in the quest for delusive treasures and the portrayal of ambition as the pursuit of death. So far in the dream, Clarence's soul has been calm in itself though oppressed by its sea-suffocation; but now, in the second dream, 'the tempest to my soul' begins. It seems to Clarence that he has died, crossed over Styx into Hades, where the wraiths of the two men he had wronged in the wars narrated in *III Henry VI* accost him:

> The first that there did greet my stranger soul
> Was my great father-in-law, renowned Warwick,
> Who spake aloud, 'What scourge for perjury
> Can this dark monarchy afford false Clarence?'
> And so he vanish'd. Then came wand'ring by
> A shadow like an angel, with bright hair
> Dabbl'd in blood; and he shriek'd out aloud,
> 'Clarence is come; false, fleeting, perjur'd Clarence,
> That stabb'd me in the field by Tewksbury . . .'

Naturally we recall Homer, Vergil and Dante in reading these lines and, short though the passage is, Shakespeare can meet the comparison. The three stages of Clarence's dream, beginning as an escape from everything 'England' means of present confinement and past memories, take the dreamer into an ultimate prison of deeds inescapably committed. The character who narrates the dream has

his own past to acknowledge, but the imagery of his journey is the
continuation in this play of imagery that in the preceding play was
attached to his brother Richard. Clarence's dream is, potentially,
Richard of Gloucester's as well as nearly every other character's in
these histories. The speech has therefore great general significance,
and as Clarence sleeps again (perhaps to dream again), watched over
by the sympathetic keeper whose curiosity and horror at Clarence's
revelations are the echo to our thoughts, Shakespeare brings in the
Lieutenant of the Tower to speak eight lines of comment upon what
we have just heard. He has not heard Clarence speak. The only real
motive for his words is the author's concentration upon his subject:

> Sorrow breaks seasons and reposing hours,
> Makes the night morning and the noon-tide night.
> Princes have but their titles for their glories,
> An outward honour for an inward toil;
> And for unfelt imaginations
> They often feel a world of restless cares,
> So that between their titles and low name
> There's nothing differs but the outward fame.

It would be easy to take this as commonplace or as prosy comment
on Clarence's habit of sleeping during the daytime; but 'unfelt
imaginations' refers not to the dream, which was most dreadfully
felt as suffocation and noise, but to 'titles' and 'glories', especially
the crown, the 'outward honour' rather than the inward condition
that Henry VI describes. Instead of Henry's crown of content, there
is 'inward toil', i.e. mental suffering, rewarded by the 'outward
honour' which conceals it; but the discord between the inner and
the outer being shows in 'sorrow' and its 'breaking of seasons'. The
applicability of Brakenbury's words to Clarence's condition raises
them beyond the commonplace. The dream shows what 'inward toil'
can be, as it also shows, by the continued presence of the past, the
cause of sorrow and the breaking of seasons:

> If all time is eternally present
> All time is unredeemable.

*     *     *

Sir Francis Walsingham, justifying Elizabeth's religious policy, wrote
to a correspondent that she had no liking 'to make windows in men's
hearts and secret thoughts'. She was prepared, it seems, to accept
what she and her ministers called an 'outward conformity' and a
correspondingly correct line of behaviour. Knowing what her difficulties were, some of them, we can admire her reticence; but we

can also reflect that, like any ruler forbidding certain forms of dissent, she was asking many of her people to live divided lives. To extend her metaphor a little, if the soul's windows are closed so that the policeman is not looking in, then the soul is not looking out much either. If then the state thrives at the soul's expense, what kind of thing is the state, and what is the quality of its order? Whatever we now mean by 'soul' Queen Elizabeth will have taken for granted, along with most of her subjects, that the soul was the only real thing about a man. Her metaphor implies that she thought of it as a place where things happen, just as they happen in the market-place or the parliament house. Markets and parliament houses have to be made, however, and for all their sticks-and-stones actuality they are only symbols of the causes of their making; but the soul, according to the Queen's metaphor, would be the original, given place, containing in itself all the other places.

The ramifications of Elizabeth's metaphor, of which she was by no means the inventor or sole user, are considerable. Donne's love poems alone supply material for a volume's commentary, and most of their figures are common enough in Renaissance literature to be called conventional: the soul as a prince ruling his little empire, the equivalence between the little individual world and the great general one, the eye as a window, and tears as raindrops. But of all the Elizabethans, few entered into the place of the soul as Shakespeare did. He may even have discovered it, as Columbus discovered America, in the sense that he found it to be real; he certainly found that, like America, it is an immense place, and a theatre of enormously significant actions.

It is worth dwelling a little therefore on some of the ramifications of rather hackneyed material in order to recover something of the feelings that must have accompanied it when it was quite new and betokened a changed perspective. A renewed feeling for the size and variety of the Elizabethan inner world is a corrective, for instance, to the nostalgia in much present-day scholarship that emphasises the orderliness of the Elizabethan 'world picture', dwelling upon its symmetry and especially its use of similes, analogies and correspondences. The actual orderliness of the Elizabethan world was in inverse proportion to the extent men demonstrated it and theorised upon it. When Brutus speaks of man as 'a little kingdom', our interest is surely not in the analogy itself, nor is there anything particularly comforting or picturesque in the idea. Our interest is caught by the feeling the image conveys of the soul's magnitude and unruliness; it becomes a fascinating, interesting and even dangerous place to us.

Such a direction of interest to the inner life bespeaks some dissatisfaction with the relation of the inner to the outer world, is evidence of the divided life that we more portentously call alienation. In this context the significance of Clarence's dream, apart from its relationship to the themes of the histories, is that it is Shakespeare's first extended voyage into the soul. A man sleeps, and while the daily world of local time and place continues about him, we know that he is in a place where distinctions of past and present, of here and there, lose point because through all that place's immensity the only continuing reality is the unforgiven, perhaps unforgivable act that makes the dreamer the man he is. No matter what name one uses in thinking of that place—hell, purgatory, death, space—it is where the final judgement takes place of what the man esentially is. But the place that Clarence is in is a place that is in Clarence. We feel not just the portentousness of the experience, but the unfathomable extent of its setting.

\*     \*     \*

With the entry upon the scene of the two murderers, the themes of self-knowledge, conscience, justice and redemption that arise naturally to our minds out of the dream's horrors take a grotesque and pathetic turn. As a comic pair the murderers are made in the forms of a long and still living tradition—the roles might even have been written for Bud Abbott and Lou Costello in their prime—and Shakespeare's bringing of them on to the stage is an example of the quality in his work which classicists called barbaric and which the wilder Romantics imitated. There is a Mephistophelean gaiety about the way Shakespeare uses a pair of clowns to debate the play's most serious themes.

An off-handed joke about Judgement Day sets the second murderer's conscience working, to his fellow's disgust and his own dismay:

> I'll not meddle with it; it is a dangerous thing; it makes a man a coward. A man cannot steal but it accuseth him; a man cannot swear but it checks him; a man cannot lie with his neighbour's wife but it detects him. 'Tis a blushing shamefac'd spirit that mutinies in a man's bosom. It fills a man full of obstacles. It made me once restore a purse of gold that by chance I found. It beggars any man that keeps it. . . .

This hired murderer's earnest prosecution of conscience, delivered *sotto voce* in tones of self-pity in the presence of his sleeping victim is funny because of its complicated reversal of normality. A murderer is usually thought of as the embodiment of brutish virility; and what sort of virility is it that is threatened by a 'blushing shamefac'd spirit'? There is a long-standing theatrical tradition that the tough guy, hard boy, bravo or yegg is a self-conscious actor, beefy, unintelligent and tongue-tied, of a role that is always more or less comic because it is overplayed and at the same time a caricature of real manliness. Shakespeare, like many writers before him and since, takes the joke a stage further by having a timid little man act the part. This aspect of the scene makes it all the funnier when the first murderer speaks his relief at his friend's decision to put conscience by: 'Spoke like a tall man that respects thy reputation.'

Then in his deft way Shakespeare turns the old joke about the little tough guy who cannot quite carry the part into an exposure of the misuse of power. Summoning all the courage he has, the second murderer speaks to Clarence in a voice of thunder but with humble looks; the looks, he says, are his own, the voice the King's. Our amusement at this is hardly over when the pathetic mingles with the comic. 'Wherefore do you come?' asks Clarence:

> 2 *Murd.*    To, to, to—
> *Clar.*    To murder me?
> *Both.*    Ay, ay.
> *Clar.*    You scarcely have the hearts to tell me so.

Clarence warns them of the unlawfulness of murder. His unwilling killers reply, 'What we will do, we do upon command. And he that has commanded is our King.' At that moment the implied caricature of bogus royalty speaking through the mouths of its hired ruffians shows us a view of secular power as an exercise in applied masculinity; there is an implication that politics are a low joke in the worst taste—not an unusual idea in Shakespeare—and immediately, as in *III Henry VI*, the poet brings in the religious standard by which we are to judge such secular performances:

> Erroneous vassals! the great King of kings
> Hath in the table of his law commanded
> That thou shalt do no murder.

In the argument that follows, the murderers accuse Clarence of his many crimes that might warrant punishment; but he nonetheless tries to bring home to them the wrongness of violating 'God's dreadful law':

> If God will be avenged for the deed,
> O, know you yet, He doth it publicly.
> Take not the quarrel from His powerful arm;

He needs no indirect or lawless course
To cut off those that have offended Him.

Like the argument about title in *III Henry VI*, this debate is about
the legitimate exercise of authority. It also has the form of a classic
'case' in moral theology, since Clarence and the murderers are
caught in a conflict of allegiance between divine and human
authority. There is more parody therefore in the way they list the
priorities governing their deeds:

> *1 Murd.*   Who made thee then a bloody minister,
> When gallant-springing brave Plantagenet,
> That princely novice, was struck dead by thee?
> *Clar.*   My brother's love, the devil, and my rage.
> *1 Murd.*   Thy brother's love, our duty, and thy faults
> Provoke us hither now to slaughter thee.

This question and its triple answer parodies, in a general way, the
form of question and answer found in the Church of England
catechism. But the parody is probably more exact than that. In the
catechistical lectures that Lancelot Andrewes gave to the students
at Cambridge in the 1580s, there is a passage where the catechist
gives his students a rule for resolving conflicts between laws. According to this rule, any conflict can be resolved if one sets out one's
obligations according to the proper order of priorities, i.e. the glory
of God first, followed by our own salvation second, and the salvation
of others third.[4] This threefold arrangement of priorities is so similar
to its parody in the mouths of Clarence and the first murderer that
the resemblance must be intentional. As a catechist, Lancelot
Andrewes meant to be orthodox and authoritative, not original; this
particular formula must have been quite well known.

There is, of course, no real order in Clarence's or his murderers'
priorities, and Clarence's last discovery in this long scene is that the
love of both his brothers has failed him. He warns the murderers
that it will fail them too—'they that set you on to do this deed will
hate you for the deed'—and the scene ends with all three men,
victims of grave moral disorder, facing the ultimate question:

> *2 Murd.*   What shall we do?
> *Clar.*                     Relent, and save your souls.

We are brought back to the instinctive promptings of conscience,
the 'blushing, shamefac'd spirit'. Like Henry VI's pity, it is, as the
first murderer says, 'cowardly and womanish'; but there is no way

out of Clarence's conclusion if one accepts his idea of law and conscience. When the murder happens, it is a sudden desperate act by a man who chooses to act a bad part to the end. The second murderer who asked 'What shall we do?' and in whose looks Clarence saw pity, shouts a useless warning to the Duke, and has the last word:

> How fain, like Pilate, would I wash my hands
> Of this most grievous murder!

This scene, superior in language, in range of feeling and thought, to anything else in the play, opens a window that Shakespeare does not, after this play, shut again. It shows a world where men long for escape from violence and its consequences, and it exposes the triviality of the play's larger action. Richmond by definition is his country's redeemer, God's captain, and minister of chastisement; but according to this scene, the place and deed of redemption are in the soul, and by that standard Richmond and his like are pseudo-redeemers. Such questions as

> Will you, then,
> Spurn at His edict and fulfil a man's?

have a way of overlapping their context. This kind of thing made Tudor censors nervous, and with reason, because such questions directly concern every pretender to supreme authority. For the time being however Richard and Richmond hold the stage with their allegorical battle, and the great questions are put aside, like Clarence in the malmsey butt.

# 5. The Life and Death of King John

There is general agreement that *King John*, whatever the problems of its date and its connection with *The Troublesome Reign of John* (a poor play published anonymously in 1591 which is similar in incidents and characters to *King John*), succeeds *Richard III* and precedes *Richard II* in the line of Shakespeare's histories. The play's action is about the search for legitimacy and truth, and with them for the hope of security and confidence of life. The play could be called *The Case of the Missing King*.

'Speak, citizens, for England,' says King Philip of France to the citizens of Angiers, 'who's your king?' To which their spokesman drily replies, 'The King of England, when we know the King' (II. i. 362–3). John is King *de facto*, and the play's action is plotted as a series of challenges to his *de jure* right to the crown. The first challenge is the presence of Arthur of Brittany, son to his elder brother Geoffrey; the second appears in the person of Pandulph, the papal legate; the third takes the form of a rebellion of the English noblemen; and the fourth is a revolt within King John himself, aided and abetted by the monk's poison. John's own doubts about his right to the crown do not trouble him much, at least not consciously; from first until almost the very last he acts like a man who thinks that the successful exercise of kingly power is right enough. When he yields up his crown to the legate on Ascension Day, receiving it again as a vassal of the Pope, all in fulfilment of Peter of Pomfret's prophecy, the symbolic weight of the action does not affect him. He treats it as a political move, necessary to win the legate's aid against the French. As for the prophecy, he is relieved that its fulfilment takes this harmless form:

> I did suppose it should be on constraint;
> But, heaven be thank'd, it is but voluntary. (v. i. 28–9)

It does not occur to him that the voluntariness of the act might be qualified by the fact that it happens according to a prophecy. These lines illustrate some qualities in John not much noticed, a strain of ironic humour and a laconic way of leaving much unsaid. During the long scene in which Pandulph persuades Philip to break his new treaty with England, John, after his first two speeches of disdain for the Papacy, speaks in single lines that conceal a world of inward watchfulness. 'Philip, what say'st thou to the Cardinal?' is a question that is very impressive in the way it cuts through the noisy interchange between Falconbridge and Austria; and his comment upon Philip's betrayal, 'France, thou shalt rue this hour within this hour', is a good example of his clipped ironic way of speaking.

As long as John's power is secure, he presents this appearance of control. 'Our strong possession and our right for us', he replies to the French challenge that begins the play. He decides policies equally abruptly. 'Our abbeys and our priories shall pay/This expedition's charge' (I. i. 48–9), he says, almost off-handedly; but the off-handedness in such a man is the sign of a formidable will. In fact, Shakespeare has portrayed him as a 'tough guy', very hard-boiled. This does not usually come out on the stage because actors treat the part as a poor substitute for Richard II, the epitome of the weak king in Shakespeare. They do their lyrical best with such poetry as the part offers and die expressively at the end. Yet for three acts John has not a moment's weakness. He acts with speed and confidence, confounding his enemies. He is intelligent and deals practically with matters as they arise. Among characters who talk lengthily and often to little purpose, his economy of speech is a positive, sometimes amusing quality. His pithy one-line remarks, his tendency to speak in the simple indicative tenses at important moments, imply an attitude to life as well as a distaste for talk and noise.

Laconic himself, John dislikes talkativeness in others. His first words to his mother, his partner in politics for the play's first half, are 'Silence, good mother; hear the embassy' (I. i. 6); he later tells the ebullient Falconbridge to be quiet with, 'We like not this; thou dost forget thyself' (III. i. 134), and he is also abrupt to Constance: 'Bedlam, have done' (II. i. 183). His long speech to the citizens of Angiers is full of an inner, saturnine humour, as if the utterance of so many words struck him as funny. A similar coolness shows in his defiance of the Pope; and his description of himself in that passage as a 'sacred king' (III. i. 148), one of only two occasions when he pretends to any special sanction, is for political effect. His defiance is based on political realism. It leads him to describe Papal authority as 'juggling witchcraft', interfering by fraud and blackmail with the exercise of real political power; and he assumes that churchmen are as practically motivated as he is. Immediately after the ceremony

mentioned above, in which he receives his crown back from the
legate, he turns to business: 'Now keep your holy word. Go meet the
French . . .' (v. i. 5).

Yet outward coolness is not the whole truth. Inwardly John burns
with rage. The speed with which he twice defeats the French is a
sign of the inner heat which he first expresses when France betrays
him: 'I am burn'd up with inflaming wrath' (III. i. 340). In the en-
suing battle, the 'day grows wondrous hot./Some airy devil hovers
in the sky' (III. ii. 1), and the defeated French speak in wonder of
'so hot a speed' combined with 'such temperate order in so fierce a
cause'. John's 'heat' finally kills him. 'This fever, that hath troubl'd
[him] so long' (v. iii. 3) is already threatening his life when the
monk's poison adds fire to fire: 'There is so hot a summer in my
bosom/That all my bowels crumble up to dust' (v. vii. 30–1). It is
fitting and moving that this interesting man whose ideal of life has
been a watchful, cool hardness should die longing for cold:

> And none of you will bid the Winter come
> To thrust his icy fingers in my maw,
> Nor let my kingdom's rivers take their course
> Through my burn'd bosom, nor entreat the north
> To make his bleak winds kiss my parched lips
> And comfort me with cold. I do not ask you much,
> I beg cold comfort. . . .   (v. vii. 36–41)

As this speech shows, such figurative language describes more than
the king's personal character. The play is unusual for its frequent
references to the idea of the 'body politic', the notion that the king's
body is the body of the land, the king's health his country's health.
In Act IV, scene ii, the war between John's soul and himself,
occasioned by Arthur's reputed death and the 'civil tumult' it has
caused, are spoken of as exactly the same thing:

> Nay, in the body of this fleshly land,
> This kingdom, this confine of blood and breath,
> Hostility and civil tumult reigns
> Between my conscience and my cousin's death.   (ll. 245–8)

John's weakness is that like any hard-boiled politician he acts on no
clear principle except for self-interest and opportunism. His deeds
are a series of responses to events, and this applies even to his
repentance for Arthur's death, which is only a response to the baron's
rage. The same responsiveness causes civil war when the barons,
their outrage at Arthur's death following closely their dismay at
John's recrowning, side with the French. The barons also act by

response rather than principle. Because their responses are emotional they are more justifiable, to a sentimental age like ours, than John's political responses; but the dramatist criticises responsiveness itself because, in the absence of a principle of action, it is a substitute for it and a symptom of its lack.

The question of principle, of legitimacy and illegitimacy, is the play's constant theme. There are of course any number of false principles involved. France and Austria are full of the holiness of their acts, but they are just as political as John, though less effective, and are liars as well. Even love is made to serve politics by the marriage of Blanche and the Dauphin, who expresses his 'love' in language as conventional as the play's pieties. His professions draw the Bastard's criticism:

> 'Drawn in the flattering table of her eye!'
> Hang'd in the frowning wrinkle of her brow!
> And quarter'd in her heart! He doth espy
> Himself love's traitor. This is pity now,
> That, hang'd and drawn and quarter'd, there should be
> In such a love so vile a lout as he.  (II. i. 504–9)

Even mother-love has political uses. Constance's passion over the loss of Arthur is partly genuine, although the legate's comments encourage us to see an element of performance in it: 'You hold too heinous a respect of grief' (III. iv. 90). Eleanor calls her 'ambitious', and on the whole it seems that Constance uses her son and her ostentatious motherhood for psychological and, perhaps, political reasons that have little to do with love. The misuse of the language of love and devotion is one of the play's recurrent motifs. Political corruption is obvious; emotional corruption can be just as dangerous, although we are more likely to miss it.

Just as King John hardly ever speaks in conventional pieties, so he does not pretend to emotions he does not have. His rage is real and deadly, and in looking for the causes of his and his country's sickness, we have to go deeper than the lies and manoeuvrings which are only its symptoms. The real trouble with John is that he is not really a king. He is only related to a king. Richard Coeur-de-Lion haunts his brother's play as a name and as a memory of undoubted right turned to a mockery in the person of Austria, a dim-witted braggart who wears Richard's lion-skin and parodies his crusading valour. Richard is also present in the person of his illegitimate son Falconbridge, whose first act is to take his father's name as he already has his voice, humour and figure. The Bastard figures in *King John* as something old and new, as the spirit of the dead king new-made; and because he is illegitimate he is as much outside the play's 'world' as he is in it. These paradoxes are not just abstractions thought up by the critic, either. Falconbridge is enough outside the play's society to be a chorus to the action, sufficiently inside to be one of its chief actors; he is sufficiently 'old' to stand for an idea of stability, sufficiently 'new' to be always surprising. He is an example of the unknown quantity that everyone knows. Like a mythical hero, his birth is mysterious, his behaviour unpredictable; but the mystery is an open secret, the unpredictability predictable. On the evidence of *The Troublesome Reign* and of some doggerel verse in *King John* (I. i. 169–75), it looks as though the character had a pre-Shakespearean existence in some popular, possibly dramatic tradition in which his boldness and frank speech will have stood for a national, though parochial, idea of honesty and truth. In *King John* the Bastard stands for an altogether larger idea. Because he is truly royal he rises superior to everything in the play except truth itself.

On his first appearance he is an innocent, country-bred, and a bit of a clown. His first reaction to ennoblement is delight at the thought of dignity and success. He will out-do the age's fashions, learn its deceits, even though he will 'not practise to deceive' (I. i. 214). This speech and his famous soliloquy on 'commodity', i.e. self-interest, have led readers to interpret him as a character who, according to one critic, denounces as chorus things with which 'he as a person really sympathises'.[1] One must not forget, though, that Falconbridge has given up 'fair five hundred pound a year', accepted illegitimacy, and chosen the honour of his birth instead of land. He is whole-hearted, he knows what and who he is; he is a secure, hugely amused critic of the society he lives in, and one must always be ready for irony in his speech.

Falconbridge laughs at himself as well as others. After railing upon 'commodity', he agrees with himself, or with anyone who might suggest it, that he enjoys the moral superiority of the un-tempted. He makes no claim to immunity. Instead, he puts a hypothetical case:

> Well, whiles I am a beggar, I will rail
> And say there is no sin but to be rich;
> And being rich, my virtue then shall be
> To say there is no vice but beggary.
> Since kings break faith upon Commodity,
> Gain, be my lord, for I will worship thee.  (II. i. 593–8)

Yet he does not worship gain. If kings break faith, says the argument, then lesser creatures may as well imitate them. The Bastard however is not a lesser creature; the reader has to be nimble-minded to see that the force of that last line, its grim funniness, is in its irony. His outrageous proposal, made before Angiers, that instead of quarrelling the two kings should join forces to raze the city which is the cause of their quarrel, is made in the same spirit:

> How like you this wild counsel, mighty states?
> Smacks it not something of the policy?    (II. i. 395–6)

Here are the citizens of Angiers secure on their walls, being no help at all, and two armies are about to slaughter each other under their disinterested gaze. The Bastard sees the absurdity of the case and decides to alter the situation with a heartless proposal, which however draws from the citizens a suggestion that mends the quarrel. He out-politics the politicians because, deciding to play a round of their game, he suits his play to the case, not to a mistaken idea of his own importance. 'Smacks it not something of the policy?' is funny because Falconbridge's disinterested wit is better politics than the kings' Machiavellianism.

The Bastard's rules of behaviour in the first three acts are truth to himself and loyalty to the King and to England. These qualities separate him from other characters. It sometimes happens that he talks to no one except the audience, the stage persons ignoring him, as when he ridicules the citizen's rhetoric or the Dauphin's love-talk. There are hints that his loyalty might find itself at odds with his truth. The 'commodity' speech is such a hint, but at first there is no clear conflict. When, however, he goes under orders from John to ransack churches, he finds himself for the first time playing a part his ironic humour cannot improve. He returns from the work less exuberant than he was at departing, and his one comment on the job (IV. ii. 141–6), although it shows that he has done it as thoroughly as he does everything, also shows that for the first time he has taken no pleasure in doing the King's work.

*    *    *

The attempt at blinding Arthur and his subsequent death form the play's crisis. These events show the truth of John's rule, and begin his disintegration. They test the Bastard and cause his development into a commanding and openly royal person.

John's instructions to Hubert to blind Arthur are the third act of his rage after the legate's challenge to his authority. First there is the battle (III. ii), then the sending of the Bastard to 'shake the bags of hoarding abbots' (III. iii. 7), and then the strange passion in which John, confessing to thoughts not to be uttered in daylight (III. iii. 30–55), invites Hubert to understand his wish that Arthur be murdered. John is a character like York and Richard of Gloucester, whose real thoughts are unspeakable and whose fixed idea is the imposition of his will to power despite any challenge offered by others or his own conscience. Unlike the other two characters, the laconic John does not take the audience into his confidence. He is not a self-dramatiser and, until failure exposes his weakness, he has no self-pity. He keeps an appearance of control, even of humour, until nature and authority in the persons of Arthur and the legate combine to challenge his rule. Then the inner evil breaks out, though still with an avoidance of direct speech:

> I had a thing to say, but let it go.
> The sun is in the heaven, and the proud day,
> Attended with the pleasures of the world,
> Is all too wanton and too full of gawds
> To give me audience. . . .
> . . . if that thou couldst see me without eyes,
> Hear me without thine ears, and make reply
> Without a tongue, using conceit alone,
> Without eyes, ears, and harmful sound of words;
> Then, in despite of brooded watchful day,
> I would into thy bosom pour my thoughts.
> But, ah, I will not!    (III. iii. 33–7, 48–54)

John's thoughts, which he will not put into words, emerge symbolically in the hot irons that Hubert prepares for Arthur's eyes, and in Hubert's instruction to the executioners: 'When I strike my foot/ Upon the bosom of the ground, rush forth' (IV. i 2). The hint of sadistic perversion is intentional, as it is in the earlier scene between John and Hubert. It implies that the exercise of unsanctioned power for its own sake is related to a peculiar set of emotions. The confrontation of Arthur with Hubert, whom John loves and who we later learn is an ugly man, is a characteristically Shakespearean matching of the unnatural with the natural. John's use of Hubert, however, is defeated by Arthur's affection. He speaks 'innocently' (IV. i. 25) to Hubert of his sadness at being kept prisoner, deprived of a normal child's life. Most tellingly, he wishes he had a father to love him. (He never mentions his ambitious, emotional mother.)

The appeal to natural affection wins Hubert, but the surprising thing about the scene, which has offended many critics, is the artful and 'conceited' series of speeches with which the child delays Hubert's intended speed of action until nature has turned him from his purpose. The technique is the opposite of realism (the offended readers are mainly realists), rendering intense emotion not by brevity, inarticulateness and noise, but by translating it into a correspondent intensity of elaborated language. An intense moment in time is arrested as the language winds itself into extended variations on two themes: the mystery of the eyes' fragility, so much at odds with their power to fascinate, and the child's hunting for an escape from his prison, which blinding would make complete. Straightforward terror, which some have thought should be Arthur's single emotion, has its place: 'O, save me, Hubert, save me!' But, as always in Shakespeare, the mind's mastery of the even is paramount. He intends not only to shock and appal, but to unite feeling and understanding. His technique, turning the intensity of the thing imitated into a corresponding intensity of the imitative medium (or, as his contempories would have said, turning nature into art) has a parallel in music, especially opera.

Hubert knows he 'must be brief, lest resolution drop/Out of mine eyes in tender womanish tears' (IV. i. 36). Arthur elaborates a conceit that tears will quench the anger of the fire (ll. 61–6), and he calls the cooling of the irons a compassionate 'denial of their office' (l. 119). These hot irons are part of a figurative pattern in the play that includes fire, war, blood and death as well as John's burning rage, the whole group coming together in the Bastard's speech before Angiers, a typically aloof performance, despite its energy:

> Ha, majesty! how high thy glory towers
> When the rich blood of kings is set on fire!
> O, now doth Death line his dead chaps with steel;
> The swords of soldiers are his teeth, his fangs;
> And now he feasts, mousing the flesh of men,
> In undetermin'd differences of kings.  (II. i. 350–5)

Arthur's weeping eyes are also the centre of a pattern. It includes rivers, rain, coolness, spontaneous affection, peace and mercy. Constance's hairs like 'wiry friends/Do glue themselves in sociable grief' (III. iv. 64–5) wherever a 'silver drop hath fallen'; the Dauphin also puts the imagery of the eye to conventional use in his wooing of Blanche. These peripheral examples, however, are cases of subverted language. The Dauphin is not in love, and Constance finds no society in her grief, whatever the King of France imagines to be going on in her hair. In *King John* the test of language is its issuing into action.

When Salisbury brings Constance news of the marriage between Blanche and the Dauphin, his eyes 'hold' tears 'like a proud river peering o'er his bounds' (III. i. 23); and John, after the battle before Angiers, speaks to the French king of 'the current of our right':

Whose passage, vex'd with thy impediment,
Shall leave his native channel and o'erswell
With course disturb'd even thy confining shores,
Unless thou let his silver water keep
A peaceful progress to the ocean.    (II. i. 336–40)

John, of course, has no real 'right'. The right is England's, and the
identity of the man who can call himself 'England' is the subject of
dispute. Later the mockery of the Dauphin's marriage comes out in
a misappropriation of the same imagery: 'O, two such silver currents,
when they join,/Do glorify the banks that bound them in' (II. i.
441–2). Nevertheless, the idea that 'right' is a 'silver water' flowing
unimpeded to the sea, and that its equivalent in the little world of
the body is the 'river' of sympathetic tears arising in the eye, turns
into action when Arthur's death causes the barons to rebel. Arthur's
undisputed royalty and his disputed right are nicely realised in the
intention to put out his eyes.

The King and the barons learn simultaneously of Arthur's reputed
death immediately after the barons' request for the boy's freedom
'ripens' John's passion, which the barons interpret as a boil which
must break:

And when it breaks, I fear will issue thence
The foul corruption of a sweet child's death.    (IV. ii. 80–1)

This murder which should cure John's political difficulties brings
his disease to a crisis, for it turns out that Arthur's life, being
England's right, is John's safety. Salisbury, who weeps easily, cries
tears of 'soft remorse' (IV. iii. 50) at Arthur's death, and in the act
of joining Lewis cries again, the 'honourable dew,/That silverly doth
progress on [his] cheeks' being a 'shower, blown up by tempest of
the soul' (V. ii. 45–6, 50). From here to speaking of the rebellion as a
river's overflowing is an easy transition, and Salisbury makes it (V.
iv. 53–7). There is also a suggestion that the barons are, figuratively,
England's rivers. Their return to John (V. v) is too late to do him
good; nor can his son's tears, another variant on this imagery of
rivers, relieve his pain:

The salt in them is hot.
Within me is a hell, and there the poison
Is as a fiend confin'd to tyrannise
On unreprievable condemned blood.    (V. vii. 45–8)

Whether John is really damned is known neither to us nor to him,
but the inefficacy of his son's tears to help him looks like a version of

the theological principle that a sacrament is actually dangerous to an unfit recipient. That which should cool and purify burns.[2] Yet although John dies, the body politic never dies, and Prince Henry's tears of grief turn to tears of joy at the kingdom's regeneration, purified through the return of its rivers to its burned bosom.

This very elaborate theologising strain in the imagery of *King John* is a form of Renaissance mannerism and overstatement; it builds up characters, incidents and feelings until they are heroic exemplars, absolutes of their kind. One of the peculiarities of the play, though, is that nothing turns out as planned or expected. Events do not support the weight of significance imputed to them by the figurative language. Arthur dies of his leap from the castle wall; the cause of his death is cold stone ('My uncle's spirit is in these stones'), not his uncle's fiery rage. He is the victim of John's coldness, not his heat. Had Arthur been murdered, the baron's anguish on finding his body would have been fitting :

> This is the very top,
> The height, the crest, or crest unto the crest,
> Of murder's arms.   (iv. iii. 45–7)

As things are, their response, proper enough to the hypothetical case, is mistaken, another example of misplaced emotionalism. The situation is bad and pitiful, but not in the way they think. Because the strength of Hubert's natural affection has saved John from his one act of downright villainy, the rebels are men who have lost their grip in a crisis. At the end of the play, the fire in John's belly is not hell-fire, but poison; the returned barons are not healing streams, but men undoing an error. The wish that things be more significant than they are has to be checked, as the Bastard checks Prince Henry's willingness to weep:

> O, let us pay the time but needful woe,
> Since it hath been beforehand with our griefs.   (v. vii. 110–11)

The Bastard is not an easy weeper; it is enough for him that England's 'princes are come home again'. In reading his famous last speech, we often fail to see how modest it is in comparison with the general luxuriance of language in the play, how much it is an admonition against self-flattering hysteria, how sceptical of grand and florid significances:

> This England never did, nor never shall,
> Lie at the proud foot of a conqueror,
> But when it first did help to wound itself.

Now these her princes are come home again,
Come the three corners of the world in arms,
And we shall shock them. Nought shall make us rue,
If England to itself do rest but true.

This is the rhetoric of plainness and simplicity.

\*          \*          \*

In the presence of Arthur's body the Bastard assumes an authority
of word and act that he maintains to the end, a notable contrast to
John and the barons. With every reason for thinking the worst, in
the presence of men overwrought almost to incoherence, his eye on
the pitiful object before him, Falconbridge answers the question,
'Sir Richard, what think you?' with three lines of superbly controlled
exactness:

> It is a damned and a bloody work;
> The graceless action of a heavy hand,
> If that it be the work of any hand.   (IV. iii. 57–9)

At the risk of being mistaken for an accessory to 'a villain and a
murderer', he protects Hubert, and Shakespeare represents the speed
and delicacy of his character's thought in crisis with marvellous
verse: 'Your sword is bright, sir,' says Falconbridge to Salisbury,
'put it up again.' Alone with Hubert, whom he suspects 'very
grievously', his control gives a little, but not for long:

>                            If thou didst but consent
> To this most cruel act, do but despair;
> And if thou want'st a cord, the smallest thread
> That ever spider twisted from her womb
> Will serve to strangle thee; a rush will be a beam
> To hang thee on; or wouldst thou drown thyself,
> Put but a little water in a spoon,
> And it shall be as all the ocean,
> Enough to stifle such a villain up.   (ll. 125–33)

These extravagant images, their exquisite smallness matching the
little prince's frailty and contrasting with the enormity of the supposed crime, express the extremities his mind is put to in maintaining
its sovereignty over confusion. The speech that follows, the finest
in the play, develops fully his heroic royalty:

>                    Go, bear him in thine arms.
> I am amaz'd, methinks, and lose my way
> Among the thorns and dangers of this world.
> How easy dost thou take all England up!   (ll. 139–42)

How simply Falconbridge sweeps away all dispute of the dead prince's significance! Unlike his master he is not only royal, he is also a royalist:

> From forth this morsel of dead royalty,
> The life, the right, and truth of all this realm
> Is fled to heaven.

As the weight of responsibility for England falls on him, he dwells on the paradoxical slightness of the morsel of dead royalty whose death threatens ruin, leaving nothing of the realm but 'the unow'd interest of proud-swelling state', the title no one owns, the dog-fight for 'the bare-pick'd bone of majesty' (ll. 145–8). Men have chosen to fight over the body of royalty, not to recognise its spirit, and as 'powers from home and discontents at home/Meet in one line' (ll. 151–2), the Bastard knows that an awaited collapse has come:

> Vast confusion waits,
> As doth a raven on a sick-fallen beast,
> The imminent decay of wrested pomp.
> Now happy he whose cloak and ceinture can
> Hold out this tempest.    (ll. 152–6)

'Ceinture' is the reading of the New Arden text. The Folio has 'center', and an equivocation on the word is intended;[3] Falconbridge is a man both ceintured (i.e. girded about) and centered. The phrase is a fine example of Shakespeare's conviction of the simultaneity of inner and outward being in a man of integrity. With these lines, which contain an allusion to the Psalms,[4] as with his grasp of the meaning of Arthur's death and his mention of '*this* world' (l. 141), a surprising quality of religious faith appears in Falconbridge, different from the ostentatious pieties of other characters, and it completes the picture of a soul in order.

Falconbridge is under no illusions about John ('wrested pomp'), he knows what has died with Arthur, he takes for granted the fact that 'life', 'right' and 'truth' are predicated upon a transcendent order of things, and in the light of that knowledge he knows how thorny and dangerous this world is. He neither retreats, like the barons, into emotionalism, nor into political *Realismus*. He acts as the time and his idea of the realm require. John may be a fake king, but he is the only king Falconbridge has. He is not Antichrist, and there is no other king to serve. When John, broken by rebellion, invasion and the disintegration of his own 'center', fails to rise to Falconbridge's encouragements—

Be great in act as you have been in thought.
Let not the world see fear and sad mistrust
Govern the motion of a kingly eye.   (v. i. 45–7)

—Falconbridge becomes the ruler of the country, and his pledge
of homage to Prince Henry at the end seems to guarantee an ordered
future. 'Renowned Falconbridge' is Shakespeare's first and most
complete portrait of the nobility that crisis brings out in certain
men.

Not all critics are prepared to go this far with Falconbridge, and
many never set out because they take his earlier joking about ambition, policy and commodity very soberly. Of the standard authorities, Geoffrey Bullough says that Shakespeare made the Bastard 'a
worshipper of Commodity', although he later mitigates this a little,
ascribing to the character 'simple loyalty and duty', and suggesting
that he prefigures Kent in *King Lear*.[5] E. A. J. Honigmann is much
more severe, not allowing Falconbridge to be a hero because his
'interference' does not 'make history'. John's delegation of authority
to a 'servant, a bastard, a boon companion' is a sign of his dejection;
Falconbridge's loss of his army in the Wash is 'criminal stupidity',
and whatever his 'triumphs as a bully' he fails 'as a general and
statesman'.[6] These are hard words. But if making history is the
criterion of heroism, then heroism is a material business, and some
dubious characters have been heroes. Falconbridge's business is, as
he says, to 'hold out the tempest', an altogether different matter
from making history. If he is a servant, all men are servants, heroes
included, and there is no shame in service. He is certainly not a
'boon companion', simply because neither he nor John takes a drink
from beginning to end of the play. Nor is he really a bully. His
hectoring attitude towards his half-brother and the Duke of Austria
(an absurd person strutting in Coeur-de-Lion's lion-skin) is more
akin to satire than to bullying, and we are not meant to disapprove
of it. The loss of the army is a significant event, but no one hints that
it results from stupidity, let alone criminality. In this case, as in his
remarks about generals and statesmen, Mr Honigmann speaks from
an un-Shakespearean world. Falconbridge never pretends to states-
manship. Although his one stroke of policy is successful, his only
object is to serve the King, and he does this so well that out of
total collapse he gathers an army, fights a tremendous battle in
which he 'alone upholds the day' (v. iv. 5) so effectually that the
rebel lords 'come home', and the French, with or without the loss
of reinforcements, are for the time being stopped. When the kingdom
is revived at the end it is not, as Mr Honigmann says, because John
is dead, but because Falconbridge has 'held out the tempest'.

He is, of course, a bastard, and this is the point of the story. The royalty to which monarchs pay lip-service is hidden in Coeur-de-Lion's natural son. To use one of the images in the play, the current of true legitimacy does not always flow in channels defined by the state's customary forms, but in the veins of the man who has in him the King's blood, and with it the gaiety, the courage, honesty and love of honour that are the marks of true royalty. Understanding *King John* and the Bastard's triumph needs a grasp of a basic Shakespearean quibble: the mystery of royalty is the mystery of reality, and both are hidden in the way that truth itself is often inward. Falconbridge's illegitimacy guarantees in a fairy-tale way his legitimacy, for its effect in the play is that royalty is found when it is needed; mere power and political ability are no substitutes for the real thing. Yet although Falconbridge is the only character with the authority to tell England to be true to itself, he, like Falstaff, is a fictitious character. Whatever hints of him there are in the sources, he is substantially Shakespeare's invention. That itself is a comment on historical truth, and the poet's developing grasp of it.

Falconbridge loses his army because that is what happened to John's forces. He has one comment on the event. In Act v, scene vi, he hears from Hubert of the King's poisoning and the barons' return with Prince Henry. In reply he tells of the loss of half his army, taken by the tide, and his own narrow escape. His two lines of comment apply both to Hubert's news and his own:

> Withhold thine indignation, mighty heaven,
> And tempt us not to bear above our power!

After his speech to Hubert at the play's crisis, we are not surprised to hear him speak like this. Later he repeats his news to the dying King, intending, although the situation is very ominous, to carry on the fight. He then learns that the legate has arrived, bringing peace offers from the Dauphin, whose own armies have suffered a similar misfortune.

Here Shakespeare must have been walking on political eggshells. Falconbridge and the Dauphin, both young men and impetuous, have scorned the legate's interference in the war. Yet he started it, and one cannot help suspecting that the storms that wreck the armies' hopes are somehow connected with his determination to make peace. Pandulph is kept off-stage at the end, but England's being true to itself seems to entail truth to a higher power. Pandulph claims to represent that power and, because all the antagonists admit the reality of the power itself, he has no difficulty putting them at a loss when they resist him as legate. John's reign, which in other hands was an *exemplum* of papal usurpation, seems in Shakespeare's to leave the question open.

Pandulph is a fascinating character. Falconbridge has to pick his way through the thorns and dangers of the world, but Pandulph has a path ready-made. The Church's primacy is everything to him. France's new-made treaty with England has no standing because England has braved the Pope whom France is sworn to defend. The higher loyalty supersedes the lower; France has made a mistake, and human considerations such as marriage and friendship have no place in the argument:

> All form is formless, order orderless,
> Save what is opposite to England's love . . .
> The better part of purposes mistook
> Is to mistake again; though indirect,
> Yet indirection thereby grows direct,
> And falsehood falsehood cures, as fire cools fire.   (III. i. 253–77)

So much for the thorns and dangers of the world. Pandulph's speech to Philip, a piece of virtuosity on Shakespeare's part, is an example of an argument that, once its premise is granted, is unanswerable except as the hero of J. H. Shorthouse's novel *John Inglesant* answers it:

> 'If there be absolute truth revealed, there must be an inspired exponent of it, else from age to age, it could not get itself revealed to mankind.'
> 'This is the papist argument,' said Mr. Inglesant: 'there is only one answer to it—Absolute truth is not revealed.'[7]

No one in *King John* makes that answer to Pandulph. His authority receives no check, and it is borne out by events. 'How green you are, and fresh in this old world', he says to the Dauphin:

> John lays you plots; the times conspire with you.   (III. iv. 145–6)

While Arthur lives, John is in doubt; if Arthur dies, John will have rebellion on his hands. Let the Dauphin invade England on his own and on the Church's behalf (the rights of both parties are good); John will be forced to murder Arthur to prevent disloyalty. Lewis's right will then be undisputed, and the English will rebel anyway. True to form, Pandulph takes Arthur's claim for granted, but wastes no sympathy on the child's fate. He is a chilling figure. 'You look but on the outside of this work', he says to Lewis later when the

young man refuses to make peace, and there is a world of patient
contempt in the line. No one ever beats him in an argument. If
people resort to force, 'The winds blow, and they are scattered.'

Whether Falconbridge's English royalty should yield to the larger
royalty of the Church and Christendom is a question not really
raised, although the possibility of it hangs like a large query over the
last act. Pandulph's cold logicality offends against the Shakespearean
standard of nature and kindliness, but although *King John* is not
exactly a Catholic play, it is certainly not a Protestant one, either.

This aspect of the play's meaning is bound up with the question of
its topical significance. Nineteenth-century readers first noticed the
plot's correspondence to events in the 1580s; the problem is whether
Elizabethans noticed it. Elizabeth II's right to the throne was
challenged as John's is in the play. She inherited from a sister, he
from a brother. Her legitimacy was questioned, and she was under
papal excommunication, so that the Armada of 1588 was under the
same sanction as the Dauphin's forces in the play. Mary, Queen of
Scots, like Arthur, was a legitimate claimant to the throne, supported by France and the Church. Like John, Elizabeth issued a
kind of indirect death warrant, and she disowned the state servant
who carried it out as John disowns Hubert. Shortly after Mary's
death, the Catholic powers tried to invade England and depose
Elizabeth; as in the play, the attack was beaten off by English valour,
and finally scattered by violent storms.[8]

To anyone living in the 1580s England's situation could have
seemed very dark, threatened within by religious dissent, and without by the Catholic powers. In 1586, in connection with the Babing-
ton plot to install Mary, there was a great rounding-up of Catholic
activists, clerical and lay, and the gaols were full of them. Then the
Queen herself was beheaded. The miracle of 1588 was not only the
blowing of the winds, but the kingdom's proving true to itself.
Pandulph's prophecy that the people would revolt at the approach
of the invaders was also made in 1588, but it proved wrong, and out
of confusion and dispute came a new vindication, as it seemed, of
the realm's integrity.

Before 1588 many would have found an echo to their feelings in
Salisbury's talk of 'the uncleanly savours of a slaughter-house' (iv.
iii. 112) and a 'smell of sin'. After 1588 Falconbridge's faith in the
land's integrity will have seemed to contain the truth of the matter.
In so far as Pandulph's predictions prove true, they are based on
political acumen and have nothing to do, really, with papal authority.
Where they prove wrong is in his not understanding what Falconbridge stands for. The storm that brings peace also leaves the
kingdom's relation to the Papacy exactly where it was. Pandulph is

not present when Prince Henry, putting on 'the lineal state and glory of the land' (v. vii. 102), receives the homage of his uncle and the peers.

*King John,* long known to be a successful stage play, is also a superb dramatic poem. It is Shakespeare's first history to be whole in itself, establishing its own standard of values by the completeness of an action that even governs the style of writing. Because the action is about right, truth and legitimacy, even the play's excesses of language have a purpose; we are warned by them to question men's words as well as their acts. So Pandulph checks the extremity of Constance's grief and, therefore, the words in which Shakespeare has expressed it. John reproves the Bastard's manners and his style in the scenes where he taunts Austria. The Bastard, in turn, criticises the Dauphin's bogus affection. The style is the man himself: this is the play's moral.

# 6. The Tragedy of Richard II

*Richard II* is in many ways similar to *King John*. The theme is still legitimacy, although the action concerns not the finding of legitimacy but the challenging and degrading of it. In the management of both plays' actions the strategy is to show one man yielding to another. Both plots have a kind of dialectical structure and make much use of debate, of scenes of trial and confrontation. There are also many specific resemblances, especially in the treatment of patriotism and rebellion.

Many readers have noticed how ceremonial, how emblematic this play is, and how strong an impression its technique conveys of the archaic and mediaeval. Many have thought that Shakespeare intended, by means of a formal style, to give a sense of the past; they have interpreted the play as a conflict between the old and the new, between poetry and politics or ritual and reality. The techniques themselves come from *Henry VI*, and so does much of the characterisation. The emblematic garden scene (III. iv) looks back to the scene in the Temple-garden (*I Henry VI*, II. iv), as well as to the Battle of Towton (*III Henry VI*, II. v). The treatment of Gaunt as a good old counsellor may owe something to Froissart or to the author of the anonymous play *Woodstock*, but it certainly owes a lot to Shakespeare's own Duke Humphrey in *II Henry VI*. The handling of King Henry VI, especially his meditation during the Battle of Towton and his last scene in the Tower, is the basis of much in King Richard II.

These older methods have taken new life because the ceremonial style is far more now than a means to a dramatic end; the ceremonial is inseparable from the play's theme, the 'unkinging' of King Richard.

In *Henry VI* Shakespeare treats kingship in terms of property, lineal succession and hereditary right. Possession—the king's possession of the land, of himself, and the land's possession of the king and self—is the ruling idea, its chief symbol the crown; and the criteria of right possession are tranquillity, order and peace, as in Alexander Iden's garden (II *Henry VI*, IV. x). In *King John* the intimate relation between the king and his realm, already adumbrated in Richard of York's psychology in *II Henry VI*, is a major theme. Natural images of the royal blood, of the country's rivers, of families, of the body, bear upon the idea of an organic polity rooted in nature and the primary human affections. Offences against the 'body politic', as against the bodies of men, are offences against natural order. The supernatural hardly enters into these plays, and if it does, as with the legate in *King John*, it is treated with great reserve.

Although their characters take it for granted that a supernatural order governs the natural order, the supernatural itself is not really a major theme in the early histories. As I have suggested, in *Henry VI* and *Richard III* Shakespeare's naturalism is so much at odds with the supernaturalism of his sources and popular belief that although he can give theatrical vigour to the diabolic supernatural by turning it into melodrama, he can give no life at all to Richmond's sanctity. (There is nothing supernatural about Henry VI's piety, which arises out of the simplicity and innocence of his character.) The frank theatricality of Shakespeare's diabolism in these early plays anticipates the Romantics' use of the same material; not being really believed in, it is all the more enjoyable.

That so little is made of the supernatural side of kingship in the early histories suggests that although Shakespeare took for granted the divine sanction of the monarchy, he shared with modern English readers the idea that it was for all practical purposes natural, a thing to be defined by constitutional law and political science. Anything else is 'symbolism', the chief symbolic idea being that the monarch represents an emotionally sensed national unity and that the criterion of a good reign, therefore, is the king's understanding of the realm and the unselfishness with which he serves it. The important royal symbol, after the monarch himself, is the crown, the sign of singleness in the state; and the most important moment in the king's life and the sentimental life of the state is the crowning. This is certainly the modern view, and it has shaped the modern coronation office in which the crowning is the climax. In the mediaeval rite, however, which was last used for the coronation of Charles II, the anointing is the important moment when, liturgically speaking, 'something happens', when a sacramental change in the king's person occurs making it proper to vest him with the regalia. The change from mediaeval to modern is from the strictly sacred to the almost wholly secular, from the theology and metaphysics of a sacrament to the sentimental associations of a symbol.[1]

The chief effect of this change in emphasis is that the absolute, if it is known at all in political affairs, is known through the feelings and in recording this in his histories Shakespeare, as in so many things, is a harbinger of modern times. I have argued a case for Falconbridge's royalism in *King John* because a sacramental view of the relation of king and state is certainly implied by the words he speaks over Arthur's body—how interesting, though, that it should require the pathos of a child's death to precipitate that floating, undefined content in the character of Falconbridge; and how equally interesting that the full force of Shakespeare's poetic sacramentalism, in *King John* as in *Henry VI*, should be found in passages expressing the 'natural' sacraments of tears and blood, those elemental bonds (as a Victorian critic might put it) of human sympathy. Such 'sacraments' have no existence except by analogy with the supernatural sacraments they parody. No one for instance would speak of a dying soldier sealing with blood 'a testament of noble-ending love' (*Henry V*, IV. vi. 26–7) unless he was familiar with the sacrament of Holy Communion. Yet although such a passage reveals a habit of association and feeling, it tells nothing about belief. Its subject is patriotism, here dressed out in robes borrowed from religion, and the poet who does this is probably more patriotic than religious, although the precision of his religious imagery reveals considerable knowledge. Later literature is full of such borrowings from religion, but as often as not the authors know very little about the implied field of reference, and this is a clear case of decadence; only the analogies by which theologians once taught religious mysteries seem to be remembered—the mysteries themselves are forgotten.

The effect of this reversal is that natural objects are treated as if they were supernatural, and this is the source of the sentimental emotionalism characteristic of post-mediaeval art;[2] people no longer believe in angels, but they make up for it by believing in angelic women. We can see the beginnings of this in Shakespeare. Among the great writers he is second only to Dickens in his exploitation of children's deaths. He also anticipates the Victorians and the Romantics in the weight of significance he imputes to family relationships, to sexual purity and to young women. We are probably still a little too close in the nineteenth century's passion for Shakespeare to see clearly just what it was that drew them to him, but a large part of the truth will be found in the relationship between such works as *Othello* and Scott's *Kenilworth*, between *King Lear* and *The Old Curiosity Shop*.[3]

Although Shakespeare looks forward, however, he also looks backward. *Richard II*—which comes first in the grand sequence of the histories, even though written later than the first tetralogy and *King John*—is fascinating partly because its theme, the uncrowning of King Richard, dramatises a profound change in sensibility. Richard is the only full Shakespearen portrait of a king sacred to himself and to others. True, in *Macbeth* there is a glimpse of Duncan, and St Edward the Confessor is just off-stage, but Richard is the only indubitably sacred king who is also a hero. It is as if Shakespeare, having begun his histories 'in the midst of things' with the reigns closer to the confusion and realities of his own times, worked himself backwards in time and imagination to the mystery of kingship and its loss.

\*   \*   \*

Richard II was the last Plantagenet king to succeed by undisputed lineal right, the last king whose title was naturally and religiously legitimate by his blood and his anointing; and his deposition provided Shakespeare with an ideal subject for a play about the breaking of the unity of realm and person vested in the old monarchy. In many ways, however, the play is unhistorical. Thomas of Woodstock, whose murder underlies the opening scenes, was no 'plain well-meaning soul' (II. i. 128), nor had John of Gaunt ever been notable for public spirit and high principle. Such changes of character are more damaging to the play's historical truth than are details like the alterations of Queen Isabella's and Henry Percy's ages, because they mean that Shakespeare can never treat properly the political realities of the reign. The only things Shakespeare's Richard and the historical Richard really have in common are royalism and good looks, and a good deal of material in *Richard II*, such as the wisdom of elderly counsellors and the heedlessness of the king's youth, is at odds with the play's substance, as inconsistencies in the exposition show.

The exposition, which includes all of the first two acts, is puzzling in many ways, as if Shakespeare had not made up his mind whether he was writing about Paradise Lost or Tyranny Rebuked. There is a Richard who banishes Bolingbroke, a Richard who is the object of his uncle's warnings, and a Richard whose own words and actions appear to the audience, and they are not quite the same person. The Richard who listens to Mowbray's and Bolingbroke's mutual accusations (I. i) and who banishes them both (I. iii) is a watchful, poised man who has the patience to wait out the long ceremony of accusation before attempting to make peace, and who acts decisively at the chosen moment when he interrupts the combat. He is sufficiently detached to comment impartially on the contestants' demeanour (I. iii. 54–8, 97–8), and his mastery of the affair shows in his replies to Mowbray's and Gaunt's complaints (ll. 174, 233–5). Yet the elaborate ceremony of these scenes conceals more than it reveals, not only of Richard's behaviour but of Bolingbroke's and Mowbray's too. Readers have been quick to accuse Richard of playing a part, of taking pleasure in ceremony for its own sake; and actors have often lisped and simpered through a scene that Shakespeare went out of his way to write in a single unbroken tone of high, stately rhetoric. Richard is the one person who is definitely not acting, either in this scene or any other. Besides being watchful of others, he is sincerely himself to the point of embarrassment, as when he tells John of Gaunt to his face that he is a 'lunatic lean-witted fool,/Presuming on an ague's privilege' (II. i. 115–16). The consummate actor is Bolingbroke, who hardly ever tells the truth.

The subject of these opening trials is the death of Richard's uncle, Gloucester, for which Gaunt and Bolingbroke (who, in a typically indirect way, hits at Richard through his servant Mowbray) hold the king responsible. On his side, the King must know what the trial is all about, and he must have a motive for not allowing it to proceed, and for giving unequal sentences of banishment. The Lancasters must know that Richard knows their opinion of Gloucester's death, and they must also have opinions of Richard's response to their man-oeuvres. Shakespeare however keeps all of this out of the trials, just as he later gives Richard no reply when Gaunt, in extraordinary language, accuses him of 'drunkenly carousing' (II. i. 127) in Glouces-ter's blood. For to give Richard a reply would give him, as well as his Lancastrian cousin, a motive. Instead Shakespeare introduces, in the conversation between Gloucester's widow and John of Gaunt, the idea that this murder underlying the play's action is a kind of original sin against natural and religious law. Bolingbroke (I. i. 104) has already compared the murder to Abel's when the widow (I. ii. 11–20) calls it a spilling of sacred blood, a mutilation of the royal tree. Gaunt, though, refuses to avenge his brother's death:

> God's is the quarrel; for God's substitute,
> His deputy anointed in His sight,
> Hath caus'd his death; the which if wrongfully,
> Let heaven revenge; for I may never lift
> An angry arm against His minister.   (ll. 37–41)

The duchess appeals to his sense of kinship, wishing him to avenge a crime against the royalty of his own blood. He refuses, choosing to rest in his belief in the efficacy of the sacrament of anointing. To her his patience is despair; to him her despair is blasphemy.

In these two aged people who lament the passing of an innocent time two absolutes meet, and they render questions of political motive irrelevant. Whether one chooses revenge with the duchess on natural grounds, or patience with Gaunt on religious grounds, the reason for the original murder (and there must have been *some* reason) has nothing to do with the choice. Gaunt's words imply that the sanctity of this king is in his anointing or nowhere, whereas the duchess's language implies the possibility of a nature so hurt by sin that no sacrament can amend it. This concentrated little scene veers towards the making or suggesting of some implied reference to the great theological problem of the Protestant movement in Shakespeare's time: how are men to reconcile the apparent discord between fallen nature and divine grace, between appearance and reality? The scene ends with the duchess's sad evocation of her empty, ruining house, a fit setting for 'sorow that dwells everywhere'. This passage, whose tone is reminiscent of the 'bare ruin'd choirs' of Sonnet 73, also recalls Calvin's use, to describe the condition of fallen nature, of this same image of a ruined building: 'a shapeless ruin is all that remains'.[4] However bizarre Calvin's theological extremism now seems to us, it was the result of his having perceived a difference between promise and actuality of just the kind enacted here in Act i, scene ii.

The Richard of the trial scene is as much at odds with the Cain-like murderer of his own blood as with the extravagant, foolish youth evoked by Gaunt's death-bed oratory, which is more telling as topical comment on the author's times than as a dying man's authoritative comment on the play's action so far. Gaunt is a repetition, in his old age, uncleship, and midnight care for sleeping England (II. i. 77) of Gloucester in II Henry VI; but whereas Gloucester's warnings are justified by matter in the play, Gaunt's are not. There are no signs of extravagance and folly in Act i, scenes i and iii. The decisions to go to Ireland and to meet sudden expense by arbitrary taxation (I. iv. 42–52) seem tacked on to a scene whose chief interest is the revelation of the depth of Richard's suspicions of Bolingbroke. The seizure of the Duchy of Lancaster is hastily carried out, but because of Richard's suspicion of the Lancasters (I. iv. 20–36) and his blunt retort to York's assurance of Lancaster's 'love'—

> Right, you say true. As Hereford's love, so his;
> As theirs, so mine; and all be as it is.   (II. i. 145–6)

—the affair of the Duchy, like Gloucester's murder, needs a political explanation. Only if one takes the Lancastrian point of view unquestioningly can one see Richard as Gaunt sees him.[5]

The object here is not to defend Richard, who in Shakespeare's hands is a fictitious character anyway, but to observe uncertainties in the play's exposition. The most peculiar discrepancy between what Richard is shown to be and what is said about him is in the matter of flattery. Everyone, it seems (Lancaster, York, Northumberland, the gardener and Bolingbroke), says that Richard is misled by flatterers. Yet Richard, who comes to believe that kingship itself is an enormous and tragic flattery of mortal man, never attends to flatterers (or to anyone else) himself, and has a sharp eye for others' susceptibility to them. He even suspects his own ability to affect men by words. There is an illustration of this when, seeing how much he has moved Aumerle, he turns his eloquent passion into conceited prettiness and so turns his cousin's tears to smiling: 'Well, well, I see/I talk but idly, and you laugh at me' (III. iii. 160–71). The flattery is on the other side. Northumberland flatters Bolingbroke outrageously (II. iii. 2–18), and Bolingbroke in his turn flatters young Henry Percy. Bolingbroke's willingness to give and to receive flattery causes some of the sharpest moments of differentiation between him and Richard, who rebukes, even taunts him for it (III. iii. 190–210, IV. i. 305–8). Richard's own 'flatterers', as far as this play is concerned, go to their deaths faithfully, defying the usurper.

Shakespeare therefore seems to have started the play without a clear idea of the causes of Richard's failure, whether it was political error, faults of character or something like original sin. Or perhaps the idea of the play was strong enough, but the historical material, fact and interpretation together, proved incompatible with the idea. In *Richard II* the imaginative is stronger than the historical. All the conventional explanations of royal weakness—arbitrary behaviour, bad counsel, extravagance, youth—are picked up, but none of them is firmly realised in the plot. The one quality that persists in Richard from the start, which receives no 'choric' comment but is there for the audience to see and the intelligent actor to represent, is a watchful separateness from others arising from his consciousness of being king and therefore alone. His remarks about Bolingbroke's flattery of the common people (I. iv. 23–36) could suggest a sinister contempt for his subjects; but in the context he is commenting on their fickleness. The harsh sarcasms of Richard's conversation with Aumerle in the same scene are the ironies of an intelligent watcher who knows as much of the inward significance of events as anyone. At the same time, there is a pride of intelligence there that combines with the pride of the monarch to make him oblivious of what others say to him. York's long expostulation (II. i. 163–85) goes completely unheard, for instance, and the separation this shows between Richard and his surroundings is more than a simple contrast between the man and the king, between an actor and the part he plays. There is something wrong in the whole position of the man who is required to act and to observe, to control events and to watch them at the same time. Whatever faults of character Richard may have are insignificant if the essential idea is to be that the king's office transcends the capacities of any man, if, in effect, the sacred unity of the king within himself and with his realm is already by the nature of things divided into the secular loneliness of the one and the many.

Richard's isolation has its counterpart in the suggestion carried by the Duchess of Gloucester's imagery (I. ii. 10–21) and Gaunt's (II. i.

40–51) of an original unity broken. To both the speakers, Richard is the cause of the break, but their language describes an event transcending any one man's act: sacred blood spilled, a royal tree hacked, a sceptred isle (a demi-paradise, Eden, a blessed plot, a little world, a teeming womb) become a common farm or tenement. All these images conjure up the familiar idea of a paradise, walled and secluded, now breached and given up to gross and vulgar exploitation. An innocence out of time is spoiled by an act of original wrong which brings it into the complications of timely existence. Both the speakers are old, themselves dying, and their evocation of a visionary, unfallen world, drawn from them in the passion of their own nearness to death, is the more moving by contrast. Death and desecration, it is implied, are very similar things. Much of this imagery will be picked up later by Richard, speaking out of his own experience of disintegration; and for him as for the dying Gaunt, there will be only a very questionable 'music at the close' (II. i. 12).

\* \* \*

With the king's departure for Ireland, the play's action begin to run clear. Away from the superintending glance of Richard's eye the nobles conspire to join Bolingbroke, already at sea with an army; and there is no doubt that they intend to depose Richard (II. i. 291–5). Whatever the King's faults, the conspiracy, formed in passion and secrecy, is sinister from the start. Northumberland, the ringleader, has been in league with Bolingbroke all along. His last speech in Act II, scene i, which sends the rest galloping off to Ravenspurgh, reveals him as a manipulator whose first line to his companions, 'Well, lords, the Duke of Lancaster is dead' (II. i. 224), is intended to begin the working of their feelings to his purpose. The words in which he reveals the plot, '. . . through the hollow eyes of death/I spy life peering' (l. 270), have been glossed as a version of 'the well-known emblem-book figure of the soul trapped inside an anatomy and looking outwards',[6] hence as a suggestion of resurrection or salvation. Perhaps. But not all stirrings of life in death are blessed. In its context of shipwreck and drowning the image calls to mind Clarence's vision of jewels in dead men's skulls and suggests that the 'life' of the conspiracy is, like the *Danse Macabre*, a parody of life. With Northumberland's words death really enters the play. In the next scene the Queen repeats the motif when she says that Green's news of the landing at Ravenspurgh makes him the 'midwife' to her woes. She sees Bolingbroke as the 'dismal heir' begotten upon her by sorrow; she is the 'gasping new-deliver'd mother' of a monstrosity (II. ii. 61–6).

In the following scenes of Bolingbroke's ride through Gloucestershire with Northumberland and his meeting with the Duke of York at Berkeley Castle, the rebels perform parodies of courtesy that at moments are very nearly comical. Act II, scene iii, lines 1–67 is as gross a scene of mutual fawnings as Shakespeare ever wrote, and that it stayed in his mind we know because Hotspur's later recollection of Bolingbroke's part in it ('this king of smiles') characterises it exactly: 'Why, what a candy deal of courtesy/This fawning greyhound then did proffer me!' (*I Henry IV*, I. iii. 251–2). One has a mental picture of smiles all round, what with Northumberland telling Bolingbroke that his 'fair discourse hath been as sugar', and Ross telling him that his 'presence makes [them] rich'. Lord Berkeley, rebuked for calling Bolingbroke 'Hereford' instead of 'Lancaster' (a fault unnoticed in Northumberland thirty lines earlier), cuts through the atmosphere of smiling deceit with a fine sharpness of phrase:

> Mistake me not, my lord; 'tis not my meaning
> To raze one title of your honour out.
> To you, my lord, I come, what lord you will.   (II. iii. 74–6)

Old York will have none of Bolingbroke's gammon either. 'Show me thy humble heart, and not thy knee', he says, and when Bolingbroke tries verbal flattery, the reply is swift: 'Grace me no grace, nor uncle me no uncle./I am no traitor's uncle.' But Bolingbroke, all innocence, will not be kept from the part he has determined to play: 'My gracious uncle, let me know my fault.' When York tells him plainly he is a banished man and a traitor, he replies with an equivocation worthy of Richard III:

> As I was banish'd, I was banish'd Hereford;
> But as I come, I come for Lancaster.   (II. iii. 113–14)

No one who attends to this scene, which later includes both Northumberland's flat lie that no more is intended than Bolingbroke's restitution to his duchy as well as Bolingbroke's smiling compulsion of York to his side, can escape the fact that the rebels are portrayed as knaves and liars, with Bolingbroke the chief liar of them all. He is a type everyone has met, the man whose ruthless selfishness is concealed by a sweet-smiling, pretty-boy exterior, who knows that an engaging manner will get the better of most people, especially women and old men. Words, in the rebel party, are used to disguise intention, and readers who are taken in by Bolingbroke's courtesy, for instance to the Queen (III. i. 36), are missing the sort of linguistic perversion upon which Shakespeare has written the last word in Bassanio's great speech upon ornament (*Merchant of Venice*, III. ii. 73ff.):

So may the outward shows be least themselves;
The world is still deceiv'd with ornament.

The concealed lie, symbolised in *The Merchant of Venice* by the skull in the golden casket, is death. No efficiencies of Bolingbroke's —and many critics have a sneaking regard for efficiency—should hide the truth that his every act is tainted by disingenuousness at best, lies at worst, right up to the end and when he weeps crocodile tears over Richard's murder which he has ordered himself. When Green, illegally condemned to death, says, 'More welcome is the stroke of death to me/Than Bolingbroke to England' (III. i. 31–2), the parallel between Bolingbroke and death is backed by the poetry.

Richard's return (III. ii), therefore, is fully prepared. Having heard what Bolingbroke says and seen what he does, the audience is now to hear what the King can say, to see what the King can do. Richard very rapidly learns that, in the ordinary sense of the word, he can do nothing. He hears of the dispersion of the Welsh army, the deaths of his counsellors and the defection of York, whereupon he dismisses such forces as he has and retires to Flint Castle, a desolate place whose 'rude ribs', 'ruin'd ears' and 'tatter'd battlements' (III. iii. 32, 34, 52) reintroduce the motif of ruin from Act I, scene ii. In fact, the fallen king in the ruined castle is a true version of the emblem of the soul trapped in an anatomy that Northumberland's image of life peering through the hollow eyes of death parodies.[7] Richard has already expressed another, fuller version of the emblem in the preceding scene, in one of his most famous speeches:

> for within the hollow crown
> That rounds the mortal temples of a king
> Keeps Death his court, and there the antic sits,
> Scoffing his state and grinning at his pomp,
> Allowing him a breath, a little scene,
> To monarchize, be fear'd, and kill with looks,
> Infusing him with self and vain conceit,
> As if this flesh which walls about our life
> Were brass impregnable; and humour'd thus
> Comes at the last and with a little pin
> Bores through his castle wall, and—farewell king!
>
> (III. ii. 160–70)

Mediaeval crowns are often depicted as slender, ornamented, circular, golden walls; an impregnable wall of brass around the island of Britain was one of the legendary ambitions credited to Friar Bacon; John of Gaunt speaks of England as a fortress moated and walled by the sea. Like a series of concentric circles, the sea surrounds the island, the wall surrounds the castle, the castle surrounds the man whose flesh surrounds—the skeleton. There the series stops. The protective wall is no protection at all; if one asks what lives within the crown, the model of all these protective circles, the answer is 'death'.

Richard is much criticised for neglecting practical, political issues and meditating upon life and death instead. Yet this, not politics, is the theme of the play. There is nothing left for Richard to do but to undergo and express his fall. In his isolation, compelled by Bolingbroke's power, he is made to be the officiant of what Walter Pater called 'an inverted rite',[8] a coronation run backwards. The whole process from the landing in Wales to the last scene in prison is the unmaking of the unity, sacramental or hypothetical, depending upon one's point of view, that is the 'king'. This is an act of un-creation, and at the end Richard Plantagenet in his very person is the creature unmade.

Understanding of this process is hindered by secular habits of speech and thought. If, for instance, we speak of a 'divinely sanctioned kingship', our use of the phrase implies that other adjectives could be found, that other forms of kingship could be named, and that they might be variously sanctioned. There is to our minds no necessary connection between what we might suggest by 'reality' and any one form of government, let alone a particular kind of monarchy. Few people today except the Communists would describe any social order as 'real' or 'necessary'. The practice of politics is an art; a polity is an artefact made under specific conditions in certain times and places, and is to be judged by its usefulness: 'What's best administered is best.' True, ontological considerations have a way of creeping in, but not always consciously and often contradictorily. The pigeon-watching behaviourist turns out on closer inspection to be a Rousseauian perfectionist, the director of an oil company will speak like a Romantic nationalist, and an Irish Catholic will believe as firmly as any Communist in the autonomy of history.

The action of *Richard II*, however, takes us into a world where there is only one form of government, i.e. monarchy, only one kind of monarchy, i.e. the divinely sanctioned, and only one God to sanction it. A divinely sanctioned monarchy is therefore a polity which, in theory, conforms to absolute reality. The sacramental anointing is not an impressive fiction meant to adorn an arbitrarily chosen social system; it is not a symbol of something else. It is a deed which signifies, explains, renews and makes reality. The process of uncrowning Richard is not a 'demythologising'; on the contrary it is a 'mythologising' because it turns something into nothing, a fact into a fiction. Nor is it, as represented on the stage, a ritual (a word loosely used in criticism), but an imitation of the undoing of a ritual, similar in subject matter to unfrocking a priest, returning an officer to the ranks or stripping a man of knighthood. In all these cases a man and a function have been united by a ceremonial form of consecration, commissioning or 'creation'. The difference between them is that while priests, officers and knights are many, the King, like the Pope, is one within the sphere of his rule. Upon that one, moreover, depend all the rest. The King is the 'fountain of honour', just as the Pope, according to the Catholic view, is the rock on which the Church and the apostolic succession are founded.

Indeed, the theory of the old monarchy is a parody of the Church's organisation and not in theory 'absolute' at all. Rather it is an inverted democracy, a communion of the many in the sacred one, an idea which reached its most elaborate development (exemplified in England by the coronation rite preserved in the Westminster *Liber Regalis*) in the late Middle Ages.

When the unkinging of Richard II is over, it has accomplished a change, not so much in the definition of monarchy as in the object of the audience's perception when the word is used. The king by nature's law and God's has been 'dismembered' before their eyes, divorced first from his realm, the 'body politic', by conspiracy and rebellion, then from his own sense of his royalty, then from the consecrated ornaments of his office and person, which are passed across the stage as if they were only 'properties'. The king himself is finally reduced to an imprisoned mind in a defenceless body, helplessly conscious of failure, and unable to order even his thoughts into a coherent whole. The irreducible actuality of the scene is the passage of time reflected in the mechanism of a clock. Meanwhile another man has become king by ascending the regal throne in God's name (IV i. 113) and clothing himself in the regal ornaments.

One running line of commentary upon this process calls it a sacrilege, which it obviously is in the plainest sense, since sacred things—the king's person, royal and human included—are turned into common objects, and the extremity of this sacrilege is emphasised by a very natural analogy to Christ's passion. Richard's rebelling people are Judases, his judges Pilates (IV. i. 170, 239). 'Dust was thrown upon his sacred head' (v. ii. 30); and, most telling of all, we have York's explanation of these events:

> . . . had not God, for some strong purpose, steel'd
> The hearts of men, they must perforce have melted,
> And barbarism itself have pitied him.   (v. ii. 34–6)

The 'hardening of the heart', a phrase formerly of greater significance than now, with weighty theological overtones, is a sign of the
suppression of something vital in men, a lessening of their capacity
to feel things truly.

One of the most interesting things in Shakespeare's treatment of
this action is that, because of the dispassionateness with which he
balances Richard's tragedy against Bolingbroke's rise, the 'kingship'
—the centre and object of the conflict—in being transferred from
one man to another, becomes the reality. Separated from the man,
it then makes another man into a king. The regalia are never the
objects of irreverence even though they are separated from their
originally consecrated use; but they are put to a subtly new employ-
ment becoming, they and the monarchy with them, the sanctions of
power or, as Richard puts it, 'the strong'st and surest way to get'
(III. iii. 201). The 'king' turns into a lay-figure, like one of those
museum suits of armour that every little boy wishes to climb into.
While the mere body of the deposed king becomes a prison to him
(v. v. 1–66), the 'body' he has sloughed off becomes the habitation
of his usurper. In this way the divinity of kingship is aggrandised
at the expense of the king's humanity or, to put it another way, the
'divine humanity' is separated into its constituent parts. And so
kingship is mythologised, turned to a role, to a symbolic fiction, to
a piece of sentimental rhetoric dressing up a very workaday actuality.

When York is loyal to the new King to the extent of informing
upon his son, his loyalty is to the office, not to the man, an equivocation easily made the excuse for a multitude of treasons. This probably explains the play's political significance in its time. What is to us
an intensely royalist play, because of the lyrical power with which
the poet sings his theme of deposition, seems so because we are no
longer royalists. The royal person is not really taboo to us, but to
the Earl of Essex's supporters in 1601 the play will have been an
acting out of two deeds essential to their rebellion, the sacrilege of
the uncrowning and the separation of the monarch's person from the
monarchy. The lyricism was essential to the enactment, for it meant
that, like Henry IV in the play, they could weep as they struck.

The centre of the play's interest, then, is not in the rights and
wrongs of a political struggle, but in what happens to a king. Those
who look for an error in the character and actions of the tragic king
will find it in his sudden appropriation of the Duchy of Lancaster
followed by his equally hasty departure for Ireland. This may or may
not be a repetition of the kind of act that removed Gloucester before
the play's opening—we cannot know that—but without any doubt
the act is a 'model' (a favourite word in this play) of the kind of
thing called original sin. Gaunt's lamentations over England as a

despoiled paradise, the Duchess of Gloucester's talk of a royal tree and sacred blood spilled, like the Bishop of Carlisle's prophecy of England's future suffering, refer all acts in the play to an absolute standard of perfection. A case could be made for seeing every act in the play as an error; if Richard is guilty, so is everyone else who acts in this drama.

The chilling, even horrifying figure of the gardener makes this plain. As 'old Adam's likeness' (III. iv. 73) he rules, like a monarch, his unruly garden. He knows the necessities of governrent. The imperative mood comes naturally to him, and he speaks without pity or conscience of beheading and maiming the plants in his care. In his condemnation of Richard there is neither mercy nor sympathy. With removed objectivity he understands the Queen's unhappiness and by planting a symbolic flower gives it a place in his garden; but this does not mitigate his severity. Many have interpreted the scene as an allegorical model of a well-governed country, pointing a moral and setting a standard by which Richard is condemned, Bolingbroke excused. But the geometrical garden is a dream of legal perfection, and before we decide to dream it, we should know that in that garden we would be the plants, not the gardener. The scene's poise, the neatness and simplicity of its allegory have nothing helpful to say, really, about Richard's condition—or our's. The gardener, despite his rustic calm, represents the savagery of the Old Law. He lets us see what goes on behind the garden walls if the protected enclosure is to have the right paradisal look; his orders for binding, cutting off, wounding, and lopping tell what is necessary if nature is to be governed in a graceless world.

*          *          *

As the priest-king and the politician-king change their places, Richard's lonely suffering is dramatised in counterpoint with Bolingbroke's first moves in the government of his garden, which is by now very disordered indeed. There is a school of criticism that interprets the political scenes—the quarrel in parliament (IV. i. 1–106) and the discovery of Aumerle's plot (V. ii. 41–117, iii. 23–146)—as showing Bolingbroke's efficient wisdom in comparison with Richard's incompetence; but I cannot see that they show anything of the kind. First, the parliament scene is one of disorderly rage very different from the stately order of Richard's political scenes (I. i, iii). Second, it brings up 'that dead time' (IV. i. 10) of the Gloucester murder only to make it clear that the truth will never be known. Like Richard, Bolingbroke fixes a day of trial; but the principal witness is dead, Aumerle has as much as openly named Bolingbroke the real object of his challenge, and Bolingbroke, just as openly, says that his business is to control trouble-makers. There can be no hope that the murder will be solved and the quarrels healed. The scene is politically interesting because Bolingbroke, having become king by politics, must govern by more of the same; but it implies no decisive expression of preference for his methods rather than Richard's.

As for the scenes of Aumerle's plot, these are more funny than significant, and just as the quarrels in parliament hark back to the quarrelling scenes of *Henry VI*, so the comedy in these scenes of the York family and Bolingbroke resembles the blank verse comedy of the older plays. It is comedy of artifice and stylisation. Old York's reaction to Aumerle's plot is as overdone as his furious loyalty to the new King, and by the time we have all three Yorks kneeling, with the duchess apparently scuttling after Bolingbroke on her knees, the scene is foundering in absurdity. This method of ridiculing a subject by style appears in *I Henry VI*, and it turns up again in the very late plays. It seems to be Shakespeare's way of disengaging himself from material essential to the narrative that he wants firmly put in a subordinate place. York is acting towards Bolingbroke as he should have acted towards Richard, and the whole episode, with York playing the loyal subject, his duchess the distraught mother, Aumerle the repentant traitor, and Bolingbroke the gracious king, is an example of those fantastic tricks played before high heaven that make the angels weep. Shakespeare's disengagement in these scenes, like the ambivalence and concealment of the early scenes, concentrates attention on the essence of the action, on what happens to Richard.

Richard believes in his sanctity, and Shakespeare gives it full and magnificent expression in every scene that concerns the King, from his return (III. ii) onwards. Richard's sanctity saves neither him nor England from the politician who, knowing 'the strong'st way to get', penetrates the protective wall of ceremony around the King and the realm. The usurper has a case, of course, as does everyone, and a measure of success. After all, this is history; one king fell, and another took his place. But the usurper's reasonings cannot explain that fall satisfactorily, any more than can the fallen man's self-recrimination, his uncle's warnings, his aunt's lamentations or his gardener's hindsight. The play's action therefore turns inward, concentrating upon the experience of the fall.

Unlike later tragic heroes, Richard does not himself ask plainly, 'Why?' Rather, the play's construction in the form of a conflict based upon an unsolved mystery forces the audience to ask the question, and to look to Richard for an answer. He, at the end as at the beginning, is the only man who has inward knowledge of the King's acts. Brought up against that 'Why?' the King's royalty is as much a pose as Bolingbroke's popularity. For many the play's issue is a choice of roles. Since Richard's and Carlisle's prophecies both prove true, one can lament the usurpation, fearing and understanding the turmoiled future. On the other hand, one can take the tough view that nothing fails like failure or succeeds like success, choosing simply not to dispute facts, and preferring to have one's grievance against an imperfect world redressed by Bolingbroke, warts and all. Shakespeare however has already undercut the tough view by his portrait of the rebel party and by his analysis of power-neurosis in the earlier histories. Even if one takes the view that Bolingbroke is the best of Shakespeare's politicians, his lies a form of courtesy, his acts just in their rough way, his usurpation leads to the wars of Henry VI, and ultimately to his own despair in *II Henry IV*.

*Richard II*'s 'Why?' disposes of both roles, the sacred and the profane. In Richard's final scene in prison, Shakespeare analyses the former as he has already analysed the latter in the characters of York, Richard III, Clarence and King John; and he ends with the same result. This prison scene is the beginning which has in it the end of Shakespeare's narrative of English history. Lyrical, expressive, icon-like, it stands, like Gaunt's speech and the Duchess of Gloucester's mourning, somewhat removed from the flow of events. It has the stillness and abstractedness of thought, as Richard in the prison of the realm and time, in the prison prepared by his captor, and in the prison of his own body, anatomises 'the grief within', bringing us to the centre of all the concentring circles of ceremony and symbol, and finding—nothing:

> But what'er I be,
> Nor I nor any man that but man is
> With nothing shall be pleas'd, till he be eas'd
> With being nothing.   (v. v. 38–41)

All the poetry in the play opposes itself to that blankness. This is the Shakespearean pessimism described by T. S. Eliot,[9] which so few readers are prepared to see. The fall of Shakespearean man is not, like the theological fall, from knowledge into ignorance but from protective ignorance into bleak and appalling knowledge. This fall awaits Hamlet in the ghost's beckoning towards 'the dreadful summit of the cliff/That beetles o'er his base into the sea' (*Hamlet*, I. iv. 70–1); it awaits Othello when he foresees his death as a dizzying plunge from bliss into a volcano (*Othello*, v. ii. 274–80), and it awaits Claudio as he imagines his spirit 'blown with restless violence round about/The pendent world' (*Measure for Measure*, III. i. 125–6). In *King Lear* Edgar reproduces with remarkable, vertiginous detail the new aspect of things seen with a downward look from a position of isolated objectivity when he describes the cliff 'of high and bending

head' at Dover. Even Bolingbroke, broken by war and anxiety, has
his vision of a vast encircling absurdity when he thinks of the ship-
boy sleeping, carelessly ignorant, 'upon the high and giddy mast . . .
In cradle of the rude imperious surge' (*II Henry IV*, III. i. 18–20);
and this thought leads him to a sense like Hamlet's of life as an
enormous, pointless process of change to which he responds with a
deep yielding towards death:

> O God! that one might read the book of fate,
> And see the revolution of the times
> Make mountains level, and the continent,
> Weary of solid firmness, melt itself
> Into the sea! and, other times, to see
> The beachy girdle of the ocean
> Too wide for Neptune's hips; how chances mock,
> And changes fill the cup of alteration
> With divers liquors! O, if this were seen,
> The happiest youth, viewing his progress through,
> What perils past, what crosses to ensue,
> Would shut the book, and sit him down and die.          (ll. 45–56)

The humane reasonableness of Warwick's reply to the man who is
now Henry IV cannot touch the root of that melancholy, though it
stirs the King to a stoical, stylish action which is the hallmark of these
Shakespearean men: 'Are these things then necessities? Then let us
meet them like necessities.'
     Richard II, though, was there before Henry IV:

> Down, down I come; like glist'ring Phaeton,
> Wanting the manage of unruly jades.
> In the base court? Base court, where kings grow base,
> To come at traitors' calls and do them grace.
> In the base court? Come down? Down, court! down, king!
>                                        (III. iii. 178–83)

A lot of readers have agreed with Northumberland that 'Sorrow and
grief of heart/Makes him speak fondly, like a frantic man.' As so
much modern scholarship shows, the elegiac sweetness in Shakespeare's evocations of an ordered cosmos speaks eloquently to us who
need no poetic or prophetic imagination to see its loss; but we can
only wonder at the noble rage with which his men tread upon the
verge of that other cosmos, bleak and infinite, lying around and
within them.

# The Secular City:
## *Pericles, Prince of Tyre to Timon of Athens*

PART ONE

# Unpath'd Waters

# 7. Pericles, Prince of Tyre

The chronologers are generally agreed that *Pericles* was written sometime in 1607 or very early 1608; and although like most Shakespearean dating this conclusion is not supported by absolutely firm evidence, it seems to be as reliable as any. The play is therefore a successor to *Macbeth* and *King Lear,* roughly contemporary with *Antony and Cleopatra,* perhaps earlier than *Coriolanus.* We should also add *Timon of Athens* to this list of *Pericles'* contemporaries since although *Timon* is not really datable at all, and is just as puzzling in its own way as *Pericles,* various kinds of internal evidence have led the majority of scholars to date *Timon* around 1607.[1] At the time he wrote *Pericles,* then, Shakespeare was by no means wedded to any particular kind of play. Were a modern dramatist to write six so different plays in a period of three or four years, most reviewers would be thoroughly confused by the third year. From the biographical point of view these years, like Shakespeare's first years in the theatre, are among the puzzles of his life.

There is no evidence that three of these plays—*Timon, Antony,* and *Coriolanus*—were performed in Shakespeare's time. Absence of evidence does not mean that the plays were definitely not performed, but it does not allow us to take performance for granted either. As for *Timon,* its text is badly printed; and the play's construction is so tentative in places that there is now a consensus that it is an incomplete work printed from the author's draft. Should this be so, one would like to know how Heminges and Condell came to have Shakespeare's incomplete manuscript in 1623. Did the family turn it over, or had Shakespeare given it to the company for someone else to finish? This seems unlikely because *Timon* is too nearly finished to look like the surviving part of an unfinished collaborative work; but I raise the possibility because collaboration is still a live issue in connection with Shakespeare's later work. The case for dual authorship in *Henry VIII* still has advocates, and even if one dismisses the lost *Cardenio,*[2] acted at court in the winter of 1612–13, as a phantom addition to the list of Shakespeare's collaborations with Fletcher, there is still *The Two Noble Kinsmen,* ascribed on the title-page of the 1634 quarto to Mr John Fletcher and Mr William Shakespeare.

Shakespeare's part in this play is now universally allowed, but so far Paul Bertram's energetic argument for Shakespeare's sole authorship has not drawn much support.[3] In the case of *Pericles*, the most inexperienced reader would suspect that at least two men wrote it.

The disintegration of Shakespeare's early plays now strikes most people as a curiosity of Victorian criticism, and we can read them reasonably confident that Shakespeare wrote them. Disintegration of the later plays still stands because it is based on stronger evidence: in *Pericles*, a marked difference in style; in *Henry VIII*, a difference in style less well-marked, but supported by verse tests which still impress many; in *The Two Noble Kinsmen*, a difference in style, verse tests, and a title-page. None of this evidence is conclusive, whether in detail or in accumulation; but there has been no dramatic advance in scholarship to overturn it as Pollard's and Alexander's work overturned the assumptions underlying the disintegration of the early plays. A reader, whether he likes it or not, needs to bear in mind that in the opinion of many only about half the lines in these three plays are Shakespeare's.

If, however, Shakespeare wrote these plays in collaboration with someone else, the result is dual authorship of an unusual kind in the Elizabethan theatre; for each play has a marked unity of tone and theme which is determined by the part everyone agrees to be Shakespeare's. Whether the second author was John Fletcher or the hypothetical unknown who may have provided the first two acts of *Pericles*, his role was a minor one. The result suggests that like certain painters, Shakespeare completed all that part of the work upon which the wholeness of effect depends, and left the remainder to a subordinate writer. There must have been advice or supervision, because Fletcher never wrote so much like Shakespeare as in the two plays where, according to disintegrationist scholarship, he was writing with Shakespeare.

Unfortunately the text of *Pericles* is so mutilated that no one would wish to rest an argument on any single detail of it. Heminges and Condell missed it out of the Folio. They may have forgotten it, there may have been no text available, or they may have known it was not wholly Shakespeare's. Equally unfortunately the Quarto published in 1609 has all the earmarks of a piracy, its text extremely corrupt and badly printed. Most scholars have assumed that the stylistic differences between the first two and the last three acts are evidence of dual authorship. More recently, however, Philip Edwards has argued that the stylistic differences are evidence that the text is the work of two reporters whose vagaries do not necessarily reflect the nature of the original text. This argument, which Professor Edwards has developed further in his recent edition of the play, leads one to be sceptical of all the authorship theories based upon the Quarto text.[4]

In general, however, there is no doubt of Shakespeare's authorship of the major scenes which determine one's sense of the play as a whole; and so the problem of authorship is not terribly important for a reader except as it affects one character, the poet John Gower who appears throughout the play as narrator, presenter and commentator. Gower speaks eight choruses. The first four and the seventh are in octosyllabics; the fifth, sixth and eighth (the epilogue) are decasyllabic. The general assumption has been that the decasyllabic choruses are Shakespeare's, the others the work of an unknown coadjutor; and since the use of Gower largely determines the treatment of the plot, the argument has followed that Shakespeare's work did not go beyond the finishing off of someone else's play. That play, in turn, might be an old play revived or a new one incompetently written, and there is no end to the entities that subtle bibliographers can multiply between those alternatives.

On the whole the choruses, with the exception of the sixth, are a consistent stylistic group despite the variation of metre. Even the sixth as it proceeds takes on more of the archaic tone of the others. Whether one prefers the decasyllabics or not, the change in metre alone tells nothing except that someone, whether a reviser or the original writer, neglected to maintain the archaic style. Should one try to explain this by assuming that Shakespeare wrote the decasyllabic choruses as additions, revisions, or as part of his allocated share of a collaborative work, then the assumption will beg the authorship question.[5]

Of their kind, and allowing for textual corruption, the choruses are good, their tone and content suited to their formal purpose, their syntax well adapted to stage speaking (important because octosyllabics, though an easy metre, are not often suited to speaking aloud). Although neither critics nor editors have paid much attention to Gower, except to remark on the crudity of the character as a device for turning a narrative into a play, his purpose is to frame the action, and his part requires considerable stylisation to separate him from his narrative. Even in his earliest work Shakespeare was adept at putting a distance betwen a play and its audience or between one part of a play and another by means of stylistic difference. His favourite method, similar to that used here in *Pericles*, was to use a more artificial style, particularly an archaic one. Sometimes the result is a language so quaint in comparison with the normal style of the play that many readers have suspected the presence of a second author. Notable examples are the play scene in *Hamlet* and Posthumus' dream in *Cymbeline*. Less striking, but important because of the use of octosyllabics, are Hymen's speech in *As You Like It* and one of the Duke's speeches in *Measure for Measure*; and there is always Puck in *Midsummer Night's Dream*.

Gower is even an interesting character. He has the self-effacing modesty of the mediaeval author. He woos the audience's imagination gently and unobtrusively, bringing in the dumb-shows and the action so quietly that while they seem to be the creatures of his imagination they also take on the heightened reality of successful magic. His presence, the limitations of his simple speech, and his homely moralisings keep the illusionary characters firmly within the time and place of the stage. If we form conclusions about the play's story different from Gower's, we should have no doubt that this is the work of our own imagination rather than the intent of the teller. Indeed Gower is an interesting artistic invention, and those who dismiss him as a crude device have hardly thought about him. His presence shapes the play's form, making us conscious of it as a tale in the telling and of the dramatist as storyteller.

These effects are inseparable from the great simplicity of Gower's story. The arrangement of its incidents is chronological, and there is no necessary connection between one incident and another. Although Pericles leaves Tyre a second time for fear of Antiochus, there is no reason why he should call at Tarsus. In this example there is a general motivation, but not a specific one; sometimes there is no motive of any kind, as when Pericles gives no reason for leaving Marina at Tarsus, or when Thaisa gives no reason for entering the temple at Ephesus. The plot's resolution begins when Pericles arrives by accident at Mytilene; and although he proceeds to Ephesus in response to a vision, he has no idea what he will find there. In a tale so lacking in motivation the characters represent ways of being that we take for granted, not persons who become what they are through choice. The language is also simple, and never more so than at the climactic moments.

The simplicity of *Pericles* is intentional, as much of a virtuoso performance in its way as the complexity of *Cymbeline;* and, despite the mutilation of its text, the play is a consistent whole. If Shakespeare finished someone else's work, then he ratified its plan; but there is always the possibility that the plan was his from the start. The change in Gower's choruses at the end may be a way of blending Gower in more completely and subtly with his story towards its conclusion. Like all such problems, the authorship of *Pericles* will remain in part an unsolved mystery; but at least we have reason for believing that Shakespeare's mind shaped the design of the play.

*          *          *

In the early sixteenth century it was commonly accepted that the founding masters of English poetry were Gower, Chaucer and Lydgate. Of these three, Gower was the forerunner, praised for his matter and his morals, but criticised for the simplcty of his language:

> Gower's English is old
> And of no value told
> His matter is worth gold
> And worthy to be enrolled.[6]

Later poets, including Lydgate, took Chaucer as their model for style and form, drawing especially on his dream visions and the *Troilus*. All three poets, of course, were thought of primarily as narrative poets, and this critical tradition was strong enough in the later sixteenth century for Spenser to continue it with *The Faerie Queen*. Through the *Mirror for Magistrates* the tradition exercised a direct and, in the minds of many, baleful influence on the drama. An Elizabethan poet who was at all conscious of English poetic tradition would see his writing as being in descent from, or in reaction to, the three great mediaeval masters of narrative and style; and if a poet chose to use a story from Gower, having the character of Gower present it himself in archaic octosyllabics, then he was almost certainly reverting, consciously, to the source of his tradition.

Gower the storyteller stands at the source of English poetic tradition, but the story he tells and his reason for telling it take us into a wider tradition. The tale of Apollonius of Tyre as we know it is mediaeval, though presumably derived from a Greek original. It survives in over a hundred manuscripts in Europe, and virtually every European nation has translated it into its own language. It became a popular tale, too, although it is not one that has survived into modern times by being included in children's collections. There is incest at the start of it, and its heroine has experiences that even modern children are not quite ready for.

This story, the same but for a few minor variations as the story of *Pericles*, is one of the great typical narratives. It is morally typical, telling of an unexpected discovery of evil, of the flight away from it, and of the desire to possess the good and the beautiful. It is psychologically typical in translating evil into sexual perversion. Its inconsequentiality is typical, the way it tells of a life lived in sea-voyaging without clear destination, of storm and calm, good fortune and bad. Above all it moves and satisfies us because it spans great distances, a long tract of time, and because it treats of extremes in character and behaviour. Our temptation is to allegorise it, and any number of allegories lie ready for use; but neither Shakespeare nor his character Gower shows any allegorical tendency whatever. At the end Gower

draws a simple moral from his tale; at the beginning he says he tells
it because it will do us good:

> To sing a song that old was sung,
> From ashes ancient Gower is come,
> Assuming man's infirmities,
> To glad your ear and please your eyes.
> It hath been sung at festivals,
> On ember-eves and holidays;
> And lords and ladies in their lives
> Have read it for restoratives.
> The purchase is to make men glorious. (i. i. 1–9)

We shall never know just how much Shakespeare owed to an older
England, already passing away in his time, of storytelling and ballad
singing. It is possible that some of his plots that we trace to books,
and that he perhaps verified in books, first came to him from fireside
storytellers. In Gower's opening words there is a theory of the uses
and the occasions of storytelling that most of us have only heard of,
if we have heard of it at all, in connection with Celtic, especially
Irish traditions; but the same ideas must once have circulated in
England too. Gower says that he has returned to tell a story that was
formerly told on feast days and on the eves of fastings, that was read
by lords and ladies for their souls' health, and that brings a grace to
the reader or the hearer.

Similar things were said about the 'noble' or 'primary' tales
formerly recited by Irish poets. One of the three wonders attaching
to the *Táin bó Cuailnge* (*The Cattleraid of Cooley*) was 'a year's
protection to him to whom it is recited'. There is a legend about
another tale, *The Fosterage of the Two Methers*, that St Patrick
ordained its many virtues:

> I shall leave these virtues
> For the story of Ethne from the fair Maigue.
> Success in children, success in foster-sister or brother,
> To those it may find sleeping with fair women.

Men are advised to hear the *Fosterage* before a voyage, before a
judgement or a hunting, when bringing home a wife, before going
into a new banqueting house. If told to a king 'to a musical instrument':

> He gets no cause to repent it,
> Provided he listen without conversation.

If told to the 'captives of Ireland', 'it will be the same as if their locks and their bonds were opened'. Similar virtues were ascribed to the tales of ancient Indian tradition.[7]

Another aspect of the old tradition of storytelling has a bearing on *Pericles*. In Ireland the poets learned the stories as part of their training; the master poets or ollaves were expected to know three hundred and fifty of them accurately. In the *Book of Leinster* the *Táin* ends, 'A blessing on everyone who will memorise the *Táin* with fidelity in this form and will not put any other form on it.' One result of this fidelity to the stories is that Irish scribes in the later Middle Ages preserved older forms of the language in their writing. In more modern times, storytellers in Scotland have been known to recite from memory passages of verse which neither they nor their listeners could understand, so archaic is the language. The closeness of *Pericles* to its source and the directness with which the tale is turned into the play, are part of the tradition to which the writer is evidently paying homage.

The chief effect of Gower's presence is that narrative is restored to its ancient pre-eminence over character. A character like Hamlet embodies the notion, which is a very modern one, that the self is autonomous: 'Before me,' he seems to say, 'nothing is.' Pericles, however, is obviously the creation of another mind. Indeed, as Gower insists, Pericles is as much the creature of our imaginations, almost, as he is of Gower's. His reality depends upon an agreement between the storyteller and his audience that things should be so, and the tale is older than either of them. Second, *Pericles* reveals the essential history of the Elizabethan drama as an etymology reveals the history of a word. As Gower turns his narrative into dumbshow, and then into spoken action, we see the art of the storyteller turning into the art of the dramatist, and the Elizabethan drama is above all a narrative art; as Edwin Muir said, it was the successor to the long mediaeval tradition of narrative.[8] If Shakespeare intended these effects, then *Pericles* is an experimental play, an attempt to restore the drama to a pure narrative form.

Whether the drama ever had such a purity is another question, and if the case were to be successfully argued, one would have to speak only of poetic drama. Anyone can write a play or tell a story and anyone, if it comes to that, can write a poem. What mediaeval tradition valued, and what Shakespeare restored in his last plays is the uniting in one work of the arts of the poet and the narrator. Drama itself, freed from the constraints of such customs as ruled the theatre of Athens, of China and Japan, has more in common with the aims of the mountebank, the journalist and the side-show than with any high art. There was always a strong element of mountebankery in the Elizabethan theatre because it was a crowd-pleasing, money-making business; and although in recent years it has been fashionable to praise the Elizabethan audience very highly, there is evidence in the *Sonnets* and in *Hamlet* that Shakespeare, like other dramatists, resented his audience's vulgar streak.

Characters like Richard III, Hamlet and Falstaff have to please 'the gentlemen understanders' (as Ben Jonson ironically calls them) by soliloquy, direct address, confession, wit and a fine, bold style of speaking. In so far as a silk purse can be made out of a sow's ear, Shakespeare made one, as Dickens did when he turned 'a certain sixpenny something' into *The Pickwick Papers*. Yet the taint of origin remains, affecting the form. There is plenty of gloriously bad, ranting verse in Shakespeare, not all of it ironically meant.[9] The more conscientious dramatists knew that their artistic difficulties arose from the forms of popular theatre. Ben Jonson, the most influential theorist among them, tried to discipline his audience with neo-classical theory and practice. Shakespeare, with that artistic instinct which is one of the most remarkable forms of intelligence, chose to experiment within the native tradition of poetic narrative.

It would be interesting to know the sources of his ideas. Besides personal experience of storytellers, he must have known Sidney's description of the true poet:

> ... with a tale, forsooth, he cometh unto you, with a tale which holdeth children from play, and old men from the chimney corner; and, pretending no more, doth intend the winning of the mind from wickedness to virtue.[10]

Several of his fellow dramatists shared his interest in narrative drama, too. Someone revived the old comic romance *Mucedorus*, giving it a new opening written in the style of Shakespeare's own early comedies. Heywood's *Four Prentices of London*, Beaumont and Fletcher's *Knight of the Burning Pestle*, and some of John Day's work, are signs that dramatists in search of subjects were turning to the theatre's own past. But the result was a sophisticated primitivism dabbled in for its own sake, whereas with Shakespeare there can be no doubt that he aimed at a Sidneian nobility from the first experiment onwards.

Of all the tendencies leading Shakespeare towards writing *Pericles*, the strongest and closest to him are revealed in his own *King Lear*. That play, which draws on material from Sidney and Spenser for its plot, has many qualities of Romantic narrative. Different characters are from time to time presenters, narrators or commentators, and the plot draws its strength from two ubiquitous themes of ancient narrative: the wicked sisters and the neglected child. Like many old stories, *King Lear* has an action spread over wide tracts of time and place, and it includes many people; it is remote, set far away in time, but it is also as close to us as our own feelings.

Fictions, like arguments, have their axioms governing what follows. King Lear's great age, which is so much at odds with the energy of his will, is the basis of the tragedy. With a capacity for life barely diminished, Lear has nothing to live for. 'Is there any cause in nature that makes these hard hearts?' he asks, and the story has its answer: old age and death. *King Lear* is about loss so complete that in the end it includes even the capacity to feel loss. Cordelia's death, which is *really* pointless, vindicating no principle whether of good or evil, is necessary because it finally destroys the old man's spirit as nothing else could. It also objectifies the dark fears that drive the play to its exhausted, blank conclusion.

The story of these imaginary people can move its hearers as if it were real. During the time of their story's enactment we watch them as we might watch something in the street; the play over, we go home, conscious ourselves of being different people in different roles, in a different world. Although conventional distinctions are made between the unreality of a play and the reality of a street, the more one thinks about it the more the distinction (from a spectator's point of view) tends to disappear. Men have called out warnings to Othello, have nodded in reply to Hamlet's questions, have wept with King Lear; in the street they have foiled criminals, listened to a stranger's story, wept at someone else's misfortune. Some men show sympathy neither in the street nor in the theatre, and there are streets, like plays, that inspire little conviction in the passer-by. Conventional notions of immediacy have little to do with it. In the Highlands of Scotland, a man telling a story of Finn MacCool would lean forward at an interesting stage of the narrative, touch his listener on the knee and wink as if the legendary hero were his next neighbour and the story happened yesterday. Even aesthetic distinctions can disappear, since a street event may have the completeness of a play and might, like an ancient battle, be turned into narrative on the spot.

Another characteristic of narrative is that, as the proverb says, 'One tale's good till another's told.' Having laughed at Sir Toby Belch today, we may weep with Hamlet tomorrow, and this fickleness in the spectators applies equally to the author, since Shakespeare wrote *Hamlet* and *Twelfth Night* at approximately the same time. Furthermore, one story leads to another, a natural fact that provides the structural framework for some of the most famous collections of stories. One of the qualities of *King Lear* is that it makes one wish to hear another story, one larger and less confining. As several critics have noticed, the frame of reference in *King Lear* is intentionally restricted. In so far as the action concerns human experience and feeling, it is drawn on the largest scale; but in so far as it deals with the meaning of experience, it is drawn very small. A story set in Ancient Britain by an author who, like his contemporaries, believes that all learning comes from Greece, Israel and Rome, is going to be very bare of philosophical, theological or cultural reference—and intentionally so. At several points in the play general statements about life's meaning (or meaninglessness) arise out of events, e.g.,

> When we are born, we cry that we are come
> To this great stage of fools. (iv. vi. 186)

Such passages are more emotional than intellectual; they show what uninstructed nature can achieve, but on reflection they are 'overstated understatements', saying with great emphasis rather less than one had thought. The author restricts his characters' thoughts with stringent discipline. The most famous instance is Gloucester's statement, which many have seized on, 'As flies to wanton boys, are we to 'th' gods' (iv. i. 38). Edgar will have none of this; as he later says, 'Men must endure their going hence even as their coming hither; Ripeness is all' (v. ii. 10). This gnomic naturalism persists through the play's last scene where Lear, finally broken, lapses into madness, which is a sort of kindness or grace in nature, like the panic that anaesthetises.

It is not that a larger frame of reference would necessarily, in the long run, make more sense of the story; simply that readers feel the restriction after a while, and long for a way out. Everyone knows the famous story of the Old English wise men who told the Christian missionaries that until their coming life was to them like a sparrow flying out of the darkness into a lighted hall and then, very soon, finding itself in the dark again. *King Lear* puts its readers back into such a world. There are two hints in *King Lear* of a way into another story, two suggestions of something knowable yet distinct from the natural order. Neither of them is qualified, like Gloucester's pessimism or Lear's mad antinomianism, by another character's comment. They occur in Lear's meeting with Cordelia, where their mutual recognition is presented as an instance of what we have learned to call blessedness; and in Lear's evocation, using some of the most mysterious words in the play, of a superintendent order of beings:

> Upon such sacrifices, my Cordelia,
> The gods themselves throw incense. (v. iii. 20–1)

No hint is given as to the significance of 'sacrifice' in this context. All the emphasis is upon the gods, spectators whose incense is the reflection of the human audience's applause and admiration but not —if one is to stay within the play's text—of their morals, beliefs or tears. Nor is Lear's and Cordelia's blessedness related to any express belief or principle; it is an interpretation put upon a natural affection, and what we make of it is our own affair. Yet these two things, the meeting of father and daughter and the presence of the supernatural, provide the climax of *Pericles*. Whatever one's critical judgement of *Pericles* (and both the state of the text and Romantic notions of the transcendence of tragedy make judgement difficult), its story is a larger one than the story of Lear, which is tributary to it, and out of which it grows; and its hero is a more typical man than the old king.[11]

\* \* \*

The misfortunes of Pericles begin in young manhood when he leaves his native place, and at first they coincide with youth and ignorance. His marriage lasts only a year, after which, on a voyage back to his own land, his wife apparently dies in childbirth during a great storm. He then loses his baby girl when he gives her out to fosterage, and this loss seems final when, on going to reclaim her fourteen years later, he is told she is dead. She meanwhile, having escaped from murder into slavery, is undegoing the trial of temptation in a brothel. The reunion of father and daughter occurs almost simultaneously with her betrothal, and is the prelude to the reunion of Pericles and his lost wife.

Just to go over the main outline of the story will suggest to anyone with experience of life and fiction that there is something decidedly typical about it. Without being either allegorical or realistic, the story is like life in the brevity of its joy and the length of its sorrows as well as in the kind of experience it encompasses. Stories, however, do not succeed by being typical. From its first scene at the court of Antiochus, *Pericles* is a succession of images inscrutably strange and unexpected: the severed heads at Antioch; the fishermen catching Pericles' armour; Pericles' entrance after shipwreck, wet, and his arrival at the tournament in rusty armour. These oddities awaken our interest in the unexpected, accustoming us to the strangeness of things and to violent contrasts. If the story is typical, well then, the typical is marvellous, and appearances are riddles. The imaginary vision of Queen Thaisa dead, 'lying with simple shells', overwhelmed by 'the belching whale and humming water' (III. i. 62–5), so mingles death with life as to make it seem other than it is; and when the same queen, richly dressed and jewelled, lives again, revived by music and incense, the scene is a challenge to one's capacity for imagining marvels.

The heroines of these romantic stories are always wholly beautiful —that much we take for granted—although in each of Shakespeare's romantic plays the special quality of the heroine's beauty arises from the story. When Marina, so named because she was born at sea, reappears in Act IV at the age of fourteen, she enters gathering flowers by the seaside for her nurse's grave. The flowers' fragility and their association with death, her own birth in a storm, and the violence of the world are the subjects of her first speech:

> No, I will rob Tellus of her weed,
> To strew thy green with flowers. The yellows, blues,
> The purple violets, and marigolds
> Shall as a carpet hang upon thy grave
> While summer-days doth last. Ay me! poor maid,
> Born in a tempest when my mother died,
> This world to me is like a lasting storm,
> Whirring me from my friends.   (IV. i. 14–21)

Gower, speaking of her needlework and her singing that 'made the night-bird mute' calls her 'absolute Marina', and her first speech vindicates him. Her beauty is the visible form of an elegiac lyricism associated with birds, flowers and music. It may seem a vulnerable beauty, but it survives storms, and shows a quiet, rooted strength. 'Thou dost look', says Pericles later,

> Like Patience gazing on kings' graves, and smiling
> Extremity out of act.   (V. i. 138–40)

The classicism and monumentality of this famous image evoke an inward strength that radiates moral power. Like Pericles' comparison of Marina with her mother in the same scene, its language is in contrast with our general impression of her slightness and simplicity.

> My dearest wife was like this maid, and such a one
> My daughter might have been. My Queen's square brows;
> Her stature to an inch; as wand-like straight;
> As silver-voic'd; her eyes as jewel-like
> And cas'd as richly; in pace another Juno.   (V. i. 108–12)

The comic scenes in the brothel, however, are also very important in giving us a clear sight of Marina's moral power. Victorian critics who rhapsodised over Marina as an embodiment of ideal womanhood objected to the scenes because of their indecency. Modern critics who find the play as a whole unreal welcome them as proof that Shakespeare was still in touch with actuality, but balk at the climax when Marina discovers to Boult, the brothel servant, the truth about his life:

> *Marina.* Thou hold'st a place for which the pained'st fiend
> Of hell would not in reputation change.
> Thou art the damned doorkeeper to every
> Coistrel that comes inquiring for his Tib.
> To the choleric fisting of every rogue
> Thy ear is liable; thy food is such
> As hath been belch'd on by infected lungs.
> *Boult.* What would you have me do? Go to the wars, would
> you, where a man may serve seven years for the
> loss of a leg, and have not money enough in the
> end to buy him a wooden one? (IV. vi. 173–84)

Whether one takes the view that the brothel scenes are meant to show Marina 'moving unsullied through the lowest depths',[12] or that they are there simply to provide comedy, these words will seem out of place. Boult's question, says John Danby, cannot be answered 'out of the Arcadian book'.[13] In other words, *Pericles* is a romance, and serious questions should not be asked in romances. But whether the question can be answered out of the Arcadian book or not, Marina answers it:

> Do anything but this thou doest. Empty
> Old receptacles, or common shores, of filth;
> Serve by indenture to the common hangman.
> Any of these ways are yet better than this . . . (IV. vi. 185–8)

There is no *a priori* reason why Marina should not speak as she does of prostitution, and none why she should not answer Boult. She survives the brothel because she knows what it is, not because of some mysterious, untouchable virtue given her by the genre called romance; and her reply to Boult is based on a knowledge of life superior to his.

The comedy that critics praise so highly in these scenes is largely owing to Boult. He may be a brothel doorkeeper, but he has the breath of intelligent and subtle life in him. Only an odd sort of sentimentality or snobbishness would object to Marina's trying to save Boult as well as herself from the brothel. He has no more business there than she has. Of course his question can be answered, and although it is very doubtful whether he acts upon Marina's words, his last speech to her is moving in the way Shakespeare's comedy can move one, surprisingly and suddenly:

> Come, I'll do for thee what I can; come your ways.

One can laugh very heartily at Marina's effect upon the brothel and its customers and still see, when the climax comes, that she is absolutely right to say that any job is better than selling one's fellow creatures. The great joke of the brothel is that values are there turned topsy-turvy; but our laughter is only secure and hearty if we know that:

> *Bawd.*  Ay, and you shall live in pleasure.
> *Marina.*  No.
> *Bawd.*  Yes, indeed shall you, and taste gentlemen of all fashions. You shall fare well; you shall have the difference of all complexions. What! do you stop your ears?
> *Marina.*  Are you a woman?
> *Bawd.*  What would you have me be, and I be not a woman? (IV. ii. 81–9)

\*          \*          \*

Unqualified distinctions of right and wrong are, as we know, characteristic of the old stories, and in *Pericles* and other late plays, Shakespeare welcomes them. The report of his daughter's death is the worst of Pericles' misfortunes, and his sorrow entrances him so that he barely lives. The recovery of his daughter will be the recovery of his life, and looked at with the limits of the character's knowledge, this recovery will seem to belong to the natural order of things. From the viewpoint of the audience, however, who already know Marina to be wholly good and beautiful, the reunion of father and daughter will seem more than the securing of a natural bond; and indeed the great power of the recognition scene, which all modern critics agree in interpreting as a kind of theatrical epiphany, arises out of Pericles' discovery that the singing girl of Mytilene is, besides being his daughter, good and beautiful almost beyond hope. The simple miracle of the coincidental meeting blends in the king's mind with the wonder of her beauty to give him a sense of life's beginning again; and that sensation transcends knowledge of joy or sorrow, pleasure or pain:

> O Helicanus, strike me, honour'd sir;
> Give me a gash, put me to present pain,
> Lest this great sea of joys rushing upon me

O'erbear the shores of my mortality
And drown me with their sweetness. O, come hither,
Thou that beget'st him that did thee beget;
Thou that wast born at sea, buried at Tarsus,
And found at sea again! O Helicanus,
Down on thy knees, thank the holy gods as loud
As thunder threatens us. This is Marina.   (v. i. 192–201)

The scene is as intense as the meeting of Lear and Cordelia but, because of its place in the story, gathers power as it proceeds until this climactic moment when Pericles seems to be experiencing something absolute in the form of a natural, human relationship; then the absolute itself breaks into the play. As Pericles, enthralled by his good fortune, talks to Lysimachus, Helicanus and Marina, he asks off-handedly in the midst of his other talk, 'But, hark, what music?' Two and a half lines later, receiving no reply, he asks again, 'But, what music?'

| | |
|---|---|
| *Helicanus.* | My lord, I hear none. |
| *Pericles.* | None? |
| | The music of the spheres! List, my Marina. |
| *Lysimachus.* | It is not good to cross him; give him way. |
| *Pericles.* | Rarest sounds! Do ye not hear? |
| *Lysimachus.* | Music, my lord? I hear. |
| *Pericles.* | Most heavenly music! |
| | It nips me unto listening, and thick slumber |
| | Hangs upon mine eyes. Let me rest.   (v. i. 225–36) |

Whereupon Pericles sleeps and receives the vision of Diana that directs him to her temple at Ephesus and his lost wife.

Of all Shakespeare's many *coups de théâtre*, this could be the boldest. As everyone remembers from *The Merchant of Venice*, the music of the spheres is the heavenly music that has its echo in immortal souls:

But whilst this muddy vesture of decay
Doth grossly close it in, we cannot hear it.
                    (*Merchant*, v. i. 64–5)

Pericles is in a blessed, visionary state that comes upon him without his knowing it, and perfectly naturally. He first asks about the music as if someone were playing in the next room; only as he attends to it, does its true nature dawn upon him, and then, almost immediately, it puts him to sleep. Of course, no one else on stage hears it.

Shakespearean editors have a habit of putting stage directions for music into this scene because, as the New Arden editor says, 'As this music is real to Pericles, it must be shared by the audience from the beginning, to avoid the absurd impression of Pericles being deluded.'[14] But if Pericles and the audience hear the music, then everyone else on stage is deluded, including Marina. At Stratford-upon-Avon in 1958 the audience laughed when Helicanus said that he heard no music; they heard it, and knew that it prefigured *musique concrète*. If a director is rash enough to supply music, even of the purest diatonic harmony and intonation, his audience will be bound to doubt the divinity of the sounds they hear, especially since unlike Pericles they remain (one hopes) awake.

The music of the spheres is inaudible to all save the blessed dead and a few living saints; it is inimitable and incommunicable. For five acts of *Pericles*, Gower has persuaded us to bring his tale to life by lending our imaginations to his art, and this is the moment when we and the play are tested. For a few seconds, in complete silence, we watch the hero as he claims to hear the unhearable. If the scene has worked, it will never occur to us to doubt him; moreover, as we watch and listen, we come to know what he is hearing. By imagination we conceive how faith fills the void made by the unimaginable.

After this the play moves swiftly and, it must be said, perfunctorily, to its conclusion. Perhaps the finding of both mother and daughter set Shakespeare an insoluble technical problem, requiring him to bring the play to a double climax; yet, if there was a technical problem, Shakespeare solved it by making the discovery of Thaisa into an epilogue. The truth seems to be that by the time Pericles arrives at Ephesus, Shakespeare's interest in the story is finished, and he hardly tries to do more than round things off. The repetitions of the story grow mildly comical, and one feels that the rhetorician rather than the poet is behind the words that have been so powerfully suggestive in earlier scenes:

> *Thaisa.*                    Did you not name a tempest,
>             A birth, and death?
> *Pericles.*                    The voice of dead Thaisa!
> *Thaisa.*    That Thaisa am I, supposed dead
>             And drown'd.
> *Pericles.*    Immortal Dian!    (v. ii. 33–6)

Not for the first time, a Shakespearean conclusion shows signs of impatience and slapdash.

Despite its text's mutilations, *Pericles* can be intensely moving either to read or to see. The play communicates a definite emotion, describable by the now archaic word 'joy'. Although it is difficult, not to say distracting, to translate emotion into ideas, it does seem in retrospect as if the joy of the play's last two scenes lightened the whole of the narrative, being the destination of Pericles' wanderings, its causes lying hidden all along in the nature of the tale. 'O, if it prove', says Viola in *Twelfth Night*,

Tempests are kind and salt waves fresh in love.    (III. iv. 419)

The condition is typical of *Twelfth Night*, which begins with a condition, 'If music be the food of love. . . .' In *Pericles* music *is* the food of love, and life, and tempests *are* kind. There is nothing conditional about it.

To speak of *Pericles*, as so many do, as a play of acceptance, patience and reconciliation misses the vitality of the play's emotion; and such readings will be generally found to be based on a sentimental allegorising of Marina. There are many varieties of the allegory, but in all of them Marina is the symbol and agent of the creative, 'redemptive' forces in the story, and Pericles is the passive object of her graces. The facts of the story, though, are that Marina is as much redeemed by Pericles as he by her (his great vow and his immense sorrow keep him in his wanderings until he comes to Mytilene where Marina is still a brothel slave in urgent need of redemption from her surroundings), and that the theological idea of redemption does not enter the play.

*Pericles* may be written from what we may call, in a large and general way, a religious point of view; but there is no need to make a religious allegory out of it. It tells a story of voyaging and discovery, full of the freshness of the sea and the coolness of sea winds. Even in its corrupt state the text reveals an abounding lyrical delight in natural things. At the climax, when the great sea of joys breaks over Pericles' heart and he hears the music of the spheres, the boldness of the conception is out of reach of any conventional allegorising.

In every way, in technique, plot, language and thought, *Pericles* strives to dramatise essential, originating truth. The poet's thought and art may have their analogues in theology, but that is another matter altogether. Meanwhile, the form of *Pericles* invites us to pay it the tribute that Beethoven paid to Handel, 'the unequalled Master of all Masters': Go and learn to produce such great effects by such modest means![15]

# 8. Cymbeline, King of Britain

Cymbeline is a most peculiar play by any standards; by classical standards it has been found ridiculous. Dr Johnson's phrase describing it is well known: 'unresisting imbecility'. This calls up an image of a drunk, helpless in the gutter as policemen prod and question; but although the phrase is a marvellous one, it is also very misleading because there is nothing helpless about *Cymbeline*, which is one of Shakespeare's most artful plays. Its offences against classical standards of economy in design, of probability in the story, of decorum in the language, are intentional and put a clear choice: *Cymbeline* or classicism.

In *Cymbeline*, as in *Pericles*, narrative is more important than character. Like *Pericles*, *Cymbeline* is a narrative *tour de force*; but whereas the earlier play makes its effects by primitive simplicity, *Cymbeline* is extravagantly complicated. The plot is really quadruple, being made up of four separate stories: (1) the story of Imogen's marriage to Posthumus, a tale of rivalries within Cymbeline's family involving the queen and her son Cloten, (2) the story of Posthumus' wager with Iachimo, (3) the story of the abducted princes, and (4) the story of Britain's war with Rome. These four stories blend into one in the astounding last scene, a sequence of revelations and dénouements unparalleled in Shakespeare's work. Readers will differ over the exact number of revelations, but there are approximately twenty-five. There is an equally surprising range of place, from Cymbeline's Britain, including Wales, to Augustus' Rome; and Shakespeare has extended the range of time so that Ancient Britain blends with Jacobean Britain, Augustan Rome with Renaissance Italy. At Cymbeline's court there are some very modern courtiers, and at Rome, besides the Roman Philario, there are Iachimo the Italian, a Frenchman, a mute but clearly recognisable Dutchman, and a Spaniard. There is a similar extensiveness in characterisation, which demonstrates a wide range of technique, including the fairy-tale wickedness of the queen, the pastoral idealism of the lost princes, the garrulity of Belarius and Iachimo, and the reserved gentlemanliness of the Romans Philario and Lucius.

Occupying the central positions in the range of characters are the

major persons, Posthumus, Imogen, Iachimo and Cloten. Each takes
its outline from the fiction. We easily recognise Posthumus' simplicity
and directness, Imogen's romantic charm, Iachimo's Italianate joy in
deception, and Cloten's boorishness. Each character also has its
psychological interest. In Posthumus there is a loneliness that leads
him through the confusions of wager and war to a melancholy readiness for death. Imogen, for all her romantic sweetness, has a tongue
that can be as sharp, sometimes, as Beatrice's; she is a demanding,
censorious young woman.[1] Iachimo is an aesthetic as well as a
villain. His most peculiar trait is that when under stress he finds
it difficult to finish his sentences. Cloten, finally, besides being a
comic boor is an uncannily accurate portrait of a paranoid schizo-
phrenic, more convincing psychologically than more famous mad
characters.

The play's language reveals the same wide range of technique.
Each element of the plot has a style suited to it, and the play's
language as a whole is unusually rich and complex. Iachimo's description of Imogen's bedroom is a well-known example of poetry
rich even to decadence, and there are less famous but equally
striking examples of the same artful stylishness. Consider for instance
the opening scene between the two gentlemen, in which the trochaic
cadences hint at a milieu and a style of speech so sophisticated that
the lines seem to droop with elegance:

> His daughter, and the heir of's kingdom, whom
> He purpos'd to his wife's sole son—a widow
> That late he married—hath referr'd herself
> Unto a poor but worthy gentleman. She's wedded,
> Her husband banish'd, she imprison'd; all
> Is outward sorrow, though I think the King
> Be touch'd at very heart.   (I. i. 4–10)

When Posthumus describes the battle (v. iii), his self-disgust, his
contempt for the man he is speaking to, as well as the violence and
strangeness of the battle are revealed in a style correspondingly
abrupt and disjointed.

These are only two examples of an attentiveness to style that
makes the play into an anthology of Shakespearean verse. It is also
an anthology of Shakespearean themes. Almost every play he wrote
seems to have its echo in *Cymbeline*. One has no sooner decided
that *Othello* is a major 'ghost' in it than one realises there is as much
of *All's Well* or *Much Ado* in it as of *Othello*—or of *Twelfth Night*,
or *Romeo and Juliet*, or *King John*. *Cymbeline* forms a web of
allusion spun from the whole Shakespearean *œuvre*.

*Cymbeline* may be what Polonius would call 'tragical-comical-historical-pastoral, scene individable, or poem unlimited', but for all its ostentatious peculiarities, it has nothing accidental or naive about it, nothing tentative or hesitant. Whether it was a challenge to Shakespeare's audience we cannot know, but comprehending its wholeness, finding a way of responding wholeheartedly to it, is certainly a challenge to us. Is it worth meeting? One thing is certain about the play; it radiates a feeling of the author's delight in his own creative power. Such pleasure in creation has for corollary a sublime confidence that the theatre would be full, the audience fascinated.

\*     \*     \*

Shakespeare's Ancient Britain is not a land of blue-painted savages, but a place civilised to the point of decadence. The First Gentleman (I. i) is a dandy, and although it may be conventional in fairy tales to attribute perfection to heroes, the virtues he ascribes to Posthumus derive from the courtier's habit of exaggeration, not from the simplicity of old wives' tales. Sophistication is an important element in *Cymbeline*; Shakespeare's use of fairy-tale conventions to frame his very sophisticated art gives the play some of its eerie tone. The queen is a wicked stepmother whose asides require the actress to do a certain amount of mugging, yet nothing could be more up-to-date (especially in a Jacobean play) than her interest in poisons and vivisection (I. v. 18–23). Her son Cloten is like many a spoiled, stupid child in the old tales, but in the atmosphere of the court his stupidity is corrupt. Shakespeare portrays him as a grown man with the brain of a retarded adolescent. Flattered by his mother and his hangers-on, he thinks he is normal, but as his puny brain grapples with life's complexities, a horrifying as well as a comical character emerges. As Imogen's suitor, he is an obscene lout (II. iii. 15), and as a patriot he is a coarse, provincial bully (III. i. 34). Imogen's refusal disturbs his fantasy picture of himself—'It is not vain-glory for a man and his glass to confer in his own chamber' (IV. i. 7)—driving him into a paranoid rage that begins as grotesque comedy when he seizes on a phrase that Imogen speaks in anger, exasperation and distraction:

> *Imogen.*                    His meanest garment
> That ever hath but clipp'd his body, is dearer
> In my respect than all the hairs above thee,
> Were they all made such men. How now? Pisanio!
> *Cloten.*   'His garment!' Now the devil—   (II. iii. 138–42)

In Cloten's later soliloquies (III. v, IV. i) we see that this insult has come to obsess him, and his crazy, sadistic design (of dressing up as

Posthumus, murdering Posthumus, raping Imogen and 'footing' her home) gives an alarmingly real insight into a form of criminal lunacy.

The courtly sophistication of Cloten's environment does not cause his sickness, but influences the direction it takes. In *Cymbeline* sophistication itself, whether a theme of the play or an aspect of Shakespeare's art, is neutral of value. As a theme it is a quality of social life, affecting the way characters speak, dress and furnish their houses; it gives them the confidence with which they move in the world. In a less well-bred society Imogen, despite her beauty and honesty, might appear rather shrewish; but at Cymbeline's court her high temper and censoriousness turn to wit.

In Cymbeline's Britain the sophistication of Shakespeare's contemporary England and of his own art meet, and the result is a play of exquisite complexity, written for a courtly, aristocratic and rather libertine audience. The play's characters undergo difficulties of perception and understanding, and its art sets the same kind of difficulties before the audience. It is often hard to know just what response is expected. Posthumus' soliloquy on hearing Iachimo's report, Imogen's soliloquy on waking by Cloten's decapitated body, and Posthumus' dream: each of these is so handled that a simple response is impossible. In each example a serious emotion or a spectacularly surprising discovery is undercut by an element of burlesque—and the burlesque, in turn, is undercut by the seriousness. Some critics have doubted that Shakespeare wrote the 'vision'; some have said that he failed in Posthumus' soliloquies, and it has also been said that he was unchivalrous towards Imogen. Audiences too lose their nerve and start laughing uneasily, especially during Imogen's lamentations over Cloten's trunk.

Like Byron's *Don Juan, Cymbeline* often requires a suspension of involvement or detachment in favour of a sympathetic curiosity. Judgement must be suspended; until the end the dramatist diverts every tendency to a simple response. The too-ready recognition of evil and good, the easy sympathy with one's own projected prejudices, the tendency to jump to a conclusion: Shakespeare diverts them all, chiefly by a running counterpoint of simplicity against sophistication, a technique brought to a focus upon Posthumus, Shakespeare's most maligned hero after Bertram in *All's Well*.

Posthumus is a famous patriot's orphan son whom Cymbeline has reared at court. He secretly marries the king's only daughter, Imogen, and is immediately banished from Britain. He goes to Rome, where his first act is to enter into a wager on his wife's chastity. Then, believing he has lost the wager, he arranges to have her murdered, and writes her lying letters. After an absence during two whole acts, he returns to the play and his country in the uniform

of Rome, but then fights against the Roman army in the clothes of
a Briton. Finally, dressing himself again as a Roman, he gives himself up to captivity, repentance and the prospect of immediate death.

Just to recapitulate Posthumus' activities shows that he is an
unusual hero. The first thing we hear about him is his marriage,
and from the First Gentleman's description of the match, and our
first sight of Imogen, we realise that decision and choice in the
matter have been more hers than Posthumus'. He may be all that
the First Gentleman says he is, yet owing to his dependent circumstances and his stolen marriage he is an odd man out in Britain.
Not until he arrives in Italy do we see him in a situation where he
can talk to others on an equal footing, yet even here rumour precedes
him. The gentlemen gathered in Philario's house are the Jacobean
international set, a pack of chatterboxes. Iachimo is their leader,
seconded by the Frenchman. They size up Posthumus very quickly,
and start to 'smoke' him. Posthumus' language, in contrast to the
Italian's, is plain, clipped and direct, and he gives an impression of
honesty and simplicity; but there is also a prickliness about him
that betrays him into exposing his love for Imogen as soon as the
Frenchman shows signs of baiting him about it. The same indefinite-
ness already seen in his bearing in Britain makes him an easy victim
to Iachimo. He accepts the wager on Imogen's fidelity without realis-
ing that it is really a wager on his own integrity. One sympathises
with Posthumus, partly out of faith in Imogen's choice, partly out of
dislike for Iachimo and his gang, but as always in this play, interest
and curiosity are as strong as sympathy.

Iachimo tests Imogen, as he baited her husband, as if it were a
practical joke. He plays the role of deceiver with a mixture of buffoonery and effrontery that makes him very interesting. For instance,
he begins by slandering Posthumus, pretending amazement that
anyone having the choice to make would prefer a whore to Imogen;
but he overdoes his amazement, and the implied slander, difficult
enough to follow without preparation, escapes Imogen who asks,
'Are you well?' He then rids himself of Pisanio with a touch of
invention that shows how superior to Posthumus he is in his grasp
of a social situation:

> Beseech you, sir, desire
> My man's abode where I did leave him. He
> Is strange and peevish.
> *Pisanio.*                    I was going, sir.   (I. vi. 52–4)

Nonetheless, he is a bit of a fool and although, unlike Cloten, he
recognises beauty when he sees it, Imogen is right to call him 'a

saucy stranger' with a 'beastly mind'. He has a knack for such phrases as 'diseas'd ventures', 'boil'd stuff' and 'variable ramps', all of them kennings for 'whore'.

The character's subtlest quality is his detachment, separating perception and intelligence from affection and will, which Shakespeare dramatises in the play's most curious and haunting scene. Iachimo's entry into Imogen's bedroom from the trunk is an event of fairy-tale surrealism superimposed upon a scene of the most exact realism. The dramatist names the time, 'almost midnight', the length of Imogen's bedtime reading, 'almost three hours', and the time of her morning call, 'by four o' th' clock'. As she sleeps, the trunk lid opens and Iachimo steps into the silence of her room:

> The crickets sing, and man's o'er-labour'd sense
> Repairs itself by rest. Our Tarquin thus
> Did softly press the rushes ere he waken'd
> The chastity he wounded.   (II. ii. 11–14)

('*Our* Tarquin' is a nice touch.) With a connoisseur's enthusiasm, he notes down the details of the room and the sleeping woman, not forgetting his business in the pleasure of the scene:

>                 The flame o' th' taper
> Bows toward her, and would under-peep her lids
> To see th'enclosed lights, now canopied
> Under these windows white and azure, lac'd
> With blue of heaven's own tinct. But my design,
> To note the chamber.   (ll. 19–24)

Some readers believe that Iachimo kisses Imogen when he says:

>                 That I might touch!
> But kiss one kiss! Rubies unparagon'd,
> How dearly they do't!   (ll. 16–18)

Surely the point is that he does *not* touch, no matter how close he comes, that even his expression of a wish to do so is a figurative comment upon Imogen's beauty, not upon his desire for it. 'How dearly they do't' means 'How dearly they kiss one another'. Iachimo's refined voyeurism has its climax in the famous description of the five-spotted mole on Imogen's left breast, 'like the crimson drops/I' th' bottom of a cowslip', an image telling as much about Iachimo as about Imogen's breast. Then, as if by afterthought, he notices her book:

> She hath been reading late
> The tale of Tereus; here the leaf's turn'd down
> Where Philomel gave up.   (ll. 44–6)

The trochaic droop in mid-line characteristic of late Shakespearean verse, joined to the euphemism 'gave up', is a perfect expression of elegant corruption.

Although Iachimo's presence in the room begins and ends with references to violent rape, he does Imogen no harm. He only praises her beauty and takes notes. Yet the scene is oppressive, like his later description of the room with its winking cupids, its Diana bathing, its Antony and Cleopatra. The air is thick with sex. There is sex on the walls, in the book, on the intruder's mind. As Iachimo returns to his trunk Shakespeare, momentarily abandoning characterisation, makes him the chorus to his own escapade in remarkable imagery:

> Swift, swift, you dragons of the night, that dawning
> May bare the raven's eye! I lodge in fear;
> Though this a heavenly angel, hell is here.   (ll. 48–50)

There is no overt connection between that eerie image of the raven's eye and the rest of the scene, but the imagination makes one. In Iachimo's own words about the 'cloy'd will' (i. vi. 47–9), the raven is a bird of ill omen that, 'ravening first the lamb,/Longs after for the garbage.' The image of its small, exploiting eye opening on the world intimates a perversion of the sense that we readily link to Iachimo's invasion of a sleeping woman's privacy and to the curious disordering of reality that accompanies it. Three hours pass during Iachimo's forty lines of seeing without touching.

Iachimo's detachment is the aesthete's equivalent of the queen's scientific experiments. The extreme of both is Cloten's schizoid paranoia. Does the alternative to detachment lie in the feelings? In their subjectivity the feelings are just as detached as Iachimo with his notebook and pencil. For Posthumus, convinced by Iachimo's evidence that Imogen has betrayed him, falls like Hamlet into an emotional conviction that all the world but himself is corrupt. The audience, already invited to see the reality of Iachimo's midnight performance, has a similar opportunity to see through Posthumus' rage as he lapses into near-incoherence and absurdity:

> O, vengeance, vengeance!
> Me of my lawful pleasure she restrain'd
> And pray'd me oft forbearance; did it with
> A pudency so rosy the sweet view on't

Might well have warm'd old Saturn; that I thought her
As chaste as unsunn'd snow. O, all the devils!
This yellow Iachimo, in an hour,—was't not?—
Or less,—at first?—perchance he spoke not, but,
Like a full-acorn'd boar, a German one,
Cried 'O!' and mounted; found no opposition
But what he look'd for should oppose and she
Should from encounter guard.    (II. v. 8–19)

In imagining Imogen's infidelity, Posthumus begins by remembering
in his mind's eye the attractiveness of her modesty towards himself.
He ends by visualising in pornographic detail his imaginary betrayal,
and there is in both images an element that a modern reader recognises as photographic voyeurism.[2] His attempt to think of Iachimo
in the act is so grossly, comically short of any possible reality that
Posthumus, as he speaks it, fades from our sympathy as from the
play. Much will have to happen before we take seriously again a man
who talks of full-acorn'd boars crying 'O!' and mounting. His
decision to solve his problems by becoming a writer completes his
downfall, and he leaves the stage, it seems, to buy ink and paper and
set to work.

                    *       *       *

In the play's middle section the story of Imogen and Posthumus is a
thread in the wider story of Britain's relation to Rome and the finding
of her lost royalty. So far the action of Cymbeline has concerned
right-speaking, true perception and integrity, hinting at positives by
an abundant display of negatives, and showing a fascination with
complexity. Now, like the action of King John, it comes to centre
upon the twin roots of human affairs: the integrity of the state, and
the integrity of the individual.

In their abstract form the questions underlying *Cymbeline*'s action
would be these: Does individual integrity derive from the state or is
it the other way round? Is there such a thing as absolute freedom,
whether of states or individuals, or is all freedom dependent on a
larger, containing order? How does a person know what he really is?
In *Cymbeline*, as in *King John*, these questions take concrete form
in two great issues, the relation of Britain to Rome, and the relation
of the individual to both. Because of its remote setting and its utterly
fictional narrative, the later play is not tied to 'the truth of a foolish
world', as the early history is; its author can write free of the
restrictions and temptations that always follow obvious 'relevance'.
*Cymbeline*'s Rome and Britain are only by analogy the Rome of the
Church, divided by schism, and James I's England, divided over
issues of politics and religion and ruled by a new, partly foreign

dynasty. Similarly Jove's providence that untangles the play's confusions compares only by analogy to the Christian notion of Divine Providence. If in each instance one makes the analogy (and I am sure we are meant to), the effect of the play's remoteness from contemporary affairs is a greater freedom of thought than history allows.

Every reader has noticed that the queen and Cloten repeat the insular patriotism of the histories in their replies to Lucius, the emperor's ambassador (III. i. 11–38). We hear again the brave bombastic emotions of Gaunt, Falconbridge and Henry V; but Cloten is an oaf whom Lucius ignores, and the queen is an ambitious woman speaking out of turn. As we can clearly understand, after the training the first acts have given us in the art of perception, neither her patriotism nor her son's serves any end larger than self. Joy in the courage of British arms and the 'natural bravery' (l. 18) of the island has nothing to do with the political issue. One can be a brave Briton and still belong to Rome. The final answer to Lucius is Cymbeline's, and he has no real case to make at all, only the case of sentimental nationalists everywhere. We were free, he says, and enjoyed our own laws before the Romans came; and to this he adds lamely that other subject peoples are in arms, 'a precedent/Which not to read would show the Britons cold' (ll. 75–6).

When Cymbeline admits that he derives his knighthood and honour from Caesar, he contradicts his own argument which, as Cloten crudely puts it, is that 'Britain is/A world by itself' (ll. 12–13). The corrective to that will come when Imogen, caught between the terrors of the court and the promise of death at her journey's end, speaks from experience:

> Hath Britain all the sun that shines? Day, night,
> Are they not but in Britain? I' th' world's volume
> Our Britain seems as of it, but not in't;
> In a great pool a swan's nest. Prithee, think
> There's livers out of Britain.   (III. iv. 139–43)

Pisanio's reply, so matter-of-fact, answers her need: 'Th' ambassador, Lucius the Roman, comes to Milford-Haven tomorrow.' Dressing herself in boy's clothes, and taking the name Fidele ('faithful'), Imogen goes off to serve the Roman, finding herself like Posthumus separated from the old centre of life and security. She goes wandering in strange places, guided (like Viola and Rosalind) by the truth of her instincts.

Rome is the play's centre, its source of civility and honour. A British kingship recognised by Rome, one senses, is a larger thing than a kingship, self-sustaining, hidden in the Western mists. Nonetheless Roman nurture produces Iachimo and the other chatterboxes at Philario's house, and Lucius' defeat shows that Britain has more to offer Rome than tribute. Roman nurture has its antithesis in British nature, which Shakespeare expresses with irony as well as lyricism in the idyllic Welsh scenes.

We soon notice the ironies, taking them for absurdities, because neither pastoral innocence nor legitimacy are themes that interest us very much. Belarius' prosiness, the conventional contrast between court and country life (to which we are still committed in its post-Wordsworthian, conservationist form), and Guiderius' abrupt beheading of Cloten all tend to make us laugh. The princes' innate royalty can appear ridiculous. Yet Shakespeare is treating in ideal, symbolic form notions we accept when they are treated realistically. The princes' royalty, their contempt for bravado, even their violence, are all qualities of Falconbridge; but in his case, owing to a Romantic prejudice in favour of bastards, they seem more acceptable.

Although Belarius and his charges lead a civil, ceremonious life in the wilderness, and although the old man prefers to climb real mountains instead of the metaphorical mountains of court favour, there is nothing soft-centred about the Welsh scenes, no shrinking from the hardness of life. Violence and death, the waste of youth and beauty, and the shortness of life are among their motifs, combined in elegiac sweetness in the scene of Imogen's apparent death. The scenes also have a moral realism, spoken in brief, declarative sentences that give the whole a stoical tone:

> We have seen nothing.
> We are beastly.   (III. iii. 39–40)
> Plenty and peace breeds cowards; hardness ever
> Of hardiness is mother.   (III. vi. 21–2)
> The sweat of industry would dry and die,
> But for the end it works to.   (III. vi. 31–2)
> The breach of custom/Is breach of all.   (IV. ii. 10)
> Love's reason's without reason.   (IV. ii. 22)

These sentences, the artifice of the scenes, the ceremoniousness of the events and the writing, and the treatment of major questions of life and death in the form of pastoral song and debate, all intimate (like the closing scenes of *Twelfth Night*) a sense of life plainly seen and accepted. There is sweetness, delicacy, innocence, generosity, hope, courage and the sense of beauty; but the ground base of it all is a sad theme, elaborated in the princes' lament:

> Fear no more the heat o' th' sun,
> Nor the furious winter's rages;

Thou thy worldly task hast done,
Home art gone, and ta'en thy wages.
Golden lads and girls all must,
As chimney-sweepers, come to dust.

The last couplet with its famous pun is too sophisticated, really, to be spoken by the princes; but like so many things in the play it has the effect of suspending judgement.

Imogen's speech on awakening by Cloten's headless corpse illustrates the same technique, and its complexities require a virtuoso actress and a skilful audience. Like Posthumus' earlier soliloquy, it requires that we see things from more than one point of view simultaneously, so that unqualified sympathy yields to puzzled curiosity. The beginning of the speech is moderately simple as Imogen, waking, continues her dream of travelling to Milford-Haven until, seeing the dead body beside her and the flowers strewn over herself, she interprets them in lines that can strike one as the epitome of the idyllic scenes' whole effect:

These flowers are like the pleasures of the world;
This bloody man, the care on't. I hope I dream;
For so I thought I was a cave-keeper
And cook to honest creatures. But 'tis not so.
'Twas but a bolt of nothing, shot at nothing,
Which the brain makes of fumes. Our very eyes
Are sometimes like our judgements, blind. Good faith,
I tremble still with fear; but if there be
Yet left in heaven as small a drop of pity
As a wren's eye, fear'd gods, a part of it!
The dream's here still, even when I wake. It is
Without me, as within me; not imagin'd, felt.   (IV. ii. 296–307)

Shakespeare's words stalk the process of Imogen's fear, her bewilderment, her disorientation up to the moment when she recognises Posthumus' clothes on the corpse. With that, her language soars, operatically. Outrage and anger (beautifully in keeping with her character) follow discovery, concluding in absolute sorrow. Yet at the moment of discovery, when her tentative waverings turn to emotional fury, an element of performance enters into the writing. Because the audience knows that Imogen is mistaken in her grief, though not her fear, the over-writing draws attention to the separation of her emotions from reality. Emotional truth and actual truth are at odds, and the contradiction is so visited upon the audience that they do not know whether to laugh or to cry.

Imogen's and Posthumus' situations are now parallel. Each is alienated from the other, each is convinced of the other's death, each is separated from home and kin, and each is absolutely alone. Their loneliness and confusion are paralleled at court where the king, without daughter, son-in-law, wife or stepson, has to sustain the consequences of Cloten's words, that 'Britain is a world to itself'. For the Roman invasion has begun, and British self-sufficiency is to be tested.

* * *

The play's lowest point, the extreme of its tangle and confusion, shows schism between Britain and Rome, divided counsels and chaos at the British court, separation between hero and heroine, and even, in the errors of perception they have both made, a separation within the person between emotion and knowledge. The audience is similarly bewildered. Like the readers of a good detective story, they can have no inkling of the story's resolution, especially since they know that the author has left himself little time to make an ending. In addition to all this, the play's persistent irony has defeated their emotions just as its complexities have defeated their reason.

As Imogen joins herself to Lucius as his page, as the princes determine to join the British army and as Posthumus, disguised as a Roman gentleman, reappears in Britain, it seems that the untanglement has begun. Posthumus especially gives the impression of a man brought to the last point of retreat, and turning to fight with no more reason for his stand than a residual faith in his own integrity:

> 'Tis enough
> That, Britain, I have kill'd thy mistress; peace!
> I'll give no wound to thee. Therefore, good heavens,
> Hear patiently my purpose: I'll disrobe me
> Of these Italian weeds and suit myself
> As does a Briton peasant; and so I'll fight
> Against the part I come with; so I'll die
> For thee, O Imogen, even for whom my life
> Is every breath a death; and thus, unknown,
> Pitied nor hated, to the face of peril
> Myself I'll dedicate. Let me make men know
> More valour in me than my habits show.
> Gods, put the strength o' th' Leonati in me!
> To shame the guise o' th' world, I will begin
> The fashion: less without and more within. (v. i. 19–33)

Those last words ring like a slogan; but although much in this speech is, on reflection, an explanatory gloss on Falconbridge's words at the end of *King John* ('If England to itself do rest but true'), Shakespeare

has not done with complication. Truth is deeper and lonelier than we
can yet sense, and confusion's masterpiece is not complete until the
Roman's are defeated and Imogen and Posthumus are both Cymbeline's prisoners.

Posthumus' imprisonment recalls earlier scenes and characters.
Indeed one's memory of Henry VI, Clarence, Richard II and Claudio,
encouraging comparisons and generalities, may obscure the significance of this particular scene. For the whole point of it is that Posthumus asks to be forgiven (v. iv. 3–29). His soliloquy is mainly a
prayer; and, though his gods are Roman, his language is Christian.
As gyves fetter his body, so guilt fetters his conscience, and although
death can release his body from its literal prison as well as the
figurative prison of life and its misfortunes, only the gods' forgiveness
can give him 'the penitent instrument' that will 'pick that bolt' which
fetters conscience. When Posthumus talks of guilt as a debt that only
his life can pay, we recall the petition of the Lord's Prayer: 'Forgive
us our debts as we forgive our debtors.' Posthumus is at that frontier
where nothing short of a complete accounting will satisfy his sense of
indebtedness:

> Is't enough I am sorry?
> . . . For Imogen's dear life take mine; and though
> 'Tis not so dear, yet 'tis a life; you coin'd it.
> 'Tween man and man they weigh not every stamp;
> Though light, take pieces for the figure's sake;
> You rather mine, being yours; and so, great powers,
> If you will take this audit, take this life,
> And cancel these cold bonds. O Imogen!   (v. iv. 11–28)

Repentance must be almost impossible to dramatise because to be
convincing it must not be motivated by self-interest. A compelled
repentance or a repentance that assures the good things of this
world is always suspicious. Posthumus' repentance is unique in
Shakespeare, and it sometimes seems as if all the extraordinary
machinery of *Cymbeline*'s plot were designed to bring us to this
prison where a hero without kin, without country or wife, with no
worldly motive that he knows of remaining to him, should discover
in the experience of sorrow that his life, which is all that he has
left to him, is not his own.

Posthumus' experience, for all its religious overtones, is a natural
one. It shows nature, in extremity, asserting itself, and it has parallels
elsewhere in the play. At the approach of battle, for instance,
Belarius can no longer keep the princes to himself; their instinctive
valour drives them and him back into the active world. Iachimo finds

himself unable to fight in Britain because, whatever the justice of the Roman cause, he recognises that he has compromised his integrity:

> I have belied a lady,
> The Princess of this country, and the air on't
> Revengingly enfeebles me.  (v. ii. 2–5)

The Britons' disorder is caused by Cymbeline's subjection to his wife, and causes their initial defeat; whereas the return of Cymbeline's sons, mistaken by some in the army for angels, brings them victory. These instances, like the princes' instinctive love for their sister, are obviously fictional symbols of the supremacy of nature, which we are to accept as one of the story's facts. Posthumus' last soliloquy, however, implies that the root of these natural responses is a deeply felt truth that both human society and the gods are real, and require service.

Posthumus' feelings are immediately vindicated by the vision, a scene that has caused critics a great deal of trouble. There can be no doubt that, properly performed with adequate music and suitable formality, the vision would be immensely impressive. Even the ghosts' fourteeners, confidently declaimed, perhaps to music, would prove the critics' embarrassment unnecessary. The lines have the rhythmical interest and the laconic economy of *The Phoenix and the Turtle:*

> Lucina lent not me her aid,
> But took me in my throes;
> That from me was Posthumus ript.
> Came crying 'mongst his foes,
> A thing of pity!  (v. iv. 43–7)

(Any tendency to perform these lines with howlings, twitterings or eldritch shrieks will of course ruin the scene.) As for Jupiter, he is a splendid figure, elegantly contemptuous of the ghosts, but also speaking in the genuine accents of power:

> Poor shadows of Elysium, hence, and rest
> Upon your never-with'ring banks of flowers.
> Be not with mortal accidents opprest;
> No care of yours it is; you know 'tis ours.
> Whom best I love I cross; to make my gift,
> The more delay'd, delighted ...  (ll. 97–102)

We take the supernatural very seriously and, whether we believe
in it or consider belief an offence against decency, the theatricality
of Shakespeare's vision will probably strike us as frivolous. Shake
speare however was dealing with something that virtually everyone
in his day took for granted. His content was old, his art new and
meant to please, whereas for many of us the content is new and the
art therefore bewildering. If we attend to rhythm and syntax, we
shall hear a style, musical and declamatory, detached from ex
perience and actuality, that evokes power and beauty such as Milton
can only rival, not surpass:

> He came in thunder; his celestial breath
> Was sulphurous to smell. The holy eagle
> Stoop'd, as to foot us. His ascension is
> More sweet than our blest fields. His royal bird
> Prunes the immortal wing and cloys his beak,
> As when his god is pleas'd.   (ll. 114–19)

Although Posthumus and later the soothsayer interpret the vision
its main purposes are to delight us with a sight of the divinity
guiding the story, and to prepare us for the marvels of the last scene
This is a play, however, not a ritual. Shakespeare is not in competi
tion with the Archbishop of Canterbury, and the vision, whether i
corresponds with our own sense of reality or not, is the only part o
the story. With fine artistic tact Shakespeare follows the vision with
a comic gaoler, one of those natural men and stand-up comedians
who will never see a vision and whose vulgarity, bad taste, grotesque
humour and proverbial wisdom restore to us a humane, not to say
low, point of view. His talk of bills and reckonings, debts and
creditors, reminding us of Posthumus' recent soliloquising, shows
that a metaphor can have more than one application; and he has
the last word, before the revelations of the last scene begin, upon
the play's solemn, rather gawky hero: 'Unless a man would marry
a gallows and beget young gibbets, I never saw one so prone
(v. iv. 206).

*   *   *

The brilliance and speed of the play's dénouement have been amply
and frequently praised. As an example of sheer logic in the arrange
ment of parts, it has hardly a rival in English drama. With the
smoothness of a film played backwards, complication yields to order
and at the end the play's discrepant parts fit together like Chinese
boxes or the spheres of the Ptolemaic heavens: Posthumus and
Imogen at peace within themselves, their marriage contained in
the new-made family of Cymbeline; that family contained in a

reinvigorated Britain; Britain contained in Rome, and all contained in the *primum mobile* of Providence:

> The fingers of the powers above do tune
> The harmony of this peace.... (v. v. 466–7)

>           Laud we the gods;
> And let our crooked smokes climb to their nostrils
> From our bless'd altars. Publish we this peace
> To all our subjects. Set we forward. Let
> A Roman and a British ensign wave
> Friendly together. So through Lud's town march;
> And in the temple of great Jupiter
> Our peace we'll ratify; seal it with feasts.
> Set on there! (ll. 476–84)

Moved by the triumphant harmony of this ending, an eager spectator might be forgiven for seeing in those 'crooked smokes' ascending to the gods an emblem of the play's action whose end seems to have been making straight the crooked.

Nevertheless, *Cymbeline* is absolute play, a thing made that delights us, engaging our imaginations; its author, to quote Sidney again, 'nothing affirmeth'. The plot and the characters might reflect a way of seeing the causes of disorder and evil; disorders are resolved into an aesthetic harmony which one might take as a myth or plot of recovery and centredness. But this is art, not action. Disorder in the real world of action and suffering lies quite beyond the scope of any art, however subtle and complex. The gaoler's melancholy aloofness as he directly addresses the audience reflects the moral modesty of the whole play:

> I would we were all of one mind, and one mind good. O, there were desolation of gaolers and gallowses! I speak against my present profit, but my wish hath a preferment in't.
>
>                               (v. iv. 211–15)

# 9. The Winter's Tale

Most readers feel that *Pericles, Cymbeline* and *The Winter's Tale* are the same kind of play. They are about the same themes: about sorrow turning to joy through the working of Providence and time; about the reunion of families and kingdoms, and the renewal of life in the succession of generations. In these plays evil is inward and concealed, erupting like the onset of a disease. Goodness, as deep as an imagined centre of things and as high as their circumference, converges upon men's lives with the inevitability of growth and sunshine, transfiguring life in moments of recognition and wonder. Time is a part of the environment, like place, and the characters live in it without being of it. The narratives that embody these themes have more in common with fairy tales than with novels, and critics brought up to regard realism as the only really adequate way to imitate life have thought that Shakespeare was as uninterested in his stories as they are; but the plays' art centres upon the art of their narratives.

Comparable as they are to each other, the plays have no real parallel elsewhere in Elizabethan drama, either as to their form or their contents. Because their content is somewhat similar, readers have naturally suspected that the plays' constant quality would prove to be some personal preoccupation, that they would turn out to be covert autobiographies. This view underlies the simple designation of them as 'Last Plays' which, for many users, is a term implying that Shakespeare intended them to be his last word. 'Romance', the currently fashionable term, undercuts the biographical approach by suggesting that Shakespeare intended to write a certain kind of play, as no doubt he did. The trouble is that one can no more imagine Shakespeare seriously intending to write a play like *The Four Prentices of London* or *The Rare Triumphs of Love and Fortune* than one can imagine him writing a closet tragedy. A genre consisting of four plays by Shakespeare and such things as *The Rare Triumphs* or even *Philaster* is hardly worth bothering about. One might as well deal with *Die Zauberflöte* by calling it a pantomime. Shakespeare's later plays cut across boundaries of genre. In fact, considered simply as literature, they have more in common with *The Faerie Queen* and *Arcadia* than with other English plays.

Classroom definitions aside, the wholeness or unity of a work of art depends upon a tacit agreement between author and audience that the work should be an image of their common experience—and in any society, the styles and forms of art are part of the audience's experience. Art is a co-operative enterprise, and overly rigid notions of form like the neo-classicists' may interfere with the subtle relationship between author and audience. (This does not mean that rules based on the practice of successful artists are not a necessary stage in the education of artist and audience alike.) Shakespeare's late plays come at the end of a twenty-year-long relationship between author and audience. They are bound to be complex, allusive, and inclusive.

All art is in some sense autobiographical. In an earlier generation this observation would have seemed so obvious as to be not worth making, but modern teaching often gives the impression that Shakespeare wrote his plays as dispassionately as men manufacture Pepsicola bottles, and as unconsciously as they dream. It sometimes seems as if years could pass in the teaching of Shakespeare without it occurring to someone to say that the plays deal with such matters of common, and personal, experience as parents' love for their children. If the life of the play arises partly out of the relationship of author and audience and if, to make its effect, the play requires the audience to draw upon its experience of life, then it must follow that the play also arises out of its author's own experience. The attempt to see works of art as self-subsistent *objets trouvés*, like stones in a field, is mistaken.

These reflections arise in connection with *The Winter's Tale* because, in the first place, its formal quirkness requires the most agile co-operation from the audience; and in the second place, the author concentrates upon the play's themes with an intensity that many readers have taken as a sign that the material came close to his own experience. This seems to be a reasonable inference, whatever the excesses of sentimental critics; but it is one thing to make a general statement, another to apply it to one's reading.

A reflective spectator watching a play will translate his aesthetic pleasure into his knowledge of life. A mature man contemplating Leontes as he recovers his wife might for instance find his adult life passing in memory before him. Anything a spectator can do, an author can do. Were we able to talk to Shakespeare, and were he disposed to be communicative, he might be able to translate his play for us into its natural particulars. We, however, can only impute to him such general experience as the play communicates to us.

*          *          *

Like *King Lear* and *Cymbeline*, *The Winter's Tale* begins with a short scene of prose conversation between a pair of courtiers. Extravagant, conceited and complimentary, their language hovers somewhere between an ideal courtliness and frank theatricality, and the scene is a prologue, drawing the spectators' attention to the stage. The brief mention of the two kings and Mamillius has a framing effect, and the talkative, prosy courtiers are really presenters of the play that follows. As this begins with Polixenes speaking to Leontes (in a speech reminiscent of the player king in *Hamlet*), one notices a marked change of style requiring a different kind of attention from the audience. On the stage there is a speaking picture, remote, intensely artificial—and also enigmatic, because the connection between the words spoken and the things seen is, to say the least, peculiar.

The presentation of action as a speaking picture goes back, as we have seen, to Shakespeare's earliest plays. In *Pericles* its use gives an intentional effect of primitive simplicity, and much of *Cymbeline*'s eerie, enhanced tone arises from the same technique. In this first major scene of *The Winter's Tale*, Shakespeare again uses the technique, this time exploiting the audience's readiness to see a difference between what is seen and what is said:

> Nine changes of the wat'ry star hath been
> The shepherd's note since we have left our throne
> Without a burden . . .   (I. ii. 1–3)

Whether one altogether likes to admit it or not, the time mentioned (nine months) and the word 'burden' connect in the mind with the spectacle of the visibly pregnant queen,[1] and it is even possible that for a moment at the start of the play an audience might think that Hermione was Polixenes' wife. Then, as one wonders about the pregnancy (which is bound to be an item in the story, since everything in a story has its point) and expects some reference to it, one is bound to feel sooner or later, as the long argument about Polixenes' departure winds on, that there is a surplus of words over matter; and this will lead to other speculations. Leontes, for instance, talks very little whereas his wife talks a lot; and Polixenes, the man who would like to go home after a nine months' absence, speaks under some kind of constraint.

As the scene proceeds, Hermione begins to give an impression of flirtatiousness, and her talk grows slightly suggestive when she assumes (correctly as it turns out) that by the 'doctrine of ill-doing' (I. ii. 70) Polixenes means sex. The conversation that follows would be a little titilating anywhere. In reply to Leontes' question, 'Is he won yet?' Hermione's 'He'll stay, my Lord' leaves no doubt that

Polixenes' change of mind is a female victory. Nor is there any doubt about Hermione's pleasure at her success. After all, these are young people still, and full of life. At the same time this is a courtly, well-mannered society, and speech is indirect, playful and evocative. The game is by concealment to reveal and by revelation to conceal.

The sexual undertone to Hermione's talk comes out more clearly as she angles for compliments from her husband:

> you may ride's
> With one soft kiss a thousand furlongs ere
> With spur we heat an acre. But to th' goal . . .
> Nay, let me have't; I long.  (i. ii. 94–6, 101)

This is verbal love-making, and in public too. Leontes' reply, which is brief and sincere, could easily suggest, in the mouth of a good actor, both reluctance to make a public avowal of feeling and reproach that this woman who speaks so readily to others was once so coy to him:

> Why, that was when
> Three crabbed months had sour'd themselves to death,
> Ere I could make thee open thy white hand
> And clap thyself my love; then didst thou utter,
> 'I am yours for ever.'  (ll. 101–5)

Hermione either senses nothing in his tone or, if she does, neglects it:

> Why, lo you know, I have spoke to th' purpose twice:
> The one for ever earn'd a royal husband;
> Th' other for some while a friend.  (ll. 106–8)

This is so ambiguous that neither critic, actor nor spectator can be certain of the tone. At the word 'friend' (so commonly used with sexual innuendo in Jacobean English), Leontes' control breaks down. By a stroke of superb theatrical technique, Shakespeare detaches him from the others to speak his suspicions aside while he watches the sociable picture of Hermione's behaviour towards Polixenes. This is the picture the audience has been watching all along, and Leontes' rage translates into action the idle speculations so cunningly encouraged by the dramatist.

Leontes, of course, is wrong, and Hermione and Polixenes are innocent. But is the audience also wrong? Does the depth of Leontes' rage and the horror of its consequences clear Hermione of all criticism? There is a falseness, a suggestiveness in the courtly chatter which may be innocent in the sense that Leontes' interpretation of it is wrong, but which in itself is different from real innocence. Polixenes' nostalgia for innocent boyhood is open to the same criticism. The image of the two boys as 'twinn'd lambs that did frisk i' th' sun,/And bleat the one at th' other' (ll. 67–8) tips over into absurdity because Polixenes is thinking of lambs, not boys, and his description of innocence by negatives reveals more a distaste for the present than a clear memory of the past. His yearning has as little connection with reality as a Valentine card.

The nearest thing to real innocence in the opening scenes is Leontes' memory of himself as he scrutinises his son,

>               my dagger muzzl'd
> Lest it should bite its master, and so prove,
> As ornaments oft do, too dangerous.   (ll. 156–8)

Here is literal innocence, something neither hurting nor hurt, but it is still not essential innocence. Muzzled or not, the dagger is there, and the seeds of later guilt are already present in Mamillius as we realise from his prattle with the ladies about their make-up.

There is no essential innocence anywhere in the first three acts of *The Winter's Tale*. At her trial Hermione is shocked by disaster into exact and heroic speech; yet as a defence of *herself*, of her own innocence, her speech never rises above the notion of innocence as the negative of guilt. She has been continent, chaste and true (III. ii. 35); she has loved Polixenes as her husband commanded her, and life 'can be no commodity' to her deprived of her three joys: her husband's love and her two children. In Hermione's defence we see an image of a good life, even, in the common use of the word, an innocent one; but it falls short of the splendour of her own presence and person. We expect a fuller, finer life for a woman who speaks like this:

>               For behold me,
> A fellow of the royal bed, which owe
> A moiety of the throne, a great king's daughter,
> The mother to a hopeful prince, here standing
> To prate and talk for life and honour 'fore
> Who please to come and hear.   (III. ii. 38–43)

In these first three acts, goodness is a form of asceticism, innocence a kind of ignorance. Leontes claims to rule his kingdom, but its real, unacknowledged monarch is the sense of guilt. Whatever the cause of irrationally guilty feelings may be, a sense of guilt must have a pretext to which it can fasten itself; and in *The Winter's Tale* that pretext is sex. The force that by making new life can at least temporarily assuage guilt turns by some perversion into the imagined cause of guilt. A good life like Hermione's, or the innocence of a child, seems a small clearing in a forest, threatened by wild growths and savageries.

The sign that some perversion is involved and that Shakespeare has poetic mastery of it shows in his having so written the opening scenes that the *double entendres* provoke the audience's own guilty knowledge. Sicily is a state of mind, its limits for the time of the play being the walls of the theatre; and each spectator finds himself a natural-born citizen of it. At its dark centre the death's head rules in hiding until, just as it possesses Othello, it speaks its obscenities through Leontes' mouth. This time there is no medium of possession, like Iago; the process is direct and entirely subjective:

> And many a man there is, even at this present,
> Now while I speak this, holds his wife by th' arm,
> That little thinks she has been sluic'd in's absence
> And his pond fish'd by his next neighbour, by
> Sir Smile, his neighbour.   (I. ii. 192–6)

Hamlet's disgust, Othello's jealousy, Lear's rage all have their place in the pathology of Leontes' disease. In the end, like Macbeth's nihilism, it issues in infanticide:

> My child? Away with't! Even thou, that hast
> A heart so tender o'er it, take it hence
> And see it instantly consum'd with fire.   (II. iii. 132–4)

\*        \*        \*

Technically *The Winter's Tale* up to this point contains the elements of an experiment upon the audience. In three acts, with speed and concentration, Shakespeare has narrated the progress of a habit of lying from its first relatively innocent consequence of artificial chatter to its appalling conclusion in child-murder. There is no possibility of a tragic resolution to the plot; it has been more the history of a disease than of a hero, and its timing and emphases are not those of tragedy. Besides, Shakespeare has so handled the hero, Leontes, that like Posthumus he is more the object of curiosity than sympathy. Although the play's tone has veered from the boisterously comic to the tragic, there has been no real relief from concentration on the action, and a spectator or reader, with a growing feeling of impatience, begins to long for an alternative to Leontes' Sicily.

Having created the appetite, Shakespeare then satisfies it. As if

remembering Hamlet's comparison of Claudius with his father—
'Look here, upon this picture, and on this'—Shakespeare's method
is to juxtapose the false with the true, and the contrast is by no
means mechanical. Truth grows out of the lie as a body responds to
disease by making antibodies against infection. The process begins
with Paulina's entry into the play and her delivery (ii. ii) of the new-
born baby from prison:

> This child was prisoner to the womb and is
> By law and process of great Nature thence
> Freed and enfranchis'd, not a party to
> The anger of the King nor guilty of,
> If any be, the trespass of the Queen.   (ll. 59–63)

In noble language Paulina makes the exact legal point that the gaoler
has no grounds for detaining the child in prison with its mother,
and the meaning of her words takes in more than the immediate
situation. 'By law and process of great Nature', she says, there is
no inherited guilt. These words are the first sign of a rallying in the
kingdom against the infection. Paulina never takes Leontes' jealousy
seriously, but in season and out of season she rebukes it:

> Fancies too weak for boys, too green and idle
> For girls of nine.   (iii. ii. 182–3)

When Hermione swoons upon the news of Mamillius' death, Paulina
speaks chorus-like a sentence that sums up the drift of the play's
first part:

> Look down
> And see what death is doing.                    (iii. ii. 149–50)

As in the story of the Sleeping Beauty, a death-like stillness comes
over the kingdom with the death of Mamillius, the seeming death
of Hermione and the passing of Leontes' rage. But unlike the Sleeping Beauty, the princess who is to be the centre of attention, having
escaped the womb and prison, now escapes her father's kingdom,
given over to mourning and tears, and arrives storm-borne on the
coasts of an imaginary Bohemia. Her escape is dramatised in a
remarkable and beautiful scene of transition. The storm that sinks
Antigonus' ship and the bear that eats him up are partly correspondent to the turbulent evil that has wasted Sicily and partly a
punishment for it. Whether one agrees or not with the mariner that,
'The heavens with that we have in hand are angry' (iii. iii. 5), one is

not really surprised either by the storm or the bear because both seem poetically just. The surprise is in the attitude that Shakespeare, using the manipulatory techniques already apparent in *Cymbeline*, has designed for his audience towards both of them.

The bringing of the bear upon the stage, no doubt in the form of a man in a bearskin, turns the horrible to the laughable; and the tone of the play, already teetering on the edge of bathos during Antigonus' account of his dream of Hermione, turns into downright burlesque. By making us laugh, even nervously, at Antigonus' fate, Shakespeare dissolves the pattern of our feelings towards Leontes' Sicily. His method is as bold, as strange and as sudden as an enharmonic modulation in music. The bear's antics having prepared us for the comic point of view, the clown's tale of disaster on land and sea forces it upon us. The old shepherd's monologue, meanwhile, has introduced us to a place, an age and a view of life that can take storms, bears and foundlings as they come. As so often in Shakespeare's plays, the wisdom of fools is about to confound the wise.

It would take a long analysis to follow in detail the artistry of the scene between the shepherd and his son. The visual imagination behind it is similar to that found in those panoramic Flemish paintings that depict several events occurring upon different but related planes. A reader needs to let his imagination move freely from the storm at sea and violence on land to the tiny, close-up centre of interest—the foundling baby, its bearing-cloth and its gold. Nor should he resist too much the feeling of mental vertigo as he tries to comprehend it all in one piece. As intelligence does its best to grapple with the closeness of death and life, tears and laughter, the feelings resolve into a sense of joy associated with the discovery of a great simplicity:

Heavy matters! heavy matters! But look thee here, boy.
Now bless thyself; thou met'st with things dying, I with things new-born. Here's a sight for thee; look thee, a bearing-cloth for a squire's child! Look thee here; take up, take up, boy; open't.

(III. iii. 115–20)

\* \* \*

*Pericles* appeals to a fundamental delight in the consecutiveness of things, *Cymbeline* to delight in magic and duplicity. *The Winter's Tale* appeals to its audience's joy in paradox. 'Truth inherent in a contradiction':[2] G. K. Chesterton's definition of paradox describes well the kind of reality that *The Winter's Tale*'s audience has to understand as the play progresses. In his best book, *The Everlasting Man*, Chesterton argues that paradox is the essence of Christian truth and therefore, by implication, a Western habit of mind. That theology is paradoxical will come as a surprise to no one; Chesterton's originality is in his argument that Christian paradox is rooted in the Christian narrative, one of the strangest stories ever written and, according to its narrators, wholly true. A formal paradox is obvious ('The fist shall be last'); the mind grows used to it as to any figure of speech. But *narrated* paradox, paradox imitated in events, is more covert and subtle,[3] and Chesterton takes the Nativity as the original paradox, universally known, if not universally understood:

> A mass of legend and literature, which increases and will never end, has repeated and rung the changes on that single paradox; that the hands that had made the sun and stars were too small to reach the huge heads of the cattle. Upon this paradox, we might almost say upon this jest, all the literature of our faith is founded ... every Catholic child has learned from pictures, and even every Protestant child from stories, this incredible combination of contrasted ideas as one of the very first impressions on his mind.... Any agnostic or atheist whose childhood has known a real Christmas has ever afterwards, whether he likes it or not, an association in his mind between two ideas that most of mankind must regard as remote from each other; the idea of a baby and the idea of unknown strength that sustains the stars.[4]

Whatever the significance of this from a Christian point of view, every reader of Shakespeare will immediately see that this eloquent comment on the Nativity touches upon one of the most famous and mysterious passages in *Macbeth:*

> And pity, like a naked new-born babe
> Striding the blast, or heaven's cherubin hors'd
> Upon the sightless couriers of the air,
> Shall blow the horrid deed in every eye,
> That tears shall drown the wind.   (*Macbeth*, I. vii. 21–5)

This is the same paradox that Chesterton finds in the Nativity; the babe striding the blast arises from the same association of apparent helplessness with irresistible strength. As Macbeth understands in a visionary way, the babe is the reality that will destroy him. To speak metaphorically, *Macbeth* is about a failed infanticide.

This paradox—Christian, Chestertonian, Shakespearean, whatever one calls it—with its attendant imagery and themes recurs in Shakespeare's work, and lies at the centre of *The Winter's Tale*'s action. The baby is not a metaphor, however, but the heroine of the tale. Numerous critics have remarked on Shakespeare's tendency in these later plays to use as incidents or characters things that had been metaphors and similes in his early and middle-period plays. The bear that eats Antigonus is an example, and so is the controversial 'clothes-line' that lures Stephano and Trinculo from their conspiracy in *The Tempest*. Thus concrete realities that Shakespeare had used figuratively to express such abstractions as appetite, usurpation, peace and ambition are now made part of the plot; and one result is that interpretation of these later plays, short of downright allegory, is otiose, a saying-over of the obvious. If threatened peace is like a sleeping child (*Richard II*, i. iii. 132–3), what is a sleeping child like? Leontes is not a usurper like Macbeth whose act, being *likened* to infanticide or patricide, is *interpreted* as a rebellion against nature. Attempted infanticide is actually one of Leontes' crimes. In *Macbeth* the imagery of Macbeth as a dwarfish thief in ill-fitting clothes, of murdered children, or of wading through a river of blood, implies the existence of other stories in terms of which *Macbeth* makes sense. *The Winter's Tale* is such a story, and it is not surprising that Caroline Spurgeon found no dominant symbol or thread of imagery in it.[5]

Despite extraordinary tehnical virtuosity, *The Winter's Tale* like *Pericles* is an example in poetry of what musicians call absolute art; it is, as we say, pure fiction. It is pointless to relate Perdita to other foundlings in fairy tales or myths, for she is simply herself. Her journey to Bohemia is the exit from Sicily's darkness that the story's design requires, and 'She-who-was-lost' is already found.[6] Sicily fades from our minds as Shakespeare substitutes for it the Bohemian shepherds and their sheep-shearing.

Contrasts between the simple and the sophisticated, the natural and the artificial, are part of any pastoral, and one of the less obvious but amusing ways of pointing such contrasts is by stylistic variation. Spenser uses the technique in *The Shepherd's Calendar*, and it is the chief source of the poem's elusive humour. Sidney uses it in *Arcadia*[7] and, as S. L. Bethell first recognised, Shakespeare uses it in *The Winter's Tale*, where he varies both poetic style and theatrical technique.[8] A tendency to burlesque in the first three acts has already been noticed; it disappears during the long scene of the sheep-shearing, and then reappears after it. When Polixenes' outburst against Florizel's love for Perdita sets the narrative moving again (iv. iv. 427), it proceeds with a series of asides so obviously theatrical that they invite overacting and therefore laughter. As Florizel and Autolycus change clothes the story grows increasingly absurd, and a climax of absurdity arrives when Autolycus, wishing to talk *solus* to the spectators, rids himself of the shepherds by pretending to 'look upon the hedge', i.e., to relieve himself. The burlesque strain continues into the fifth act, for when Leontes, Paulina and the rest reappear it seems that for sixteen years nothing has happened in Sicily. Under Paulina's supervision, Leontes has kept his vow of daily mourning, and the result has been an existence as remote as the worst and clumsiest art from what the word 'life' usually signifies. We find ourselves smiling therefore when Leontes speaks lines drawing attention to the staginess of his performance as actor as well as king:

> Nor more such wives; therefore, no wife. One worse,
> And better us'd, would make her sainted spirit
> Again possess her corpse, and on this stage,
> (Where we offenders now appear) soul-vex'd,
> Begin, 'And why to me—?'    (v. i. 56–9)

The element of stylistic clowning in the play is not only, as it would be in a play by Day or Fletcher, a show of self-conscious cleverness; it is also a way of putting inessential matter in its place and implying a scheme of values. The complications of the story, charming and necessary as they are, are shown to have mainly an entertainment value. 'The pretence to want to relieve himself', says J. H. P. Pafford about Autolycus, 'is merely a dramatic device (chiefly for the groundlings) . . . .'[9] And so it is, but there is no need to be snobbish about it. The asides, the clothes-changing, the overwriting, the bear, even Father Time, they are all dramatic devices, all amusing and interesting, holding our attention while guiding our understanding of the kind of attention that is being held. In listening to a story we are all groundlings, and perhaps for that reason few critics have tried to explain the workings of narrative. C. S. Lewis, however, was an exception, and among his many comments on narrative technique the conclusion of his essay 'On Stories' bears directly upon Shakespeare's technique in *The Winter's Tale*:

> . . . the art of story as I see it is a very difficult one . . . . To be stories at all they must be series of events: but it must be understood that this series—the *plot*, as we call it—is only really a net whereby to catch something else. The real theme may be, and perhaps usually is, something that has no sequence in it, something other than a process and much more like a state or a quality. Giantship, otherness, the desolation of space, are examples that have crossed our path. The titles of some stories illustrate the point very well. *The Well at the World's End*—can a man write a story to that title?[10]

No reader or spectator of *The Winter's Tale* can doubt that the end or purpose of its narrative comes out chiefly in two scenes: Perdita's handing out of flowers, and Hermione's return. Although these incidents are part of the plot, the form they take has no necessary connection with it. Perdita does not have to hand out flowers, nor must Hermione return as a statue. These are lyrical scenes, in Lewis's words the 'something else' caught by the net of the play's narrative. Technically they are like Posthumus' repentance and dream, Pericles' finding of Marina and his hearing the heavenly music. In all these cases reality, the moment of discovery and truth, is shown coming to men from sources outside the sequence of cause and effect that is usually, and has been in Shakespeare's own work, the stuff of drama.

Those sources are two, and virtually simultaneous, seeming to be echoes of one another. The first source is *in* nature as we normally understand it, and is not so much an action as a state of what we call 'the heart'; the second is *outside* nature, and its narrative form is an act of Providence. In *Cymbeline*, totally alone, Posthumus repents, and his vision appears to him. In *The Winter's Tale*, the gods disclose their providence, and the finding of Perdita fulfils it.

Perdita however is never really lost. From the delivery of the oracle, the narrative is under the gods' superintendence. Its presentation and arrangement are the work of their servant Time who, as Shakespeare so frankly says, can do anything (except go backwards). The audience is in the secret; they know all about Perdita and, measured against that fact of the story, all its complications seem absurd. Indeed one of the pleasures of this story is that our knowledge of Perdita gives us the illusion of having a sane grasp of life. The characters on stage know nothing of this; their ignorance and the audience's knowledge give its piquancy to Perdita's argument with Polixenes about hybrid flowers.

Some readers have made heavy weather of this miniature treatise on the relation of art and nature—a theme as common among Renaissance critics as horn jokes among Renaissance comics. One is tempted, upon first encountering Polixenes' speech in favour of hybridisation, to head for the library, but there is no harm in resisting. The argument is conventional, and it is only really important because of Perdita's answer. She, it will be remembered, explains that she has no carnations or gillyflowers in her garden because they are 'Nature's bastards', produced not by 'great creating Nature' alone but partly by the gardener's art. Polixenes answers with what has become the standard reply of the technologist and experimenter to the accusation that his work is 'unnatural':

> Yet Nature is made better by no mean
> But Nature makes that mean; so, over that art

> Which you say adds to Nature, is an art
> That Nature makes.   (IV. iv. 89–92)

And of course, like a lecturer, he illustrates his point. Hybridisation
is like marriage; we breed a 'gentler scion' with 'the wildest stock',
and, 'This is an art/Which does mend Nature'. Provided one means
by Nature 'whatever I do and whatever I think', this argument is
unanswerable. Perdita therefore replies, 'So it is.' 'Then', says Polixenes, triumphant over the shepherd's daughter,

> . . . make your garden rich in gillyflowers,
> And do not call them bastards.

Nevertheless Perdita means by 'great creating Nature' something
quite different from the self-projection (megalomaniac or complacent
as the case may be) which the word 'nature' signifies to Polixenes.
Like Cordelia's love, Perdita's own naturalness exists independent of
talk about it, and expresses itself in actions, not words. So she offers
no argument to Polixenes, saying simply:

> I'll not put
> The dibble in earth to set one slip of them.

Her only explanation is spoken to Florizel as she turns to him:

> No more than were I painted I would wish
> This youth should say 'twere well, and only therefore
> Desire to breed by me.

Any thought of falseness disturbs Perdita who is nonetheless
herself disguised for the day as the queen of the sheep-shearing. Yet
though her disguise embarrasses her, the audience knows it is really
no disguise at all. Like Falconbridge's, Perdita's royalty may be
disguised by her seemingly common birth, but her beauty and goodness are as royal as they are natural. The point of the argument is
not to settle the ethics of the laboratory, but to tell the audience how
they should judge the play's character's. Because Perdita refuses to
answer Polixenes directly, and because the audience sees her momen-
tary pain at the imagined feeling of insincerity, they know there is
something contemptible about Polixenes' glibness. Only a little while
later his rage at hearing of his son's wish to marry the shepherd girl
exposes the shallowness of his talk. He is one of those people who
will experiment with any child but his own. Meanwhile Perdita's
interrupted welcoming of her guests continues, and as she comments

on her flowers, the difference between Nature's children and the bastards fathered upon her by human ingenuity comes clear. Her own children express her irreducible beauty, but the bastards express men's continual absorption in trivialities and appearances. We know that we are in the presence of an image of absolute naturalness and integrity when Florizel, enraptured by Perdita, expresses not just the wish that the moment of seeing her be infinitely extended, but an understanding that somehow, in his joy, it *is* infinite:

> What you do
> Still betters what is done. When you speak, sweet,
> I'd have you do it ever; when you sing,
> I'd have you buy and sell so, so give alms,
> Pray so; and for the ord'ring your affairs,
> To sing them too. When you do dance, I wish you
> A wave o' th' sea, that you might ever do
> Nothing but that; move still, still so,
> And own no other function. Each your doing,
> So singular in each particular
> Crowns what you are doing in the present deeds,
> That all your acts are queens.   (IV. iv. 135–46)

Perdita's innocence is one of the greatest compliments ever paid an audience. Assuming that people on the whole, provided they do not have to write examinations on the subject, know what is meant by nature and what by art, then an audience's pleasure in Perdita is a sign of a wish satisfied, a wish to see goodness so represented that the art of its representation seems as natural as the act of seeing it. Our pleasure in Perdita as she hands out her flowers is surely meant to be as immediate as the shepherd's on first finding her. In the spectacle of the princess disguised as a shepherdess disguised as a rural princess, nature and art cancel each other out, and the eye is educated in the innocent perception of innocence.

* * *

Leontes' recognition of his daughter and his reunion with Polixenes are reported (v. ii), and the common explanation is that Shakespeare, not wishing Hermione's recovery, like Thaisa's, to be an anti-climax, this time decided to solve the problem of a double ending by excluding its first part from the stage. This may be so, but there is a better reason. To dwell upon Leontes' finding of Perdita would be superfluous because such a scene could add nothing to what we know of Perdita, who has already been thoroughly found by the shepherds, by Florizel, by Polixenes, and by the audience.

To dramatise in addition all seven or eight reunions would bury the play's proper ending in a distracting tangle of theatrical business.

Instead, by dramatising the effect of Perdita's finding upon Leontes' court, and not the finding itself, Shakespeare puts the incident exactly in its place; it is the means of bringing Sicily up to date with the rest of the world, the necessary, fore-ordained prelude to the play's true, single ending: Leontes' recovery at the end of the wife he lost at the beginning. His loss originated in mistaken perception, to which Shakespeare made the audience a party; after sixteen years' penitence, Leontes now sees her again, and the audience is once more a party to the discovery since it knows no more than Leontes does of Hermione's preservation. The king and his audience are as much in the dark at the end as they were at the beginning.

It is really a matter of perception. Having been prepared for a statue by 'that rare Italian master, Julio Romano' (v. ii. 105), we find ourselves looking at something so true to nature that it might be alive, years in the making, just finished, and as new in its way as a new-born infant. Art triumphs first, then, over time. Inception and completion join in the finished work, and the interim is lost. In the case of this statue, however, every moment of the interim has its record in the marks of age on the figure's face:

> *Leontes.*                    But yet, Paulina,
>   Hermione was not so much wrinkled, nothing
>   So aged as this seems . . . .
> *Paulina.*   So much the more our carver's excellence,
>   Which lets go by some sixteen years and makes her
>   As she liv'd now.   (v. iii. 27–32)

Besides, the statue is only this moment completed; its paint, it seems, is still wet. Should it set, then Hermione will in a way die again, for the life of art is the death of its subject. As he looks at the supposed status, Leontes is seeing a life in which he has had no part, frozen and motionless before his eyes. Once again he has the power of life and death over her, but without knowing it. We, unfortunately, can imagine a travesty—though surely Shakespeare could not—in which Leontes turns from Hermione, not in passion but in boredom. As it is, she has the power over him; the sight of her sixteen years' life fascinates him, and if the state in which the status stands represents death, or if his sense of its reality is madness, then Leontes would choose either to what he now has of life.

It makes no difference that Paulina has staged reality to make it

seem a fiction. There is art in Hermione's figure, though not Julio
Romano's:

> What was he that did make it? See, my lord,
> Would you not deem it breath'd, and that those veins
> Did verily bear blood?   (v. iii. 63–5)

>                    What fine chisel
> Could ever yet cut breath?   (l. 78)

According to the play's plot, the artist is Time, and Time is the vicar
of the gods. The play is a work of art, however, and Time and the
gods are part of it. For all his unclassical wildness, there is one rule
of decorum that Shakespeare never breaks, although in this late
play he comes near to breaking it: stage people are not real people,
they neither sleep real sleep nor die real deaths. Similarly, stage gods
are not real gods. If there are real gods, then like sleep and death
they can only be imitated. If there are no gods, then (to paraphrase
Sidney) art, not being captived to a foolish world, can make a
golden one and invent them.

   Shakespeare was an old hand at recognition scenes, yet he dramatised Hermione's return with an intensity that has hardly a parallel.
To put it mechanically, the scene requires that we look concentrat-
edly at Paulina's 'statue' for the space of more than eighty lines.
When Hermione finally speaks, the play comes as near to breaking
through the veil separating art from life as anything in Shakespeare:

>                 You gods, look down
> And from your sacred vials pour your graces
> Upon my daughter's head!   (ll. 121–3)

If a miracle is being dramatised here, what is it? That husbands do
indeed have wives, wives daughters, and daughters mothers? That
human relationships are real, integral to individual life, not accidental?

                              *       *       *

*The Winter's Tale*'s effect—if indeed it can still make its effect—
depends not upon the suspension of disbelief, however willing, but
upon the stirring of faith. Not long ago no reader of Shakespeare
would have questioned that in imitating the art that makes nature,
Shakespeare had decided to bring within the bounds of his art and to
recreate according to its laws the devinely ordered universe that he
and virtually all his contemporaries took for granted. Whether he
believed in the things he imitated or whether they are themselves

real are questions lying outside the bounds of either art or criticism, and not to be settled by the witness of William Shakespeare on either side. We have no justification for recreating the man in the image of our own disbelief, and at the same time the decorum of criticism requires that critics should not play at theology. It is enough in the present instance to define the action of *The Winter's Tale* as 'finding the lost'; for the principle of decorum in art and criticism alike is related to two ancient and complementary proverbs: 'A word to the wise is enough'; but 'a nod is as good as a wink to a blind horse'.

PART TWO

# Landfall

# 10. The Tempest

*The Tempest* is a very beautiful play but, mainly for historical reasons, a rather difficult one to see clearly. *Tempest* criticism really begins with the Romantics, whose expectations of poetry in general and of Shakespeare's poetry in particular have shaped the world's idea of *The Tempest* for nearly two centuries. Even a critic writing in conscious reaction against Romantic tradition is still under its influence, his perspective determined, in ways he does not always recognise, by the Romantic point of view.

The charm and the excitement of Romantic criticism lie in its subjectivity, its habit of overstatement, and its intentional non-rationality. Coleridge, probably the most important English Romantic critic of *The Tempest*, said of the play that 'It addresses itself entirely to the imaginative faculty'; and in the same essay he adumbrated a characteristic Romantic approach by identifying the poet with his hero.[1] To us the Coleridgean language is commonplace, and so we do not see how provocative it really is; but what Coleridge is saying is that *The Tempest* eludes common understanding. On his view the play is a world by itself, organically whole, brought into being by the miracle of imaginative creation; and the imagination alone can comprehend what imagination has made. In Coleridge's vocabulary, of course, 'imagination' means far more than it does in common usage. It signifies an occult creative agency operating in men, nature and the universe. As a modern critic in the Romantic tradition has said, 'imagination' means in Romantic usage something like the theological concept of divine grace.[2]

Coleridge and his contemporaries set fantasy free, and turned *The Tempest* into a romantic work, as much a part of the Romantic canon as Keats's *Letters*, Wordsworth's 'Preface' to the *Lyrical Ballads*, or Coleridge's own *Biographia Literaria*. At the same time they could hardly avoid turning the author into a Romantic poet. As the play's form exemplifies the creativity of the imagination, so its fiction represents, in the ideal form of a poetic fable, the spirit of the poet. Interpretation of *The Tempest* as symbolic autobiography is inseparable from the Romantic approach, and indeed gives it its status as a Romantic document.

As time passed and Romantic rebellion became academic ortho-
doxy, an impressive frame of scholarly apparatus gave an appearance
of solid actuality to the Romantics' convictions. By the end of the
nineteenth century there was general agreement that *The Tempest*
was Shakespeare's farewell to poetry and the theatre. From a scholarly
point of view the argument supporting this reading was, as so often
in Shakespearean matters, rather circular. All that was known for
certain was that *The Tempest*, a late play, had its first recorded
performance at James I's court on Hallowmass night, 1611. This,
however, taken in association with arguments against Shakespeare's
sole authorship of *Henry VIII* and with the absence of any other
wholly Shakespearean play definitely dated between 1611 and 1616,
seemed to justify reading the play as a personal allegory. The
argument is circular because one cannot be sure whether Prospero
must represent Shakespeare because the play is the last, or whether
the play must be last because Prospero is so obviously Shakespeare.
As with all circular argumentation, the basic assumptions lie outside
the ostensible process of reasoning.

Three hypotheses, therefore, seemed to have the status of fact.
These were that *The Tempest* is (1) comprehensible only by the imagination, (2) personal and (3) final. The interpretation that emerged
from the application of these facts is interesting, even a little alarming, and in one variant or another has dominated criticism. According
to it the play is a fable showing the artist (Prospero) inhabiting a world
alone (the island) which he rules absolutely by the power of imagination (Ariel and the lesser spirits), holding in subjection his and our
lower nature (Caliban). By the confluence of destiny and his own
power he brings to the island the men who drove him from his
former dukedom. In the confrontation that follows, the purity of the
artistic imagination meets the rapacity of the ordinary man of the
world. In righteous indignation the artist reproves the worldlings,
showing them images of their guilt while at the same time, by means
of imaginary wonders, giving them a sight of a redeemed existence.
Then, taught by his own imagination to feel a humane sympathy
with his suffering enemies, the artist changes his justice to mercy,
forgiving them all. Meanwhile, by marrying the natural, spontaneous
humane innocence that is the child of his own being (Miranda) to
the purged and cleansed son of his enemy (Ferdinand), the artist
works a kind of secular redemption of the everyday world, to which
he now returns, his task accomplished. His last work is to return the
spirit of imagination (Ariel) to nature, whence it came. Then, step-
ping forward to speak the Epilogue, half in character, half out of it,
he explains the significance of the story: the artist-hero is the author;
the island is the theatre of his many triumphs; Milan, the dukedom

to which he is restored, is the consummation of his life and art, the goal of his earthly voyage; and his exit from the stage is his retirement from poetry and drama.

This thrilling exposition makes Shakespeare the spokesman for the Romantic attitude to art and life which can be summarised as follows:

(1) The artistic imagination is transcendent, and every artist is God of a world of his own making.
(2) That world is separate from and superior to the world inhabited by other men.
(3) The signs of its superiority are three. (*a*) It is governed by occult, supra-rational forces; (*b*) they are revealed by its continual newness and originality; (*c*) a change of life is enforced upon all who enter it.
(4) It is the duty of the artist, by means of his visionary calling, to offer others the redemption of their lives through citizenship of his 'brave new world'.

This is an exciting reading because it seems to make poets and their readers into supermen. It is alarming because the same ideas, translated into secular politics, have produced the 'metapolitics' of totalitarianism, whether of the left or the right.[3] The literary significance of these ideas, however, lies chiefly in their being a parody of religion, and a sign of fantasy and wishful thinking.[4]

Only wishful thinking would identify Prospero with Shakespeare because, if we judge from what we know of the real Shakespeare, Prospero is very unlike him. He is a bookworm, a student who has neglected his affairs, a theoretician, solitary, irritable, absolute in his judgements; whereas Shakespeare, everyone has always agreed, was not theoretical, not particularly studious or bookish, was an able man of affairs, successful and prosperous by no magic except the intelligent conduct of business, was sociable, good-tempered, friendly and generous in judgement. One could not imagine Prospero writing a play, for his ruling interest is power. In some moods Shakespeare may have felt an admiration for the men of power, for those who live by the will; but if we go by the evidence of his plays and by what we know of his life, power conceived as a mystique either bored him, amused him or horrified him. No one will find the romance of power in Shakespeare. *The Tempest* makes romance out of abdication.

'But surely', the Romantic will object, 'Prospero is an artist, and *that* is the basis of the parallel?' Prospero, however, is not an artist in the modern sense of the word. His art is a means to power, and when he relinquishes power, he gives up art as well. Prospero's art *is* power as twentieth-century technology is power. It has nothing to do with what the Romantics called imagination because Prospero has never created a single thing. He has only used such things as lay to hand. Shakespeare made the island and everything on it, and it is as much a mistake to call Prospero an artist as to call Richard II a poet. Prospero is a magician, Richard a king; Richard never writes a poem, and Prospero never shows the least interest in art. Like many a rich Renaissance father, he provides an entertainment for his daughter and her betrothed; but as far as he is concerned the performers are 'rabble', the performance 'vanity', and as soon as he remembers more important matters he dismisses the whole show. His famous speech to Ferdinand (IV. i. 146–63) is one of the most eloquent statements ever made against the belief that art, or anything else that is made, is truth. Nihilism was never more sweetly, beguilingly put.

Hardly anyone now accepts the Romantic allegorical *Tempest* completely. For one thing contemporary criticism is too self-conscious, the critics too many, their style too muted. For another, able scholars have defended Shakespeare's sole right to *Henry VIII*, and *The Tempest*'s finality is therefore doubtful. Studies of the play's form and ideas in relation to contemporary seventeenth-century interests have given a local habitation and a name to what had looked like fantastic imaginings. Nonetheless the basic Romantic attitudes still dominate. Imaginative interpretation is still the basis of criticism, even though academic custom requires that it be footnoted; and the notion persists that *The Tempest* is an unusually portentous drama.

The trouble with the Romantic tradition of criticism is that it separates *The Tempest* from ordinary life, making it the exemplar of an art that is occult, intensely personal and accessible only to initiates. It also leads to the play's partial failure in the theatre, for in performance it never seems quite able to carry the weight of significance imputed to it.

\*    \*    \*

Superficially *The Tempest* resembles its three predecessors, with its idealised heroine, its contrasts of barbarity and civility, of nature and nurture, of true and false nobility; and of course there are general stylistic resemblances. In action, tone, and form, however, it is very different.

It is brief, compact and, in contrast with the formal freedom of its predecessors, pedantically neo-classical. It keeps a strict unity of time, place and action, and arranges its plot according to the neo-classical rules of construction. In fact it is the most academic of Shakespeare's plays since his early comedies and histories.[5] Its tone

is elegiac, sceptical and questioning, and its characteristic kind of
statement is brief and laconic:

> —O brave new world,
> That has such people in't!
> —'Tis new to thee.     (v. i. 183–4)

Important incidents—Miranda's and Ferdinand's meeting, the chastisement of the usurpers, the clowns' plot—are shortly, even sum-
marily dealt with. As for the action, its centre of interest is not an
error of Prospero's, or the love of his daughter and Ferdinand, not
even, really, Prospero's revenge upon his enemies; the focus is on
the very abstract theme of moral and political power. The play is
about a usurpation and a restoration, and has more in common with
the histories and the tragedies than with its immediate predecessors.

*The Tempest* is also Shakespeare's most spectacular play. So much
time is spent upon spectacle that most of its action is expressed in
visual symbolism. Antonio's, Alonso's and Sebastian's moral isolation
is expressed by the magical disappearance of the banquet as they
approach it (III. iii. 53). In so far as they are criminals, they are also
madmen, a thought we are shown rather than told when, after
Ariel's 'harpy' speech, they perform a kind of dance of the possessed
with wild contortions.[6] Log-carrying expresses the contrast between
Ferdinand and Caliban, and shows us the nature of Ferdinand's trial.
A game at chess signifies the quality of the young lovers' betrothal,
their absorption in each other and their attentiveness to each other's
presence. When the clowns steal the finery put out for them by Ariel,
the action shows in one swiftly understood emblem the unintelli-
gence, simplicity, incongruity and, of course, thievery of their plot.
Gonzalo's tears show his sympathy. Even the play's comedy is visual.
Stephano's drunken dealings with the four-legged beast and Ariel's
interruptions of Caliban are examples of ancient, though perennially
effective, routines. When Ariel leads Stephano and Trinculo into 'the
filthy-mantled pool' the action, besides diverting them from their
purpose and punishing them, turns them into visual images of their
own beastliness.

The play's poetry and music complement its visual imagery. Ariel's
speech to the 'three men of sin' (III. iii. 53–82) and Prospero's farewell to his magic (v. i. 33–57) exemplify a tendency in the play's style
towards a static lyricism. They are two of the most difficult passages
in Shakespeare's work for an actor to perform satisfactorily, demanding a perfect control of rhythm and breath. They are apostrophes,
accompanied by magical shows and followed by music, and they
require a delivery approaching recitative. Indeed, language is never

far from music in this play. Just as our attention is continually drawn by aptly placed choric comments to the spectacular beauty of the play's *mise-en-scène*, so it is drawn to its aural beauty in such moments as Ferdinand's description of the effect upon him of Ariel's singing and Caliban's reassurance to Stephano:

> Be not afeard. The isle is full of noises,
> Sounds and sweet airs, that give delight and hurt not.
>
> (III. ii. 144–5)

*The Tempest*'s language has the abstract aural beauty that we associate with Milton. It shows in those passages requiring the simultaneous performance of words and music[7] as well as in such explicitly 'musical' passages as Ariel's lyrics where sense and grammar are obviously subordinate to sound:

> Come unto these yellow sands,
>     And then take hands.
> Curtsied when you have, and kiss'd
>     The wild waves whist:
> Foot it featly here and there,
>     And, sweet sprites, the burden bear.
> *Burden* (*dispersedly*).   Hark, hark!
>                             Bow-wow.
> The watch-dogs bark!
>                             Bow-wow.
> *Ariel.*   Hark, hark!   I hear
>     The strain of strutting chanticleer
>     Cry, 'Cock-a-diddle-dow'.   (I. ii. 376–86)

It is no wonder that Milton was so impressed with *The Tempest* that echoes of it occur frequently in his early poetry, especially in the two masques. The pre-Miltonic Shakespeare shows most clearly in the *Tempest* masque (IV. i. 60–137) where words, music and spectacle are combined in seventy-five lines of cool virtuosity that not all readers have admired:

> Ceres, most bounteous lady, thy rich leas
> Of wheat, rye, barley, vetches, oats, and pease;
> Thy turfy mountains, where live nibbling sheep,
> And flat meads thatch'd with stover, them to keep;
> Thy banks with pioned and twilled brims,
> Which spongy April at thy hest betrims

To make cold nymphs chaste crowns; and thy broom groves,
Whose shadow the dismissed bachelor loves,
Being lass-lorn ...   (IV. i. 60-8)

One of the puzzles of criticism, the consequence perhaps of
Romantic impressionism, is the view of many that because the
masque is untypical and poorly written it cannot be Shakespeare's
work. Once one has recognised the verbal cunning and richness of
the masque's style, the clue to its place in the play is that it is a
piece of genre-writing. Inevitably a brief pastoral occurring in a
poetic drama not itself in the pastoral style will have a look of
pastiche about it. Shakespeare, however, lets the genre's own stylistic
character distinguish the masque from its context without exaggeration or parody. Consequently the masque can stand by itself as the
play-scene in *Hamlet* or the vision in *Cymbeline* can not. The pastoral rules are kept, of rough metre, rustic diction and stylised subject. The result is a style neither pedantic nor naive nor silly-sweet
(the characteristic faults of Elizabethan pastoral), evoking a landscape and a tone as unmistakably English as in Virgil's pastorals
they are Italian:

> Hail, many-coloured messenger, that ne'er
> Dost disobey the wife of Jupiter;
> Who with thy saffron wings upon my flowers
> Diffusest honey-drops, refreshing showers,
> And with each end of thy blue bow dost crown
> My bosky acres and my unshrubb'd down,
> Rich scarf to my proud earth; why hath thy queen
> Summon'd me hither, to this short-grass'd green?   (IV. i. 76-83)

This style seems untypical because we do not think of Shakespeare
as a pastoral poet, even though his plays contain some of the
loveliest pastoral in English. Shakespeare the pastoralist, however,
was a strong influence in his time. This fact explains the characterisation of Shakespeare in Milton's *L'Allegro* that we find condescend-
ing:

> Or sweetest Shakespeare. Fancy's child,
> [Warbling] his native woodnotes wild.

Again, Romantic preconceptions are probably misleading. This
couplet does not mean that Milton thought Shakespeare was an
untaught countryman from Stratford. In its context it is high praise
and an expression of homage to the man who more than any other

poet naturalised pastoral in England. Echoes of Shakespeare's pastoral, especially the tone and rhythm of the late work, occur everywhere in early Milton:

> By the rushy-fringed bank,
> Where grows the Willow and the Osier dank,
> My sliding chariot stays . . .

*          *          *

In the plays that we think most characteristically Shakespearean, the comedies and tragedies of his middle years, one often suspects that the author's style of composition is chiefly improvisatory, and that anything might happen—as indeed it does in *Hamlet*, what with the killing of Polonius, the fight with the pirates, Laertes' rebellion, and Hamlet's jump into Ophelia's grave. Events outrun premeditation, and such freedom of action, falling at the end into so happily patterned an order, naturally leads to talk of Providence:

> let us know
> Our indiscretion sometimes serves us well
> When our dear plots do pall; and that should teach us
> There's a divinity that shapes our ends,
> Rough-hew them how we will.     (*Hamlet*, v. ii. 7–11)

In *Pericles* and *Cymbeline* Providence appears on the stage as a dream or vision; in *The Winter's Tale*, it still superintends the action even though it appears only indirectly.

The Tempest differs from these plays, however, in being without surprise once we have absorbed the wonders of the exposition. Everything seems premeditated. The notorious lapse (i. ii. 438) when Ferdinand mentions an otherwise non-existent son of Antonio is quite untypical of a play where the careful, planned art of its form and style have their parallel in a plot that is always, by definition, under complete control. There is little in the play to satisfy ordinary dramatic interest, and there are signs that in the attempt to make the plot more theatrical, Shakespeare has slightly confused it. If we are to judge by Prospero's arrangement of Miranda's and Ferdinand's betrothal and the conclusion of Ariel's 'harpy' speech (iii. iii. 81–2), he intends forgiveness of his enemies from the start. But at the moment of its announcement, Prospero's forgiveness is made to look as if it were the result of a sudden change of mind (v. i. 21–32). Prospero's long scene with Miranda (i. ii. 1–186) and his perturbation on remembering the clowns' plot are two more examples of a conflict between plot and character. There is no reason why Prospero should suspect Miranda of not listening to him, and there is no reason why he should react so strongly to Caliban's absurd conspiracy. The plot of *The Tempest* is so designed that everything turns out as planned, and so the play is one of the least mysterious, most comprehensible that Shakespeare wrote.

*The Tempest*'s special beauty arises from clarity, formality and impersonality. Its theme is the dream of power justly exercised upon men and nature requiring, as a condition of its working, the intellectual mastery signified by chastity. This last, which both Prospero and the spirits of the masque express, worries some who suspect any curb upon instinct; but instead of hypothesising a puritanical streak in the author, it is better to accept the theme, recognising that Miranda's and Ferdinand's chastity is absolutely secure, guaranteed by their nobility of birth and breeding. The harmlessness of any threat to their chastity is revealed in the masque by the account of their defeat of Venus and Cupid, who return penitent to Paphos (IV. i. 91–101). There is beauty in the threat, and charm in its defeat. Even Caliban, who is ur-brutishness and unchastity itself, is idealised, rendered harmless and comical. He has enough of an instinctive response to nature's beauty—which the civilised and reasonable know is a form of goodness—that he can evoke the wonder of the island more persuasively than any other character:

> Sometimes a thousand twangling instruments
> Will hum about mine ears, and sometimes voices
> That, if I then had wak'd after long sleep,
> Will make me sleep again; and then, in dreaming,
> The clouds methought would open and show riches
> Ready to drop upon me, that, when I wak'd
> I cried to dream again.   (III. ii. 146–52)

Caliban, however, should not be sentimentalised. He is a grotesque, a monster conceived in a tradition whose roots are in classical mythology, scripture, folklore and the pseudo-science of witchcraft. Like other grotesques, he is a mixture of the comic and the horrid, and like other mythological characters in Renaissance literature, his parentage explains his significance. His mother, 'the foul witch Sycorax, who with age and envy/Was grown into a hoop' (I. ii. 258), conceived him by a demon, presumably the god called Setebos whom Caliban mentions (I. ii. 374). Witches were loathed and feared exactly because they were suspected of such alliances with supernatural beings inimical to humanity. From a mediaeval/Renaissance point of view, the witch was an enemy agent, and her reputed ugliness and malignance popularity symbolised the moral consequences of her illegal traffic. Like a character in Dante's hell,

Sycorax, bent into a hoop, looks the thing she is. Sexual intercourse with a demon was the ultimate act of witchcraft, the consummation of the witch's dream of transcendent power and of the demon's dream of subversion. Each has, to speak ironically, a hope for humanity, and Caliban, the 'freckl'd whelp, hag-born' (I. ii. 283), is Shakespeare's poetic image of that hope made flesh. He is a bad copy of humanity, fertile in curses.

He is definitely not human. Brutish and untameable as he is, he is therefore not corrupt, and the pleasure we take in him is partly owing to his sincere ignorance of any other way of being than his own. His language, person and actions are all of a piece. He is unforgiveable because there is nothing to forgive; one can only put up with him, as with an unreliable dog, knowing that if one is careful the brute can do no real harm.

Because he is not human, Caliban is as likely to have anthropomorphic fancies projected upon him as is any other animal, and the process, which thrives in *Tempest* criticism, begins in the play. Prospero's attempt at educating Caliban, bringing him up with his own daughter, is the result of one such fantasy, that Caliban is an innocent, untaught savage. Events prove Prospero so utterly wrong that Caliban's curses make very effective satirical comedy:

> You taught me language; and my profit on't
> Is, I know how to curse.   (I. ii. 363–4)

That, as a joke, is worthy of Swift. (There is a similar story of a sage who spent long hours teaching a chimpanzee to paint. The poor animal's first picture was of the bars of its cage.) Stephano and Trinculo mistake Caliban for a native of the island, and in their subsequent treatment of him there is some satire on colonisers of whom the bullying, drunken butler Stephano is a strong caricature.

Caliban, however, is not a cannibal, a Caribbean or an Indian nor is he a woodewose, salvage man, satyr or Cyclops. Likenesses however compelling to the perceiver, are not identities. Caliban is himself, and his presence in the play tells us that evil has consequences that no moral order can assimilate.

Caliban's fellow-servant Ariel also comes to us out of the pages of Renaissance pseudo-science. He is one of those Neo-Platonic entities a discarnate inhabitant of our air, able to assume a body at will having power over the elements and lesser spirits, and subject under certain conditions to human control. Unlike the demon whose cold embraces begot Caliban, Ariel belongs to an order of beings with no particular wish for dealings with humanity. Control of Ariel brings

vith it control of nature, of water, wind, lightning, thunder and fire;
ut he is an unwilling servant, who must be kept under strict
iscipline. Like Caliban he longs for the freedom to be solely himself,
nd under the constraint of servitude he behaves like a disturbed
hild, playful, malicious, affectionate and sulky by turns. He can
urprise by a show of feeling that has the appearance of sympathy,
s when he prompts Prospero to feel sorry for his enemies; but this is
nly another role that Ariel has learned to play during his association
vith Prospero.

Prospero's two servants are amazing creatures, neither allegories
or symbols, but imitations of nature. If there are Neo-Platonic
aemons then they must be like Ariel; that is the proposition Shake-
peare's art forces upon us. Until very recently it was probably easier
or us to conceive an Ariel than a Caliban, whose breeding has long
een utterly ruled out by everything we know about natural pro-
esses. Now that biologists are talking of creating a special kind of
nonkey or anthropoid to do our menial work for us, Caliban will
ome into focus again, parentage and all.

Caliban and Ariel are the necessary adjuncts of Prospero's power.
Without them he would be just another Robinson Crusoe, making do
ntil help came, day-dreaming over the campfire. As it is, he has
bsolute power at his fingertips, with all his daily wants supplied,
nd a daemon to obey his commands. That, having these resources,
rospero should do so little with them for twelve years is a sign of
ie distance between his milieu and ours. The only characters who
now any interest in taking practical advantage of the island are
tephano and Antonio. Prospero's aim is solely moral, justice for
imself and his daughter, punishment for his enemies. Then, in the
our when his plans come to fruition, he abandons his whole design
xcept the betrothal of his daughter, forgiving his enemies, releasing
riel, leaving Caliban, one presumes, on his island, and sailing home
 Milan.

In *Measure for Measure*, also a play about power and forgiveness,
istice and mercy, there is as succinct a statement as one might find
f the thesis tested in *The Tempest*:

> He who the sword of heaven will bear
> Should be as holy as severe.   (III. ii. 275–6)

1 both plays, however, it turns out to be irresistibly true that 'The
rer action is/In virtue than in vengeance' (*Tempest*, v. i. 27–8),
nd in both, as a consequence, nothing really happens. The elaborate
chemes of Duke Vincentio in *Measure for Measure* leave the corrupt
ity of Vienna and its people much as they were to begin with, and

there is no sign that Duke Prospero's rehabilitation of his brother works better than his schooling of Caliban. Moreover, in developing their moral strategies both dukes somewhat compromise themselves. Vincentio is underhanded and calculating, and Prospero, disciplining himself as firmly as he rules Ariel and Caliban, grows testy and monstrously self-confident.

In Shakespeare's work, sanctity and severity repeatedly fail to mix. The idea of the virtuous prince, fundamental to Renaissance theories of government, no more came alive on the Shakespearean stage than it did in real life. In one way therefore *The Tempest* has no real ending. Swayed by the Shakespearean emotions of sympathy and pity, Duke Prospero fails once more in the exercise of power as he discovers the difference between fantasy and real action. In another way, however, *The Tempest* ends very definitely when Prospero, finally abandoning his dream of power, sets Ariel free, Caliban, the island and its spirits all fade away at the end, as Prospero forecast that they would:

> Our revels now are ended. These our actors,
> As I foretold you, were all spirits, and
> Are melted into air, into thin air.  (IV. i. 148–50)

According to this reading, the Prospero who returns home to Milan is very different from the man who left it with his robe, books and baby daughter in a leaky boat.

Are exquisite manners a symptom of melancholy? Like the Emperor Charles V, Prospero abdicates to prepare for death, but whereas the figure of the Hapsburg emperor is invested with the violent light and movement of the Counter-Reformation, Duke Prospero at his best, as when he greets his old acquaintances, is an urbane, stylish man. Deprived of his 'rough magic', he keeps an unruly world at his fingers' ends by graceful verbal conjuring; the 'discovery' (in the theatrical sense) of Prospero to his enemies and his old friend Gonzalo is the discovery of a new man, the gentleman that potent figure who will rule by style alone:

> There are yet missing of your company
> Some few odd lads that you remember not.  (V. i. 254–5)

The unquestioning and unquestionable certainty of that manner of speech rules more effectively than 'rough magic'. It tames Caliban in a trice, for it is the language that puts things in their place, even Ariel:

> My Ariel, chick,
> That is thy charge. Then to the elements
> Be free, and fare thou well! (v. i. 316–18)

In this last scene Prospero has forsaken one kind of charm for another which was to prove, prosaically and historically, much more effective, just as empirical science proved more effective than magic. Like Theseus in *The Two Noble Kinsmen*, Prospero anticipates the eighteenth century, its despots enlightened by reason and good manners, and its gentlemen.

He also anticipates its melancholy. This is the significance of the epilogue; for what Prospero really has on his mind is death. Death is as central to *The Tempest* as it was to *Richard II*, but a technique has been found, of thought and art, whereby it can be moved for the time being to the circumference. The play begins with the fear of death and ends with the expectation of its backstage visit. The interim is the players', and the formal perfection of their play, the inventiveness of its fable, the beauty of its language, music and spectacle express spirit and courage as well as imagination. But the epilogue makes us see a necessary difference between the play's ending and the ending, both as conclusion and purpose, of life:

> Now I want
> Spirits to enforce, art to enchant,
> And my ending is despair,
> Unless I be reliev'd by prayer,
> Which pierces so that it assaults
> Mercy itself and frees all faults.

Even at his most classical Shakespeare has to remind us that his work is illusory, uninclusive. His epilogue is charmingly, elegantly put, but its effect is monitory, making us think that Prospero is a real man who will really go home to die.

There is for us something elegiac in the mere fact of an ending, so unwilling are we to set a limit; and as we stand at that boundary line between a kind of being we know and another we can only imagine, we naturally tend towards self-dramatisation. Post-Romantics as we are, we see an application in Prospero's farewell to his island; for each of us is in his own fantasy a Prospero on an island of wish-fulfilment, and when the other Prospero goes home we cannot help feeling sorry for ourselves. But we have no reason for supposing that Shakespeare felt anything of the kind.

\* \* \*

*The Tempest* is rather unusual in English literature, being a work that is classical in spirit and achievement as well as in form. The essence of classical achievement is the realisation in a single work of two apparently opposed ideals: formal perfection and comprehensiveness. The former, which we associate with small-scale works, seems to exclude the latter, which we associate with large, unruly affairs such as the novels of Charles Dickens. The grand exemplars of classical art, however, are the large forms: in literature the epic, tragedy and comedy; in music the sonata; in architecture the great house, of which the temple or cathedral is the sublime instance. The joy of the classical comes from the sense of achievement within the bounds of what is reasonably possible. The barbarian, of whom Alexander the Great cutting the Gordian knot is the emblem, has neither the patience nor the modesty of the classical man. His formality excludes, and his comprehensiveness submits to no forms. Alexander weeps when there are no more kingdoms to conquer, and again he represents the barbarian, and so does Procrustes, fitting his guests to the size of his bed.

One can demonstrate the formal comprehensiveness of *The Tempest* by dwelling upon the range of style and character, by showing how neatly the plot is accommodated to the play's form. There is ample matter for commentary in the extraordinary contrasts between the absolute tempestuousness of Ariel's tempest and the equally absolute musicality of his music, between Ariel and Caliban, between the style of Prospero's invocation to his spirits and the style of Antonio's talk (II. i. 1–296). Such contrasts define a range that seems sufficient, potentially, to accommodate the scale of human experience. But there are two qualities in the play that seem to defy commentary (in our unclassical times at least) since they are only 'in' the play if an audience agrees to put them there, and they are essential to one's sense of its classicality. They are freedom and decorum, the aesthetic equivalent of the more abstract ideals of formal perfection and comprehensiveness already mentioned as necessary to classical art.

Beauty obeys no law of necessity and vindicates none. Considered as a quality in things, as being in Shakespeare what reviewers often call 'the poetry', there is no reason why it should be there at all—unless of course one begs the question by saying that art is always beautiful, or by advancing some reductive theory of what makes for 'true' art, which then becomes the condition of the beautiful. Beauty, if one takes for a moment a necessitarian view, is quite gratuitous. A building may have to be in some degree functional and a novel must 'mean' something, but neither of them has to be beautiful; and if an artist, exasperated by utilitarian necessities, imposes upon himself the anti-utilitarian necessity of being uselessly beautiful, he may find that beauty does not come at call.

In works of art beauty expresses the purest kind of freedom, the presence of an utterly disinterested delight; and its characteristic form is that element in art with which modern criticism is virtually helpless: ornament. The entire fiction of *The Tempest*, everything in it from the great idea of a magus on an enchanted island down to the exquisite detail of Ariel's songs, is conceived, in relation to its ideas and to any possible occasion of performance, as ornament. Hence the religiosity, the allegorising, the mythologising, even the scholasticising of the critics. Unable to accept the utter gratuitousness of the thing that has been made for us, to enter into the playfulness of it, we ask with the persistence of Planty in *The Horse's Mouth*, 'What does it all mean?' It is inconceivable to us servants of the modern authoritarian and utilitarian state that the play should mean simply what it seems to mean, unbelievable that any man should spend his capacities so lavishly for what in the end is only the fun of it. We therefore convert the play's beauty to some principle of our own—the transcendence of the imagination, the dominance of archetypes, or whatever—neglecting as we do so the play's other principle, which is decorum.

Decorum, the rule of what is fitting and proper, is explained by grammarians and rhetoricians as the principle according to which good writers suit style to speaker and occasion. Caliban's language is a famous instance of that kind of decorum. This however is only a classroom interpretation of a wider and profounder idea, since the principle of decorum is primarily moral and social, involving the definition of bounds, of what is acceptable.

The rule or standard of decorum in this wider sense (which validates the rhetorician's narrower sense) is based on the humane point of view itself and the fact that it is absolutely limiting. *The Tempest* is in that sense as decorous as it is free. It never exceeds the limit set by a humane point of view. All its wonders are humanly made. There are things in its environment subject perhaps to human control, but never to human possession; and there are things which to a lively imagination might imply the existence of realities beyond the natural. Ariel for instance acts the part of a Providence understood to perform its miracles through natural means, and Miranda's beauty appears godlike to Ferdinand. But 'the poet nothing affirmeth'. Everything comes under the rule of his art, and the decorum that hazards no statement outside the terms of the play's fiction has its moral equivalent within the fiction in Prospero's tempering of justice with mercy, and his return to Milan.

It is doubtful whether in our time we can see the classical *Tempest* adequately performed. The play is so spectacularly written and, to be effective, requires such splendour of properties and expense that it seems very probable that it was written, like *Love's Labours Lost* and *A Midsummer Night's Dream*, for some noble occasion, perhaps a royal one. No doubt all three plays went over well in economy-style productions in the public theatres, whether indoor or outdoor; but in the case of *The Tempest* it is hard to see how anything short of royal resources and a royal sense of occasion could do it justice. Moreover, as contemporary performances and criticism reveal, we have little sympathy with Renaissance dramatic style, and hardly any real knowledge of it.

# 11. Henry the Eighth, or, All Is True[1]

*Henry VIII* and *The Tempest* are both spectacular plays, but in other respects they are opposites. *The Tempest* is brief, spare, classically constructed; *Henry VIII* is a long, dramatic pageant, treating successive incidents in the style of a chronicle play. The plot of *The Tempest* is Shakespeare's own invention, a pure poetic fiction; *Henry VIII's* plot is taken directly from historical materials which Shakespeare follows very closely. The plays' heroes are opposites, too.

Prospero, judged by really worldly standards, is a failure. He is like one of those gamblers who work out infallible systems of wagering or investing. In their imaginations everything works perfectly, but at the moment of action nerve fails or some hidden flaw is revealed, and dreams of fortune fade. The flaw in Prospero's scheme is that his 'rough magic' cannot coerce nature beyond a certain point. It can bring Antonio, Sebastian and Alonso to the island, but it cannot change Antonio's heart against his will, nor can it make Prospero into a man of action. Whatever he had imagined himself doing to his enemies, his failure to do it puts him in the company of Richard II, Brutus and Hamlet, each of whom by a moment's yielding to sympathy sealed his own doom. Prospero's future in Milan is a very dubious one.

Henry VIII on the other hand is one of history's successes. Any politician who changes the ownership of more than half his country's land, and gets away with it, is a success. Henry's revolution, carried through with ruthless violence, still marks the English landscape, its evidences never more interesting than when his new order stands closely juxtaposed to the old which it displaced. At Fountains, the ruined monastery lies a few hundred yards downstream from the lay proprietor's house, built in 1611 in hayseed Renaissance style, and the two buildings make a contrast that Shakespeare, the poet and dramatist of contrasts, would have relished.

Just such an implicit contrast lies between the heroes of *The Tempest* and *Henry VIII*. Henry's world is a poetic version of the

Milan to which Prospero returns, his England the poet's counter-statement to Prospero's island. Prospero rules a little world of his own making, a world of foregone conclusions, complete in itself, out of the normal currents of time and change, enjoying no future. Henry, however, rules and shapes an inherited England in a time of sudden, portentous change, and his play is laden with a feeling of future events. *Henry VIII*, then, is a poetic as well as a chrono-logical sequel to *The Tempest*.

The idea that the two plays are related by the very contrast between their forms, themes, subjects and characters is only surpris-ing because somehow the tradition of criticism has taught us that in his later years Shakespeare ceased to surprise. The deeply en-trenched notion that *The Tempest* is his last and consciously testa-mentary play has so bedevilled criticism of *Henry VIII* that despite its continual success in the theatre the play has been for most of its critics something to be explained away. *Henry VIII*'s actuality, its cool truthfulness—in a word, its worldliness—have always been in-compatible with the Romantic version of Shakespeare's last years as a time of retired, semi-religious contemplation.

To explain the worldliness of *Henry VIII*, the Romantic critics brought in the hypothesis of mixed authorship. If, after stylistic analysis, it should prove that the objectionable parts of the play were by someone other than Shakespeare, then the appearance of the Romantics' idol was saved. The most popular candidate has been John Fletcher, a dramatist long considered the Noël Coward of the Jacobean theatre; and this attribution is related to another debunking hypothesis, which is that the real explanation of Shakespeare's career, when we get down to brass tacks, is the series of theatres he wrote for and the audiences who attended them. Thus one recent historian gives a lively, though not very charming, picture of Shakespeare sitting down with his business associates at the time they leased the Blackfriars Theatre to discuss what kind of play would best 'go' in the new house. This, we are told, was the real cause of the later plays coming out as they did—a theory that would be more con-vincing had the partners arrived in limousines and swapped cigars.[2]

Neither the theory of mixed authorship nor that of a calculated appeal to public taste affects the real questions about *Henry VIII*. Collaboration does not itself affect the integrity of a work, nor does an artist's wish to please an audience. Just because Shakespeare, like most artists, had a practical grasp of business affairs, there is no reason to talk about him as if he were a huckster. The answer to such theories is in the basic fact that makes them possible, which is that Shakespeare's career spans with such marvellous neatness the vicissi-tudes of theatres and companies. Like J. S. Bach, he used the opportunities that came to him. It was part of his genius to be able to do so, and it puts the cart before the horse to say that instead of using, he was used.

More recently several critics have defended the play's integrity, both of authorship and design, against the older view that it is at best a commonplace, at worst an offensive popular 'show', a kind of Jacobean *Cavalcade*. The older view takes the play much as it stands, as a medley of events, requiring of its audience no finer emotion than sentimental nationalism, no subtler political thought than that the government is always right. The defenders' case turns upon the demonstration that *Henry VIII* is a dramatic and poetic whole, and the proof, generally speaking, takes two forms. First, the play's form is compared to the tragi-comedies', with which it has much in common. Beginning darkly, it ends with the prophecy of a glorious future, the play's whole action showing the gradual emergence of Henry as true King of a new, united England. Second, this action is shown to embody the teachings of contemporary political doctrine. According to one interpreter, for instance, the play is like a political morality, in which the King finally acts the part of Mercy when he saves Cranmer.[3]

This school of interpretation is a welcome development, a sign of a return to the text as we have it from the First Folio. Unfortunately, it has the effect of defending Shakespeare's aesthetic values in a way that does little credit to his moral or political sense. Hardin Craig, for instance, explains the play's rambling form by saying that a history play need have no clear form because only God's Providence can shape history.[4] Translated into practical English and applied to *Henry VIII*, however, this means that Shakespeare was a totalitarian. After all, the actual cause of Buckingham's, Catherine's and Wolsey's falls, as of Cranmer's rise, is the King. One might wish to say that in some sense eluding either his or our knowledge, Henry is an agency of Providence; but good taste, not to mention stronger considerations, should rule out an identification of Henry and Providence. Nonetheless:

> If God alone is stable, he has a kind of high-priest on earth, in the person of Henry.... When he administers the law himself, justice as of heaven operates.... Once the power of Rome is quelled in England, the King assumes his rightful dominance, and Cranmer symbolically kneeling to Henry, demonstrates the true idea of a protestant kingdom.[5]

There were undoubtedly some Tudor subjects prepared to say as much as this. There were also others who carried their refusal to say anything of the kind as far as the block and the gallows. Did the author of *King John* and *Richard II* really end up as a kind of Jacobean Eisenstein, glorying in the megalomania of the new regime and the helplessness of its victims? If *Henry VIII* is really the play its scholarly defenders say it is, then at the end of his career Shakespeare turned his intelligence and his humanity over to the state; the poet who questioned the moral basis of existence had no questions to put to the King:

> If his treatment of Katherine leaves a feeling of uneasiness in the modern mind, it is largely Henry's character as fixed by history, rather than by the play to which this is due ... there is no question of a morally false equation between her downfall and Wolsey's. He is abandoned by God, she suffers only the loss of a husband.[6]

These are high regions where the loss of a husband is as nothing to the loss of God. Besides, if Henry is God's high-priest on earth, then Katherine loses God as well as her husband and there is indeed an equation, morally false or not, between the two falls, and the dramatist, not 'history', is responsible. But the critic's eye is not on the object before him. Just as *Henry VIII* has nothing to say about quelling Rome's power or about the true idea of a Protestant kingdom, so it says nothing about God's abandoning Wolsey. On the contrary, both the dramatist and his source see in Wolsey's fall an act of divine grace that saves his soul:

> His overthrow heap'd happiness upon him;
> For then, and not till then, he felt himself
> And found the blessedness of being little;
> And, to add greater honours to his age
> Than man could give him, he died fearing God.   (iv. ii. 64–8)

The average reader, given the choice, would no doubt rather read *Henry VIII* as a prototype of *Cavalcade* than of *Ivan the Terrible*. Aesthetic unity is not so important an artistic virtue that ordinary decency as well as the play's text have to be sacrificed to it. There is however a third way out, offering an escape from an unpleasant choice. Neither the play's attackers nor its defenders have much to say about the irony which provides a continual, running commentary on its action and which, once perceived, alters its whole aspect. Nor is there anything hidden or esoteric about it. Like all irony it works on the assumption that we will take certain implicit contrasts, such as that between *The Tempest* and *Henry VIII*, for granted and that, duly prepared, we will take a hint.

*          *          *

*Henry VIII* brings us closer than any other play to Shakespeare's sense of his own times. It does not make covert allusions by analogy and figure or settle great questions with a myth. Shakespeare is here writing about the England his parents and grandparents knew, about the events that decided the quality of his own times, that may even have influenced his own life. He is writing moreover with the expertise of a lifetime's work as poet and dramatist. He is the master of subtleties of construction and tone that no other writer can approach. He will need all his skill, too, for as the subtitle announces, he has set himself an extraordinarily difficult task. *All is True*: what kind of title is that for a poet's invention? Sidney defended poets against the charge of lying by saying that since the essence of poetry lay in the art of making fictions, no poet pretended to tell the truth; the truth of poetry lay in its imitative relationship to real life and character. Shakespeare's tragi-comedies, perhaps consciously and intentionally, exemplify Sidney's doctrine. His earlier histories seem to belong to a genre outside Sidney's scope, but even in them Shakespeare found a way of so mingling history and fiction that, whatever conclusions his audience might reach, he was himself left largely uncommitted.

*All is True*, however, is a challenge and a boast. While it would certainly draw in the customers, it would also make Shakespeare liable, in the minds of thoughtful spectators, not just for his facts (always allowing for the compression enforced by dramatisation), but for his interpretation of them. At the same time, it challenges the spectators because the sentence 'All is true' inevitably suggests that although 'all' may be true, it will also be incredible; and, as always, the moral challenge of the incredible is whether one should be amazed or appalled. The object of this boast or challenge was, in addition, the difficult subject of recent English history.

The problem of Shakespeare's subject was ideological because its real theme was the schism with Rome and, with it, a schism in national life between past and present, between Protestant and Roman Catholic, between, in concrete terms, man and man, between descendants and ancestors. Tudor government, persistent nationalism, skilful propaganda and the crude foreign policies of Spain and the Vatican had prevented the English schism from turning into civil war, and had also kept repression to comparatively mild levels. But the threat of a real national division was always present, and no Tudor government could tolerate criticism or even disinterested enquiry, whether in the press, the pulpit or the theatre.

A play like *Henry VIII*, subtitled *All is True*, would not have been allowed in Elizabethan England, but by the time of its production (1613) the earlier anxieties were over and after ten years of James I's rule the atmosphere was a little freer. There was a pro-Spanish peace party at court and in the Church; the persecution of Roman Catholics had quietened down, and the most violent Protestants were (for the time being) under control. Flurries of anxiety could awaken persecution, and the mob could always express dislike of its masters by accusing them of Popery; but on the whole, and especially within range of the court's political and religious atmosphere, there was more toleration. One interesting sign of this, already mentioned,[7] and close to Shakespeare's interests, was the tendency to rehabilitate Richard III. Another was *Henry VIII* itself, with its sympathy towards the government's victims and its persistent irony towards both the government and those who let themselves be drawn within the field of its influence.

Perhaps our times have taught us lessons in political realities that our immediate predecessors, born into a fundamentally civilised and decent world, lacked; yet one does not have to be especially sensitive to political nuance to see the ironies of *Henry VIII*, both the open ones and those more slyly implied. The open irony sets a standard of interpretation, putting a control upon the way we take words, and it begins in the first scene. Buckingham, with one sharp sentence, challenges Norfolk's account of the Field of Cloth of Gold as well as Cardinal Wolsey's part in it:

> What had he
> To do in these fierce vanities?   (I. i. 53–4)

His open contempt, as we learn from Norfolk's advice to him, is dangerous; but is has the effect of immediately setting forth a case, not just against the Cardinal, but also against the state he serves. It later appears that Norfolk shares Buckingham's opinion, his enthusiasm for the splendours of the two kings' meeting not affecting his assessment of its political result which 'not values the cost that did conclude it' (l. 88). But he is a cautious man, and his reply to Buckingham's downright attack on Wolsey (whom he calls a 'keech', i.e., a lump of suet) is a smooth sarcasm, the first explicit piece of irony in the play:

> Surely, Sir,
> There's in him stuff that puts him to these ends;
> For, being not propp'd by ancestry, whose grace
> Chalks successors their way, nor call'd upon
> For high feats done to th' crown; neither allied
> To eminent assistants; but spider-like
> Out of his self-drawing web, he gives us note
> The force of his own merit makes his way—

> A gift that heaven gives for him, which buys
> A place next to the King.   (i. i. 57–66)

This cunning, intense rhetoric hints at much unspoken fear as well as contempt, and it is characteristic of *Henry VIII*'s irony in that it grows to a climax of open sarcasm in the last lines, implying that Wolsey has corrupted heaven as well as the commonwealth. In this play Shakespeare often makes an irony explicit by means of such a sting in the tail.

Norfolk's cautious speech also introduces a more covert form of irony, depending upon euphemism or intentional vagueness for its effect. He warns Buckingham that his quarrel with Wolsey has been noticed by 'the state', a word which may signify a body like the Privy Council, but which in the context more probably refers to Henry himself. Norfolk then tells Buckingham that Wolsey's hatred 'wants not a minister in his power', and this also, upon reflection, can only mean Henry. The first hint suggests that the King, acting independently, has observed the quarrel; the second suggests that the Cardinal has Henry in his pocket, and this equivocation raises the most important question in the play's first part: does the Cardinal rule Henry or not?

This first scene's atmosphere of ironic suggestion demands the closest attention of the audience, whose participation as a kind of mute chorus to the play is as necessary to the success of *Henry VIII* as to that of *The Winter's Tale* or *Cymbeline*. The scene prepares the audience, or rehearses it, for its understanding role in the play to come; its irony is expressed with a lightness that shows us how much Shakespeare came to rely upon his audience's responsiveness, knowing that on the day they would be there following him.[8]

The court scene that follows shows political lies in the making. In its first part Wolsey, forced by Queen Katherine's appeal to the King to remit an unjust taxation, instructs his secretary to announce that the remission came through his intercession. In the second part the false witness of the Duke of Buckingham's surveyor begins his master's end. The formal arrangement is important. In both parts Henry and Wolsey act as a pair, with the emphasis on Wolsey in the first part, on the King in the second. In both parts Queen Katherine advocates the truth. This balancing of roles shows that the notion of Henry's early dependence upon Wolsey exists more in the critics' imaginations than in the play, where Henry is his own man from the start. At first he operates through his ministers. At the play's end, in the vacuum left by Wolsey's fall, when the Council begins to show too much independence, he puts out his own authority undisguised when he protects Cranmer.

The scene also makes it clear that Divine Providence and royal justice are not the same thing. If anyone speaks for truth it is Katherine, who checks Wolsey—'My learn'd Lord Cardinal,/Deliver all with charity' (I. ii. 142–3)—and tries to discredit the false witness. At the scene's end, when Wolsey and Henry are intent upon Buckingham's destruction, her cry 'God mend all!' is more than a sentimental interjection. Henry's final speech exposes his injustice plainly enough:

> If he may
> Find mercy in the law, 'tis his; if none,
> Let him not seek't of us. By day and night,
> He's traitor to the height.   (ll. 211–14)

This is a grim, cruel joke because mercy, which is part of the King's prerogative, is not to be found in the law. One can go further and say that to anyone with a normal sensitivity to hypocrisy Henry's reply to Katherine's complaint about taxation carries no conviction:

> Taxation!
> Wherein? and what taxation? My Lord Cardinal
> You that are blam'd for it alike with us,
> Know you of this taxation?   (ll. 37–40)

Wolsey's extremely tactful reply says that others are responsible besides himself, but also implies through its vagueness that he only did what he was told to do:

> Please you, sir,
> I know but of a single part in aught
> Pertains to th' state; and front but in that file
> Where others tell steps with me.   (ll. 40–3)

There is an element of suppressed comedy in the smooth performance of King and Cardinal as each of them shifts the blame for an unpopular act and angles for the credit of revoking it. Wolsey's order that Katherine's intervention be kept secret typifies the fate of truth at this court.

Buckingham's downfall exposes completely the league between King and Cardinal as well as Katherine's isolation. Here lies the connecting link between the opening scenes and the divorce scenes. In proceeding directly from Buckingham's death to the royal divorce, Shakespeare passes over more than a decade and makes a connection, implicitly causal, explicitly moral, between the two misfortunes.

Katherine's outspokenness somehow leads to her downfall and that in turn causes Wolsey's fall in which he, and we, discover plainly the King's service is not God's.

We first hear of an impending divorce between Henry and Katherine when two gentlemen, in the scene of Buckingham's death, speak of it as a machination of the Cardinal's 'out of malice to the good Queen' (II. i. 157). This is repeated in the next scene when Norfolk says that Wolsey, wishing to hit at the Emperor Charles, has dived into the King's soul and wrung his conscience over his marriage to his deceased brother's wife (II. ii. 24–37). At the trial, however, when Katherine accuses the Cardinal of having 'blown this coal', Henry relieves Wolsey of all responsibility. His story (II. iv. 167–206) is that his 'conscience first receiv'd a tenderness' during a conference with the Bishop of Bayonne.

There are, then, two theories current explaining the origin of the divorce. Either the King's conscience grew tender all by itself or else Wolsey irritated it; or, to take a third way out, agreeable to the Cardinal's and the King's habit of appearing to act in concert, they both had the same idea simultaneously, if for different reasons. There is no mystery about Wolsey's part in the divorce, since Shakespeare has shown the Queen's antagonism to him. The King's motive is the problem, both as a matter of historical fact and of practical dramaturgy, and Shakespeare's treatment of it is continuously and subtly ironic. First, he employs a mute irony of inference. For instance, he shows Henry flirting with Anne Boleyn before there is any mention of divorce (I. iv); and his constant hinting at Henry's independence bears fruit in the divorce scene where the King's exculpation of Wolsey (II. iv. 155–209), which at first seems like a royal favour, proves in the end to be the first stage in Henry's dismissal of Wolsey. Second, Shakespeare uses explicit verbal irony to put the King's talk of conscience in doubt.

Shakespeare's irony in fact centres on 'conscience', beginning with a comment aside by the Duke of Suffolk upon the official story of the King's motive:

> *Chamberlain.* It seems the marriage with his brother's wife
>     Has crept too near his conscience.
> *Suffolk.* [*Aside*]                    No, his conscience
> Has crept too near another lady.   (II. ii. 17–19)

There are the makings here of an obscene *double entendre* on the word, but before it appears in its full force there is a most significant little scene when Henry, professing to be about his 'private meditations' (II. ii. 66,) rebukes the nobles for interrupting him but immediately welcomes the two Cardinals, Wolsey in particaular, as 'the quiet of my wounded conscience'. There is a bitter irony here because the nobles, who do not altogether understand what is going on, have a more Christian care of the King than do the Cardinals. They stand by, watching, as Henry, having welcomed Campeggio, says to Wolsey:

> My good Lord, have great care
> I be not found a talker.

Many think that this instruction means only that Wolsey is to see that the visitor is well entertained. But since the whole point of the scene is that the Cardinals have arrived to put through the divorce, it is more likely to mean that Henry is giving more important instructions: 'Now that I have come so far, you must see this thing through.' This explains Wolsey's reply:

> Sir, you cannot.
> I would your grace would give us but an hour
> Of private conference.

It is however characteristic of this political play that a statement can be so completely ambiguous. The talk that follows, about 'the voice of Christendom', 'this just and learned priest', and so forth (ll. 86–98) is pure state fiction; and in case anyone should miss the point Shakespeare includes a conversation between the Cardinals about Wolsey's treatment of one Doctor Pace who, it seems, had shown more independence than prudence. 'He was a fool,' says Wolsey, 'for he would needs be virtuous':

> Learn this, brother,
> We live not to be grip'd by meaner persons.

'Brother' is beautifully placed there. But the real bite follows, one of those stings in the tail of a speech or scene already mentioned, when Shakespeare, having disposed of the Cardinals' Christianity, similarly disposes of the King's conscience:

> O, my lord,
> Would it not grieve an able man to leave
> So sweet a bedfellow? But, conscience, conscience!
> O, 'tis a tender place; and I must leave her.

This has the true canting ring to it, since 'able' also means sexually able, and 'conscience', described as a 'tender place', begins to sound like obscene slang.

In the next scene (II. iii) Anne Boleyn and an old lady discuss the Queen's misfortune. 'By my troth and maidenhead,' says Anne, 'I would not be a queen.' To this the old woman, reminiscent of Emilia in *Othello*, replies, 'I would,/And venture maidenhead for't; and so would you':

> ... which gifts,
> Saving your mincing, the capacity
> Of your soft cheveril conscience would receive
> If you might please to stretch it.   (II. iii. 30–3)

After this, it would be too obvious to have anyone mention the 'prick of conscience', yet in the next scene the phrase appears, suitably muted and cushioned from sounding too coarse an irony:

> My conscience first receiv'd a tenderness,
> Scruple, and prick ...   (II. iv. 170–1)

If one compares this line with its original in Holinshed, 'a certain scrupulosity that pricked my conscience',[9] one sees the mischievousness of Shakespeare's alteration. He has turned the innocuous verb 'pricked' into a suggestive noun, placing it third of a series so that it takes most emphasis; and he has neutralised the perfectly respectable 'scruple' by putting it between the dubious pair 'tenderness' and 'prick'.

Meanwhile the scene between Anne and the old lady also has a sting in its tail which deflates Anne's protestations:

> *Anne.*                              It faints me,
>    To think what follows.
>    The Queen is comfortless, and we forgetful
>    In our long absence. *Pray, do not deliver*
>    *What here you've heard to her.*
> *Old Lady.*                    *What do you think me?*

Wolsey's motive is power, and he over-reaches himself, for in ridding the court of Katherine he brings into it, along with Anne Boleyn, Cranmer and his Protestants. Henry's motive is partly, if not fundamentally, sexual; and he also over-reaches himself because, as everyone who watched the play knew, Anne Boleyn turned out more sexual than he bargained for. As the play moves towards its specifically pre-Elizabethan material, its ironies are not so explicit. But there is one climactic moment of ironic revelation that throws its dubious light retrospectively and prospectively over the play's story

when Henry finally abandons all pretence of legality and piety and
decides to govern his own kingdom in his own way:

> *King. (Aside)*                I may perceive
>    These Cardinals trifle with me; I abhor
>    This dilatory sloth and tricks of Rome.
>    My learn'd and well-beloved servant, Cranmer,
>    Prithee, return.            (ii. iv. 235–40)

Naturally, the speech is spoken aside, since history does not preserve
such moments for us; we can only infer them from the record.

This moment of revelation is also the moment of Protestantism's
inception in England. There have always been Clotens in the
audience who miss the point, and cheer the name of Cranmer and
hiss the name of Rome; but Shakespeare is saying, as plainly as he
could in 1613, that his England came into being because of Henry
VIII's unmastered passion for a young woman.

\*    \*    \*

As the reward for honesty and plain-speaking Buckingham and
Katherine receive, one a beheading, the other divorce and abandon-
ment. The fortitude and patience of their deaths shows the courage
of their lives. Considered as dramatic characters, they undergo no
last-minute discovery, no sudden reversal of belief or understanding.
They are open to criticism therefore on the ground that since the
essence of drama is conflict, the final scenes of their lives are undramatic. The drama, though, is in the counterpointing of their fall
with others' rise. The opposition of Queen Katherine's 'crowning' by
the Spirits of Peace just before her death to the great show of Queen
Anne's state crowning is bound to make one reflect upon the 'fierce
vanity' of the latter. It makes visible the distinction made from the
play's opening scene onward between divine justice and state justice.
The same is true of Wolsey's fall, opposed as it is to Cranmer's rise.

In misfortune Wolsey shows courage and dignity, as when he
replies to the nobles (iii. ii. 203–372) They, when it is safe to do so,
turn on him just as they abandon Katherine (iii. ii. 41–71). Although
Wolsey's repentance in misfortune follows a familiar pattern, Shakespeare was following his sources in treating it as he did. The Cardinal's
most famous words, explicitly separating the service due to God and
the King, are almost a direct quotation from Cavendish's *Life of
Wolsey*:

> Had I but serv'd my God with half the zeal
> I serv'd my King, He would not in mine age
> Have left me naked to mine enemies.   (iii. ii. 455–7)

An old tradition gives to a man's last words the credit of truth, and in Wolsey's speeches after his fall even the word 'conscience' is rehabilitated. It occurs in a passage praising Thomas More; the lines are almost a prayer and, in the circumstances, rather chilling:

> May he continue
> Long in his Highness' favour, and do justice
> For truth's sake and his conscience, that his bones,
> When he has run his course and sleeps in blessings,
> May have a tomb of orphans' tears wept on 'em!   (III. ii. 395–9)

('Run his course' is a liturgical phrase, still to be found in the *Book of Common Prayer* at the last Collect of the service for consecrating a bishop: 'that, faithfully fulfilling his course, at the latter day he may receive the crown of righteousness.') Wolsey's advice to Cromwell, that he should serve the King faithfully, without ambition, is also portentous; not only did Cromwell come to the block, but he neglected his master's advice against ambition, thoughts that come to mind when we hear of his great advancement (IV. i. 109, v. i. 33). Unless Shakespeare intended to remind the audience of further deaths beyond the scope of *Henry VIII*, there would be no purpose in these references. There is also a foreboding of Anne Boleyn's death (v. i. 22).

Most important, Katherine, hearing of Wolsey's death, forgives him. At the beginning of this scene (IV. ii), the most finely written in the play, Katherine is still tangled in the loyalties of life and the world. Although she forgives Wolsey and sympathises with his suffering, she cannot forget the evils of his life:

> i' th' presence
> He would say untruths; and be ever double
> Both in his words and meaning. He was never,
> But where he meant to ruin, pitiful.   (IV. ii. 37–40)

Wolsey's doubleness is a quality of the world itself which Shakespeare has imitated in the characteristic irony of this play, and even Katherine is touched by it since her forgiveness is mingled with censure. Complete forgiveness of Wolsey immediately follows when Katherine's servant Griffith undertakes to 'speak his good':

> This Cardinal,
> Though from an humble stock, undoubtedly
> Was fashion'd to much honour from his cradle.
> He was a scholar, and a ripe and good one;
> Exceeding wise, fair-spoken, and persuading;

Lofty and sour to them that lov'd him not,
But to those men that sought him, sweet as summer.
And though he were unsatisfied in getting,
Which was a sin, yet in bestowing, madam,
He was most princely: ever witness for him
Those twins of learning that he rais'd in you,
Ipswich and Oxford! one of which fell with him,
Unwilling to outlive the good that did it;
The other, though unfinish'd, yet so famous,
So excellent in art, and still so rising,
That Christendom shall ever speak his virtue.

This disinterested speech, plain and declarative, gives like Prospero's epilogue, an effect of literal actuality. Katherine calls it 'religious truth and modesty', and it leads her to meditate upon 'celestial harmony'. There follows the vision of the Spirits of Peace. Their white robes symbolise purity and salvation, their garlands of bays symbolise lasting honour on earth, and their garlands of palm symbolise eternal triumph and honour. In saluting Katherine they recognise her to be one of themselves. As she tells Griffith, their dance invites her 'to a banquet', and the garland they hold over her promises 'eternal happiness'. In comparison with the vision music is 'harsh and heavy'.

Not much is said about this vision. One could I suppose take it as an example of the tribute vice so readily pays to defeated virtue, interpreting it as a pretty, generous and effective way of dismissing Katherine and her failure from the stage in order to prepare for a splendid welcome to the future. The trouble is that this quite gratuitous vision introduces an order of reality different from anything else in this very secular play. It says unequivocally that Katherine is to die blessed, and that the vision of blessedness turns secular affairs into unreality. Does the suppressed—or repressed—meaning underlying the play's irony condense here into literal statement? Are the defeats triumphs, the triumphs defeats?

In their deaths Cardinal and Queen draw together, and charity supersedes judgement in an order not of this world, where ambiguity rules to the end. The King's vindication of Cranmer (v. iii. 130–47) recalls his earlier vindication of Wolsey. His reception of the news that he is the father of a girl is decidedly ambiguous (v. ii. 158–70). Every technique, certainly, is employed to make the play's end as boisterous, as popular, as glorious as possible, but even here there is irony. Shakespeare, having required the subtlest participation of his audience, now casts them (v. iv) as a rowdy, good-natured London mob come to the christening procession as to any wonderful show:

Is this Moorfields to muster in? Or have we some strange Indian
with the great tool come to court, the women so besiege us?
                                                                    (v. iv. 33–5)

The inference to be drawn is that crowds at a procession understand
the real nature of things no better than groundlings at a theatre,
capable of nothing but inexplicable dumb shows and noise. Thus
Shakespeare provides both the popular joy and a more intelligent
reflection upon it. In the popular mind there is a causal connection
between the whole long story of Henry's reign and the birth of the
great princess Elizabeth; but in the play, there is no such connection.
Like Perdita in *The Winter's Tale*, the infant Elizabeth is a new-
found future, wholly herself, the pure gift of Providence. Her
England is as little connected with the play's England, or indeed
with any England of the historical present, as Perdita's return to
Sicily is due to any merit of Leontes'. Elizabeth's birth is sheer grace,
akin to forgiveness.

*Henry VIII* is a remarkable play, a fascinating imitation in
dramatic terms of the Gospel precept, 'Render unto Caesar the
things that are Caesar's, and unto God the things that are God's.' Its
method is objective, contrapuntal, and ironic. One can, if one wishes,
simply take it as a fine show, revelling like London crowds then and
now in the ceremonies of state; that pleasure, as far as it goes, is
proper and well-justified. But if one takes the play's irony, then
somehow one's unreflective pleasure needs to accommodate the
knowledge that between the ceremony of the state and the ceremony
of the soul there is no simple or necessary correspondence.

Indeed, the real critical question to be finally answered is whether
the action of *Henry VIII* reconciles the state and the soul or not.
Conventional criticism tells us that this play was meant to make its
audience happy, to congratulate them upon being Englishmen; but
the play's prologue tells each spectator that he must make up his
own mind:

> Those that can pity, here
> May (if they think it well) let fall a tear;
> The subject will deserve it. Such as give
> Their money out of hope they may believe
> May here find truth too. Those that come to see
> Only a show or two, and so agree
> The play may pass, if they be still and willing,
> I'll undertake may see away their shilling
> Richly in two short hours. Only they
> That come to hear a merry bawdy play,

A noise of targets, or to see a fellow
In a long motley coat guarded with yellow,
Will be deceiv'd. . . .
Therefore, for goodness' sake, and as you are known
The first and happiest hearers of the town,
Be sad, as we would make ye.

As a prologue to a play about Henry VIII, this is surprisingly detached. Some pointedly Shakespearean words (pity, belief, hope, truth) are so used as to tell certain spectators what kind of reception the author would like his play to have. But apart from dissociating his play from such vulgarities as Rowley's Henry VIII play, *When You See Me, You know Me*, and defining the general tone as 'sad', i.e., solemn, the author is cautious and tolerant. He gives his verbs 'pity' and 'believe' no objects, and puts nearly all his other verbs in the subjunctive. It is for the individual spectator to decide whether he weeps, pities, believes, finds truth or not. Like several scenes in the play, however, the prologue has a sting at the end:

And, if you can be merry then, I'll say
A man may weep upon his wedding-day.

This seems to dismiss a rather solemn prologue with a joke, but the mood is still subjunctive, and the joke is on the spectators, many of whom did of course take the play cheerfully. That being so, the implied response follows: a man *therefore* may (might as well?) weep at his wedding. True enough, if people were more reflective they would weep more at weddings, especially if they knew what led up to them and where they in turn would lead; but if they were really reflective, there would be no weeping at all because the initial mistake would not have been made, of taking things like *Henry VIII* cheerfully. 'People', says the tramp in *Waiting for Godot*, 'are bloody ignorant apes', and a similar thought, if less astringently put, could have been in Shakespeare's mind as he finished the prologue to *Henry VIII*.

Play and prologue alike exemplify a markedly Shakespearean attitude to words. The speculative tendency that leads him to pun and quibble endlessly with meanings is here extended by means of irony to the subject of an entire play. The irony of *Henry VIII*, indeed, works very like a quibble. In his verbal punning, especially of the obscene kind, Shakespeare often gives meanings that are not alternate but contrary:

Many a good hanging prevents a bad marriage.

(*Twelfth Night*, I. v. 20)

Both meanings of Feste's joke are funny, in fact there are two jokes, and in the end one has to decide which joke one is going to laugh at. So with *Henry VIII*'s irony. One's first impression is of a cool ambivalence that offers, non-committally, alternate readings of history; but the ambivalence, like punning wit, is protective, and there is nothing ambivalent about the ambivalence itself.

# 12. The Two Noble Kinsmen

*Henry VIII* follows *The Tempest* in being about power, which it distinguishes with some sharpness from Providence. *The Two Noble Kinsmen* follows *Henry VIII* in being about Providence, how it 'shapes our ends,/Rough-hew them how we will.' Another way of characterising the play is by the fictional deities who rule it; as Diana ruled *Pericles*, Jupiter *Cymbeline*, Apollo *The Winter's Tale*, so Venus rules *The Two Noble Kinsmen* in conflict with Mars. The contrast between those two deities of love and war or, in our blunter jargon, sex and aggression, their attraction for one another, their common origin in human appetites, were favourite themes of Renaissance art. In *The Two Noble Kinsmen* we see their anarchy subdued to necessary ends, their driving energy turned to the forms of civility.

The story is from Chaucer's *Knight's Tale*. Shakespeare has reduced the time taken by the plot from years to a matter of months, and he has suppressed the quarrel among the gods, which would have been difficult to stage, even in a masque. There is no hint therefore of divine discord in the play, each lesser deity's rule being a thread in the weft of Providence. *The Two Noble Kinsmen* also recalls much in *A Midsummer Night's Dream*, also related to *The Knight's Tale*: Theseus, Hippolyta; a pair of young men in love, indistinguishable in their infatuation; a heroine who remembers an innocent childhood friendship; a scene of hunting, of May-day observance.[1] It is wise to keep in mind the connection with Chaucer and the earlier play because the tendency to make downright biography of Shakespeare's later work has affected readings of this play. More than one critic takes Shakespeare's depiction of Venus and his evocations of innocence and chastity as evidence of a turning away from life, a development also alleged to show in the undramatic nature of these last plays and in what one critic calls the 'clotted rhetoric' of their verse.[2] Taken simply as themes and situations, however, Shakespeare's versions of sex and chastity in *The Two Noble Kinsmen* can be paralleled in his own earliest work as, indeed, they can be paralleled in Chaucer and the poets who followed him. What is new and, apparently, disturbing is the technique rather than the themes themselves, for once again we have the grand manner of

Shakespeare's latest work to deal with, demonstrative, detached and objective.

The objectivity, especially, is a stumbling block because the object shown has changed. In *Pericles* and *The Winter's Tale* Shakespeare shaped a means of staging in dramatic narrative the moment of visionary lyricism that transfigures life; but now the emphasis has shifted almost imperceptibly and the technique that showed Perdita now shows her antithesis, not the lyricism transfiguring life but the energy that drives it. The shift occurred, I think, in *The Tempest*, for although many read that play as if it were an extended lyric, it can also be read as a coolly reflective example of applied lyric. *The Tempest* uses lyricism as the great court entertainments (of which it may be an example) used all the arts: to glorify and ennoble something in itself perhaps not glorious at all, namely centred, autocratic authority. The lyrical element is not at the centre of *The Tempest* as it was of the preceding tragi-comedies, and the play even has a different kind of plot from theirs. Its events unfold in an orderly, coherent sequence, and its centre in the magician who controls it. In *Henry VIII* the shift continues and the difference shows in the fact that, whereas in the earlier tragi-comedies the divine vision was the threshold of new life, here it is the threshold of death, and peripheral to the main action. Once again in Shakespeare's career we seem to be at a turning point in the development of dramatic ideas, the direction now being towards a new sombreness as the tragi-comedies had been a development towards lyricism.

*The Two Noble Kinsmen* is, especially in its undoubtedly Shakespearean parts, a stern, rather dark play. The premise of its fiction is that men either rule or are ruled by their appetites. The rule of appetite is therefore the focus of interest, and an audience's sense of the play's value will depend largely upon its judgement of the strength of the appetites being ruled. Palamon and Arcite, the heroes, are more patients than agents, and have little interest as characters; the play is so designed that the audience will not prefer either of them, and the fascination of the story, in Shakespeare as in Chaucer, is that there can be neither a perfect solution granting each man his desire nor a judicial solution preferring one man's desire over the other's. The object can only be to reconcile their conflict as economically as possible, so that if each cannot have his whole desire, then each can in a way receive the thing he has asked for. The story ends with a narrator's equivalent of a witticism when Arcite the devotee of Mars wins the combat but loses the girl, and Palamon the devotee of Venus loses the combat but wins the girl. As the kinsmen's prayers are granted, we see clearly that between their desires, considered as means, and their object, considered as an end, there is an incompatibility that from one point of view might be tragic, from another comical. What has Emilia to do with either of these votaries of sex and violence, and how can such gods as the kinsmen worship do anything but irritate the unhappiness of their condition?

The conclusion, arising out of the incompatibility of means and ends, reconciles them with an irony that gives some defence against absurdity, but leaves its causes intact:

> O you heavenly charmers,
> What things you make of us! For what we lack,
> We laugh; for what we have, are sorry; still
> Are children in some kind. Let us be thankful
> For that which is, and with you leave dispute
> That are above our question.   (v. iv. 130–5)

The speaker is Theseus, and how surprising it is—and how satisfactory—that after twenty years Shakespeare should have returned to the notion of a rational duke in Athens, making him the centre and the spokesman of a state of law, justice and reason. The earlier Theseus' rationalism is too pat, takes too little account of things the most ignorant of his subjects knows all about, and that is part of the play's comedy. Theseus is ruled by Titania without knowing it, and he has no inkling of what goes on in the woods just beyond his city, nor does he guess that the wood's inhabitants invade his own house after dark. In some ways, therefore, he knows less about life than Bottom knows. The later Theseus however knows the significance of his own actions because he understands the significance of Creon's Thebes as well as the power of the kinsmen's gods. His reason takes account of the darkness within and without, is not itself the object of irony, but sums up the irony of the conclusion.

\*     \*     \*

The play begins with a conflict between two kinds of action, the free action of Theseus and Hippolyta's wedding, and the compelled action of the three queens' interruption. Both kinds have their ceremony and order. The wedding is stately, slow, the symbolism of flowers and harvest suggesting a natural ripeness in the time. There is a harmony of things usually opposed. Women lead the bridegroom, men the bride. Hippolyta's giving of herself in marriage, symbolised by her unbound tresses, is contained by the processional formality and celebrated by the garland held over her head. Then, as the song expressly says, discord and pain are temporarily banished; the attendants strew roses stripped of their spines. Into this scene of Athenian ceremony, white, garlanded, musical, there comes a counter-ceremony of three queens 'in black, with veils stained, with imperial crowns'. They kneel, each before one of the chief actors in the wedding, and the symmetry of ceremony and counter-ceremony is unmistakable.

The emblematic technique requires emblematic reading. In the queens, imperial order ruined begs redress from the Athenian duke at a moment when the civility of his rule and city are most perfectly in being. They tell of a place where Creon of Thebes has destroyed their lords:

> We are three queens, whose sovereigns fell before
> The wrath of cruel Creon; who endured
> The beaks of ravens, talons of the kites,
> And pecks of crows, in the foul fields of Thebes.
> He will not suffer us to burn their bones,
> To turn their ashes, nor to take th' offense
> Of mortal loathesomeness from the blest eye
> Of holy Phoebus, but infects the winds
> With stench of our slain lords. O pity, duke,
> Thou purger of the earth, draw thy feared sword
> That does good turns to th' world; give us the bones
> Of our dead kings, that we may chapel them.... (I. i. 39–50)

This fine speech, besides naming unsparingly the horrors of war and tyranny, shows by its stately formality that death and destruction have their ceremony too. Creon's wrath expresses itself in a symbolism as formal as that of the wedding. The foul fields of Thebes are as apt and proper in their way as the 'launds' (III. i. 2) of Athens, and so the conflict in the play is not between order and disorder, but between two kinds of order expressed here by Athens and Thebes.[3]

The contrast grows stronger with Act I, scene ii, laid in Thebes, where the kinsmen Palamon and Arcite, moved by conscience and honour, plan to leave. Under Creon, Thebes has become the opposite of what a city should be, a scene of incontinence where an unrewarded soldiery wanders through decayed streets, and 'every seeming good's a certain evil' (I. ii. 39–40). Even the phrase describing the city's lanes and streets, 'the cranks and turns of Thebes' (I. ii. 28) suggests a mean, dark, benighted place, the opposite of Athens, just as the report of Creon's rage (I. ii. 84ff.) is the opposite of Theseus' deliberation before setting out upon his campaign. Creon, according to Palamon, is:

> A most unbounded tyrant, whose successes
> Makes heaven unfeared, and villainy assured
> Beyond its power there's nothing; almost puts

Faith in a fever, and deifies alone
Voluble chance.   (I. ii. 63–7)

This describes a nihilist. Thebes is built in the image of his despair.
The man and his city represent a choice which the kinsmen refuse,
and although from an average, humane point of view their decision
to leave Thebes will seem obviously right, it would be a mistake to
underestimate either the appetites that rule in Thebes or the allure of
the city. In one line of the three queens' funeral song, 'And clamors
through the wild air flying' (I. v. 6), we can feel the Romantic thrill
that the nearness of death and terror can bring. The third queen's
concluding couplet makes the cranks and turns of such places as
Thebes an image of the world, and names its centre:

This world's a city full of straying streets,
And death's the market place where each one meets. (I. v. 15–16)

In Athens men put their appetites under the rule of reason,
and make ceremonious the passing of times and seasons. This is the
cause of Athens' nobility, yet time, appetite and violence are no less
real there than in Thebes. Theseus, about to be married, recalls on
seeing the first queen his presence at her wedding, and ends his
reminiscence on a note of melancholy fear:

O grief and time,
Fearful consumers, you will all devour.   (I. i. 69–70)

Hippolyta, we hear, was:

near to make the male
To thy sex captive, but that this thy lord,
Born to uphold creation in that honor
First Nature styled it in, shrunk thee into
The bound thou wast o'erflowing. . . .   (I. i. 80–4)

Although Athens sets bounds, the thing bounded is the same nature
that thrives unbounded in Thebes. Mars and Venus are the same
deities everywhere. To be a soldier, says Hippolyta, is not to weep:

When our friends don their helms, or put to sea,
Or tell of babes broached on the lance.   (I. iii. 19–20)

Venus too is a strong goddess. To turn Theseus, on the threshold of
marriage, from Venus' service to Mars' requires the pleas of the three

queens, and the common decision of three persons, Theseus, Hippolyta and Emilia:

> When her arms,
> Able to lock Jove from a synod, shall
> By warranting moonlight corslet thee, O when
> Her twinning cherries shall their sweetness fall
> Upon thy tasteful lips, what wilt thou think
> Of rotten kings or blubbered queens, what care
> For what thou feel'st not, what thou feel'st being able
> To make Mars spurn his drum? (I. i. 174–81)

Some have wondered what relevance this first act has to the main
action of the play, and the answer lies partly in the changes Shakespeare has made in Chaucer's opening of *The Knight's Tale*. There,
Theseus is already married when the story opens. He is on his way
home from the Amazonian war, just about to ride into his city when
the queens interrupt him, and neither he nor his people hesitate a
moment about riding off to deal with Creon. The kinsmen first
appear wounded on the battlefield. The introduction of sex and
aggression under the names of Mars and Venus is also more schema-
tically done in Shakespeare's than in Chaucer's version. In Chaucer,
Theseus is Mars' soldier, carrying the god's image on his banner; but
Shakespeare has preferred to give Theseus and Hippolyta each a
dual allegiance to Venus and Mars tempered by reason embodied in
the institution of marriage. Their love is really the love of Mars and
Venus made lawful. Shakespeare's Arcite has no rival in his devotion
to Mars.

Shakespeare also prepares for the kinsmen's love of Emilia by
similarly schematic illustration of three kinds of love possible in
Athens. Theseus and Pirithous show the comradely love of man and
man. Emilia's memory of her childhood friend Flavina shows the
innocent love of children, and Theseus and Hippolyta show the
Athenian version of married love. All three kinds of relationship are
good, but only the third includes Venus. Emilia, young and fearful of
the world, judges the quality of friendship by its unpremeditated
naturalness:

> But I
> And she I sigh and spoke of were things innocent,
> Loved for we did, and like the elements
> That know not what, nor why, yet do effect
> Rare issues by their operance, our souls
> Did so to one another. (I. iii. 59–64)

In her order of precedence, married love would come last. But as Hippolyta's firm though tender reply to her younger sister says, whatever the sweetness of childish love, Venus must some day be coped with just as Theseus and Pirithous, in their male friendship, have coped with Mars.

The counterpart of Shakespeare's opening, which is not to be found in Chaucer, between Athens and Thebes and between the two orders of reason and appetite, evidently represents his interpretation of the story's interest by means of the typical forms of Renaissance mythology. Nor does he rely upon irony or implication to declare his 'sentence'. Theseus and Hippolyta, individually and as a married couple, represent an ideal, mature and noble humanity; and when they speak we are expected to concur, for in Theseus the rule of intellect has raised man higher than the gods themselves:

> *Third Queen.*   Thou being but mortal makest affections bend
> To godlike honours. They themselves, some say,
> Groan under such a mast'ry.[4]
> *Theseus.*                    As we are men,
> Thus should we do. Being sensually subdued,
> We lose our human title.   (I. i. 228–32)

                              *     *     *

Theseus defeats Creon, the queens bury their dead, and the Theban kinsmen, gravely wounded in the battle, are taken prisoner to Athens where, like a pair of young philosophers, they decide to live a contemplative life in gaol (II. i.). But, seeing Emilia as she walks in the garden, they become deadly enemies, rivals for her love. Meanwhile their gaoler's daughter, betrothed to a decent young Athenian, has fallen in raging love with Palamon. The kinsmen's rivalry is treated, like that of Demetrius and Lysander, chiefly comically, in a tone often verging upon parody. The gaoler's daughter, too, receives a partly comic, partly pathetic treatment, and many have found the mixture offensive, mainly because the comedy is often obscene. Much in the handling of the kinsmen, of the daughter and of Emilia seems not to rise to the conception of the action as it is announced by the first act. These parts of the play, which make up most of Acts II to IV, are generally agreed to be Fletcher's contribution, and at least one distinguished critic regrets that Shakespeare did not carry out the whole of the design.[5]

One of the difficulties of *The Knight's Tale*, however, from a dramatist's point of view, is that it has no 'middle'. Once the kinsmen have seen Emilia, all that follows up to the prayers to the gods in Act v is amplification, manoeuvring and business; and much of it is, again by standards of dramatic reality, ridiculous. In *A Midsummer*

*Night's Dream* (if that play does indeed bear some relationship to the fiction of *The Knight's Tale*), the young Shakespeare solved the difficulty by a stroke of sheer invention when he translated the middle of the story into a totally different fiction of two young men and two girls at cross-purposes, the absurdity of their situation being given ideal poetic form in the nocturnal adventures of the enchanted wood.

In returning to Chaucer's tale, and evidently wishing to treat it faithfully, both as to events and tone, Shakespeare has filled the emptiness of its middle with the sub-plot of the gaoler's daughter; but much of the tale's absurdity remains because the stage cannot accommodate Chaucer's courtly sentiment unchanged. One way to treat it is by means of the detached irony found in *The Winter's Tale* and *Cymbeline*. This technique, as we have seen, goes back to Shakespeare's earliest plays, and its effect, as in the examples given from *I Henry VI* and *The Winter's Tale*,[6] is to make the characters more objects of interest than sympathy. The technique first appears in Act II, scene i, the scene of the kinsmen's first sight of Emilia. This is also the first scene to be assigned mostly to Fletcher. Perhaps the Quarto title-page is correct, and perhaps, as the disintegrating statistics show, Shakespeare deputed these scenes to Fletcher; but if he did, the technique and the plan are as much Shakespeare's as Fletcher's.

The burlesque or 'sending-up' effect is confined to certain scenes, and at vital moments in the middle of the play the design emerges clearly, untouched by parody. The gaoler's daughter for instance has two especially important soliloquies, one narrating the start of her love for Palamon (II. iii), the other being the prelude to her madness (III. ii). Both speeches, besides being very moving, advance the play's ideas. Sex ends innocence:

> Out upon't,
> What pushes are we wenches driven to
> When fifteen once has found us! (II. iii. 5–7)

It turns the gaoler's daughter into a juvenile delinquent who defies the Duke, sacrifices her father by setting his prisoner free, and runs away from home to meet a man under a bush. Driven by her obsession, she goes without food and rest, and when she realises what she has done to herself and her father, the fear of incipient madness turns her thoughts to death:

> Alas,
> Dissolve my life, let not my sense unsettle,
> Lest I should drown, or stab, or hang myself.

O state of nature, fail together in me,
Since thy best props are warped! So which way now?
The best way is the next way to a grave.   (III. ii. 28–33)

The play's tone also recovers in the doctor's long prose speech
instructing the daughter's suitor how he is to cure her by pretending
to be Palamon: 'It is a falsehood she is in, which is with falsehoods
to be combated' (IV. iii. 95–7).

One of the themes of *A Midsummer Night's Dream*, indeed the
grand joke upon which it is based, is that love is blind, really blind,
not just short-sighted. Puck's mischief exploits the lovers' plight, but
does not cause it; and things finally come right for them because
Oberon's eyes see for them. In *The Two Noble Kinsmen*, however,
where the same idea emerges from the story, the gods represent the
cause of the darkness; the night in which the gaoler's daughter goes
mad is Venus' own dark. The only illumination available comes from
human reason. Readers tend to dislike the doctor and his cure, but
the spectacle of the gaoler's daughter, as of Creon's Thebes, shows
that the rule of appetite is death; and so as Theseus fights war with
war, the doctor fights sex with sex. Both of them act for the same
simple reason, that life and sanity are to be preserved at any cost.
'Ne'er cast your child away for honesty,' says the doctor to her father,
'Cure her first this way, then if she will be honest,/She has the path
before her' (v. ii. 21–3).

The alternatives to lust and violence are reason and ceremony.
Perhaps the most famous passage in the play is Arcite's tribute to the
Athenians' maying:

> This is a solemn rite
> They owe bloomed May, and the Athenians pay it
> To th' heart of ceremony. O Queen Emilia,
> Fresher than May, sweeter
> Than her gold buttons on the boughs or all
> Th' enameled knacks o' th' mead or garden—yea,
> We challenge too the bank of any nymph
> That makes the stream seem flowers! Thou, O jewel
> O' th' wood, o' th' world, hast likewise blest a place
> With thy sole presence. . . .   (III. i. 2–11)

In this long-breathed lyricism the day, the place and the girl are
celebrated for living perfection in words that are a model of what is
meant by such a phrase as 'high civilisation'. Vitality and repose,
temperance and intensity, discipline and freedom: the ancient opposites join in an ostensive definition of what 'Athens' means in this

play; and one of the strongest ironies immediately follows when Palamon, having overheard Arcite, bursts in a rage 'as out of a bush', shackled, filthy and hungry, the image of a man subdued to brutishness by appetite.

\* \* \*

All agree that the great scenes of Act v are Shakespeare's. There the kinsmen's unyielding rivalry gives each of them the nobility of a fixed purpose, whatever the folly of its cause. Emilia, responding to their resolution and to the horror of its certain conclusion in the death of one of them, appears finally as a young woman who knows that her entanglement in the story makes choice impossible, and who therefore subdues the selfishness that governs choice. Theseus, whose decisions events and men's passions have continually overruled since the appearance of the queens at his wedding, yields again when Emilia refuses to see the tournament and, finally, at the story's end:

> The gods my justice
> Take from my hand, and they themselves become
> The executioners.   (v. iv. 119–21)

He is Shakespeare's last portrait of an absolute ruler. From the first, when he turns aside saying 'Troubled I am' (ɪ. i. 77), to the last, his absoluteness is mitigated by his reasonableness. Like Prospero he anticipates the enlightened despots of the next century, and like theirs, his rule is touched by an air of melancholy. Tolerant, urbane, a representative of an ideal man, he is also the spokesman of limitations upon human potentiality.

The true autocrats are the twin deities, sex and aggression. 'O cousin,' says Palamon over Arcite's body:

> That we should things desire which do cost us
> The loss of our desire!   (v. iv. 108–10)

Hence Theseus' melancholy. When he acts as soldier and judge against outrageous passion, he does so, like a homeopathic doctor, by fighting fire with fire. If one kinsman is to destroy another, then let him do it lawfully; but Theseus' rule cannot touch the force that drives the kinsmen. One cannot imagine a civilisation where that fact would not bring with it a certain melancholy. Within the order set by Theseus' justice, the conflicting passions are resolved at the expense of the human lives that express them. The man dies but the gods, though reconciled, are unchanged.

As for those gods, three of them, Mars, Venus and Diana, the sources of motive in the play, are splendidly realised in the prayers of their votaries, even though the characterisations have dismayed many. Emilia prays to Diana as the goddess of chastity, and in her prayer the virtue encompasses not virginity only but the suppression of the ego and therefore of desire. Her prayer is the climax of the temple scene. Its intensity of language, both of sound and sense, of musical and visual symbolism, represent the beauty and severity of life at that point where the ideal and the real meet, as Emilia, 'bride-habited,/But maiden-hearted', waits upon the moment of irrevocable change:

> O sacred, shadowy, cold and constant queen,
> Abandoner of revels, mute, contemplative,
> Sweet, solitary, white as chaste, and pure
> As wind-fanned snow, who to thy female knights
> Allow'st no more blood than will make a blush,
> Which is their order's robe! I here thy priest
> Am humbled 'fore thine altar. O vouchsafe
> With that thy rare green eye, which never yet
> Beheld thing maculate, look on thy virgin;
> And sacred silver mistress, lend thine ear—
> Which ne'er heard scurrile term, into whose port
> Ne'er entered wanton sound—to my petition
> Seasoned with holy fear. . . .   (v. i. 137–49)

This is extraordinarily static verse, giving the impression that the grammar itself is standing still, thus imitating Emilia's virgin state. Yet the goddess of chastity is also the 'general of ebbs and flows', and the fall of the single rose, accompanied by 'a sudden twang of instruments', is an eerie symbol of what theologians call necessity:

> The flow'r is fall'n, the tree descends. O mistress,
> Thou here dischargest me, I shall be gathered.

In Chaucer's version, the invocation to Diana comes second, and the story is resolved by the intervention of Saturn. Shakespeare, by putting Diana last, implies that she is the most powerful of the three gods, that her intervention is decisive. As the general of ebbs and flows she governs time, and by releasing her votaries in due time she gives to the other gods their power over human life but, at the same time, constrains it.

Arcite's address to Mars is the shortest, and as blunt as the speeches of Act I in evoking the effects of war, in expressing war's part in the economy of human life:

Thou mighty one, that with thy power hast turned
Green Neptune into purple, [whose approach]
Comets prewarn, whose havoc in vast field
Unearthed skulls proclaim, whose breath blows down
The teeming Ceres' foison, who dost pluck
With hand armipotent from forth blue clouds
The masoned turrets, that both mak'st and break'st
The stony girths of cities! ...
O great corrector of enormous times,
Shaker of o'er-rank states, thou grand decider
Of dusty and old titles, that heal'st with blood
The earth when it is sick, and cur'st the world
O' th' plurisy of people! ...   (v. i. 49–56, 62–66)

Strange to say, Arcite's worship of war has not been much noticed, even though we live in a century when war's contribution to the cure of the world's plurisy of people must be around a billion persons by now. Theodore Spencer says only that it 'is a dignified and exalted piece of writing ... more or less what we would expect in an address to Mars.'[7] His complacence turns to dismay at Palamon's prayer to Venus, which stimulates adjectives like remarkable, odd, peculiar, negative, disagreeable, inappropriate; and the critic's explanation of the offending speech is that Shakespeare, 'writing rapidly ... to get a job finished', called back the 'ghost of his almost forgotten mood of disillusionment to fill out' the speech.[8] This is romancing, but the revulsion that prompts it is common. W. H. Auden says that Palamon's examples of love's power are 'humiliating or horrid', and that the speech reveals 'disgust at masculine sexual vanity'.[9] In Philip Edwards' opinion the prayer contributes largely to making this play 'the most cynical assessment of the progress of life since the writing of *Troilus and Cressida* ... not the sort of thing one wants to associate with Shakespeare.'[10]

Shakespeare however was not alone in portraying Venus as a cruel goddess, and love as painful and absurd. The unanimous distate for the portrait on the part of three such notable critics is probably to be explained by the change in attitude towards sexual appetite that has occurred in this century. To use the mythological symbolism of *The Two Noble Kinsmen*, we now attribute to Venus effects that were formerly Diana's work, such as health of body and mind, a happy family and well-behaved children; consequently her portrait in *The Two Noble Kinsmen*, where she breaks the kinsmen's friendship and drives the gaoler's daughter crazy, is bound to look sinister, if not actually blasphemous. Palamon's address to Venus is part of a long tradition of moral satire. Like *The Merchant's Tale* to which it is

closely related in some of its images, it is not now acceptable unless
its contents can be attributed to some psychological inadequacy in
its author, not, that is, until criticism has turned it into the expression
of an unfortunate subjective mood, and thereby saved whole the
appearance of a twentieth-century goddess. The general response to
this speech reveals an interesting vein of contemporary prudery.

The scene in the temple depicts, with poetic and visual power, the
three conflicting forces or gods that the narrative has to reconcile:
sex, aggression and their opposite, chastity. If, within the bounds of
this story, a man worships aggression, then the object of his worship
must be shown to accord with the rest of the story. Arcite's Mars,
therefore, accords with what we know of war from the first act.
Similarly, if a man should worship sex, then it is necessary that the
author show what is being worshipped within the framework of his
story. Palamon's Venus drives people mad, and if one is going to
object to his prayer, then in consistency one should object to the
whole story's way of mythologising the sources of human energy. If
we do object, then we should be as honest in reviling Venus as
Palamon is in evoking her. The 'most soft sweet goddess' (v. i. 126),
'sovereign queen of secrets' (l. 77), 'that from eleven to ninety
reign'st in mortal bosoms' (ll. 130–1):

> whose chase is this world
> And we in herds thy game    (ll. 131–2)

is presented as always attractive, and to everyone. This is the point of
the prayer, as it is of her power. She is irresistible, and not only to the
young, the handsome, the rich and the normal:

> 'Twas thy power
> To put life into dust: the aged cramp
> Had screwed his square foot round,
> The gout had knit his fingers into knots,
> Torturing convulsions from his globy eyes
> Had almost drawn their spheres, that what was life
> In him seemed torture. This anatomy
> Had by his young fair fere a boy, and I
> Believed it was his. . . .    (ll. 109–17

In the context of the speech, along with the cripple flourishing with
his crutch and the polled bachelor singing love songs at seventy, this
eighty-year-old father is, of course, meant to be funny.

Palamon's Venus is not much different, really, from the goddess of
Shakespeare's *Venus and Adonis*. She has no taste, and she respects

neither persons nor times. A force than can enliven cripples and put power into dust is surely as valuable as more sober schemes for enlivening old age (as geriatric specialists are now telling our Palamonian society), although the spectacle undeniably has its funny side. But then it always was funny; the yoke men bear 'as 'twere a wreath of roses . . . stings more than nettles' (ll. 96–7), and men desire their own scourge. Surely everyone feels some yielding of the imagination at the words 'And we in herds thy game'? And isn't Arcite's 'O great corrector of enormous times' supposed to have a similar effect?

Chaucer's story and Shakespeare's interpretation of it are not for the sentimental, but neither are they for the sentimentalist's opposite, the hard-nosed cynic. *The Two Noble Kinsmen* leaves in the mind many brilliant images, of a dead king, 'showing the sun his teeth, grinning at the moon' (I. i. 100); of Emilia, 'all the beauty extant' (II. i. 207), walking in her garden; of the gaoler's daughter, 'How prettily she's amiss!' (IV. iii. 28); of Arcite's last reconciliation with his kinsman, their quarrel cured by death:

> Take Emilia,
> And with her all the world's joy. Reach thy hand.
> Farewell. I have told my last hour. I was false,
> Yet never treacherous.   (v. iv. 89–92)

One's last impressions are of civility and graciousness, of irregularity tamed by ceremony and justice, of Providence acknowledged and the gods themselves subdued to the order of a large design. The play's tone is ruled by the Athenian's maying, by the gathering and strewing of flowers, by a sense of cool winds and waters. Theseus' Athens has a temperate beauty all the more satisfying in the context of the passions it controls. The destructive elements flow through men and cities, and have the name of gods; Athens, modest, reasonable and self-limiting, is the name of our humane city.

# 13. Conclusion: Timon of Athens

*The Two Noble Kinsmen* was written and first performed in 1613. Whether it was by Shakespeare and Fletcher, as the 1634 title-page says, or whether Shakespeare wrote it alone, as Paul Bertram argues,[1] is a question that cannot be finally decided. It is certain however that of Shakespeare's datable plays it is the last that he either wrote or partly wrote. It is equally certain that there is nothing valedictory about it. Although Shakespeare had only two years more to live, and although critics write about him as if he were as old as Lear and as weary of life, there is no evidence at all, either that he stopped writing or that he expected to die so soon. There is no justification, then, for treating *The Two Noble Kinsmen* as a poetic last will and testament. It may have had a successor.

Another certain thing about *The Two Noble Kinsmen* is that it is a very beautiful play, revealing an artistic intelligence in complete control of its material. Like *The Tempest*, it shows a Shakespeare at the height of his artistic power, for whom to think is to design, to design is to think. No matter whether Fletcher wrote part of the play or not; Shakespeare's design governs the beginning, the middle and the end of the action so firmly that it can carry Fletcher's alleged contribution.

Let us imagine, then, a spectator who had followed Shakespeare's poetic career from its beginning, a courtier-poet like John Donne, a well-educated woman, a statesman or even a learned divine like that Samuel Harsnett, now Bishop of Chichester, whose book on diabolic possession so interested Shakespeare at the time of *King Lear*; let us see such a spectator in the mind's eye, coming away from a court performance of *The Two Noble Kinsmen*, done with a finish, a splendour and a fidelity to the author's intention that we, unfortunately, have almost no chance of seeing equalled. Naturally enough, having no reason to suspect an interruption in the series of plays, he wonders what Shakespeare will write next; and as he speculates his mind goes back over the recent sequence of performances.

The theme of the tragi-comedies, put simply and generally, is the saving of men and kingdoms from the consequences of evil. Although the plays have a great variety of fiction, character and motive, in all

of them, as in the major tragedies, evil works its effects through the
passions, especially through sexual passion, being sudden in the
onset, violent and disruptive in its consequences. In *Pericles*, *The
Winter's Tale* and *Cymbeline* evil is eventually contained and turned
to good by a larger, providential design of which the ultimate
authors are the gods, although we see its effects as time, nature and
patience. The plays' people see their deliverance from evil as a grace,
something miraculously given that breaks the succession of evil cause
and bad effect.

The plays, then, are an answer to *Hamlet*, *Othello*, *King Lear* and
*Macbeth*, testing or working out with the means available to dramatic art the hypothesis that in the long run, in fortunate cases, a
transcendent goodness overcomes evil. As T. S. Eliot's plays show,
this is a difficult idea to make convincing in the theatre. The long
passage of time, divine intervention, the interruption of cause and
effect, disinterestedness, virtue, simplicity, innocence: even a writer
helped initially by his audience's predisposition to believe in such
things might find that their imitation in drama, not in dogma, is
nearly impossible. *The Winter's Tale* and *Cymbeline* stretched even
Shakespeare's formidable technique.

Inevitably such concentration on the adequate representation of
an idea entails considerable criticism of it. These late plays are not
in the least naïve, Shakespeare being even readier than he was at the
time of the early histories and comedies to see an absurdity in his
material, and to disarm criticism by drawing attention to it. Readings
of the tragi-comedies as religious allegories tend to ignore this element in them, and one imagines that a Christian whose faith does
not depend on the witness of Shakespeare would find the plays, as
religious fables, too knowing and clever. Religion does not so easily
go into art, and the more sophisticated the art, the harder the
translation.

Then comes *The Tempest*, superficially similar to its predecessors,
but differing from them in an essential way: its whole scheme of time,
patience and Providence is Prospero's invention, and its gods are
imitation gods. In *Cymbeline*, Jupiter exists, therefore men are delivered; but *The Tempest* is well on the way to representing a very
different idea, that because men must be delivered, the gods will
have to exist. At a stroke, the interrelation of the natural, humane
and divine orders become a fiction. Whether an external order exists
or not is, for practical purposes, an unnecessary question.

There is no doubt that we should take it for granted that Prospero
believes in a supernatural reality. (Ariel and his fellow-spirits are not
supernatural beings, of course.) His epilogue says as much, and his
famous expression of doubt—

> We are such stuff
> As dreams are made on, and our little life
> Is rounded with a sleep—

is the expression of a moment's weariness and trouble. Even so, it is evidence that Prospero's belief is maintained by his will. Should the will to believe waver, a psychological upheaval would follow because —to trace a little the drift of an idea separated from its dramatic context—without his will to believe in a larger, Providential order that his magic imitates, Prospero would have nothing left to govern his actions but a sense of injury, a wish for revenge, and the kind of utilitarianism that inspires his pre-marital advice to Ferdinand. Should he continue in his subjective, self-absorbed habits of thinking, he would inevitably find himself in conflict with life, the exponent of a dark, ineluctable destiny. In fact he would be what we recognise as a Byronic hero. As it is he rules others by using their fear of retribution, and rules himself (in this like the Count of Monte Cristo) by devotion to the achievement of perfect power. That he uses his power for good or seemingly good ends is, I suspect, incidental to our pleasure in the fact that he has it, and uses it.

Prospero sees no visions and on the evidence of the play has no more first-hand knowledge of absolute reality than Antonio has. It comes as a surprise at the end of *The Tempest* that all that power and beauty should have been humanly directed, that Prospero's renunciation is real and that 'outside the play', as we like to say, everything is unknown. In *Cymbeline* the play's spiritual poles are Jupiter and the soul of Posthumus; in *The Tempest* there are no polar opposites whose relationship makes up reality. Instead there is a range of possibilities illustrated by the relation of Prospero to Antonio, of Ariel to Caliban, of the island to Milan.

*Henry VIII* shows, ironically and tragically, the separation of human power from a divine power that ought to correspond to the presence of Queen Katherine's goodness. As in *The Tempest*, abdication of power and the turn to religion accompany preparations for death. Katherine's vision is comparable as an idea, though not, thank heaven, as art, to the recurrent nineteenth-century notion that only in the presence of death do we know ultimate truth. Shakespeare's scene has none of the morbidity of Wagnerian chromaticism, of those Tennysonian waterscapes, the massed choirs of angels, and expiring children, but the content is not too different; death alone puts an effective case against human self-sufficiency and is, besides, the only real mystery left in life. In *Henry VIII*, however, death has a rival in the birth of the little princess which, considered in the light of seventy years' hindsight, was an inexplicable good fortune.

To think about it in relation to the play's whole action drives one back upon such things as Hamlet's 'Use every man after his desert, and who should 'scape whipping?' The play leaves one with a sense of a gift beyond deserving, and this is surely intentional. If the play was written for a patriotic occasion, such a feeling might have seemed to Shakespeare the only sane and honourable basis for the expression of patriotic pride.

In *The Two Noble Kinsmen*, Shakespeare has altered Chaucer's story in a way that makes its gods inscrutable, but at the same time turns them into projections of human passions. In this play, the gods are men's motives deified, and the fact that in the temple scene they 'speak' to their worshippers is not exactly comforting. Autonomous, beyond (or before) reason, these gods are no respecters of persons. Like many of the characters of *Henry VI*, the kinsmen are automata, but with the difference that whereas the earlier characters were automata without adequate motive, the kinsmen are all motive. The rationality and ceremoniousness of Theseus' Athens provide a theatre where the kinsmen's monomania can be contained, be observed, judged and settled. But in Athens itself ceremony is as much propitiation as celebration. The Athenians' maying is a rite *paid to the heart of ceremony*. Even so, a city of a different order is perfectly thinkable.

*The Two Noble Kinsmen* is a comedy based upon the choice between reason and passion, set in a reasonable city; and one can imagine a successor to it, a tragedy, in which Shakespeare treated with the abstraction and objectivity of his late style the idea of a world governed neither by reason nor Providence but by human motives alone. No one knows what Shakespeare was doing when he died at the early age of fifty-two, and any speculations about a final play will always be open to doubt. Nonetheless, in the early sequence of histories we have seen Shakespeare finding and dramatising a kind of melancholy that seems to have originated in the discovery of men's loneliness. In the later sequence, by reading *Henry VIII* and *The Two Noble Kinsmen* as fully Shakespearean works, we have seen the same tendency of thought and feeling reappearing, displacing its comic opposite, the joy dramatised in the tragi-comedies. One we see that Shakespeare's career continued after 1611 and *The Tempest*, the possibility of a successor to *The Two Noble Kinsmen* becomes quite real, and a genuine question arises: is there, extant among Shakespeare's plays, one that was probably written after 1614?

*   *   *

Heminges and Condell were no modern university editors. They did not publish Shakespeare's fragments, such as the additions to *Sir Thomas More*, or his non-dramatic writings. They did not even publish *Pericles* or *The Two Noble Kinsmen*. The bibliographers are agreed that they did not intend to publish *Timon of Athens* either, because it occupies space in the First Folio originally intended for *Troilus and Cressida*, a text which must have proved temporarily unavailable for some reason. Bibliographers and critics alike are now generally agreed that *Timon of Athens* is an unfinished play;[2] and this probably explains its last-minute inclusion in the Folio.

There is no external evidence at all for dating *Timon of Athens*, and the usually suggested date, 1607–8, is based on deductions from three aspects of the play, its source, its similarity to *King Lear*, and its verse. Since the chief source is North's *Plutarch*, and since Shakespeare took the materials of *Antony and Cleopatra* and *Coriolanus* from North round about 1607, then, it is thought, he will have used North for *Timon of Athens* at about the same time. Second, there are some resemblances to King Lear, generally dated about 1605. Third, the 'freedom' of the verse, defined with statistics about feminine endings and pauses, is used as evidence of a comparatively late, but not very late, date.

None of this amounts to proof. Shakespeare had used North for *Julius Caesar*, and signs of its influence show in *The Winter's Tale*. It was one of Shakespeare's favourite books, and the fact that he definitely used it for two plays circa 1607–8 would decrease the likelihood that he used it for yet a third at the same time. The similarities to *King Lear* have been much exaggerated, but even if they were stronger than they are they would not be evidence of date. As for the metrical statistics, their significance is very doubtful. The metrical character of a solitary late tragedy's verse may be rather different from that of a comedy like *The Tempest*. Furthermore, since *Timon of Athens* is unfinished, the statistics are doubly unreliable because all the other statistics apply to finished plays. There are no statistics for Shakespearean drafts. Some things in the play, like the old Athenian's complaint (i. i. 109–51), sound quite early, whereas others, like the dialogue of the poet and the painter in the same scene, sound very late indeed. In the play as we have it there seem to be layers of style, and some passages, like the brief scene of the soldier-messenger (v. iii), are obviously no more than rough first jottings.

The real reasons for dating *Timon of Athens* in 1607–8 have little to do with evidence. The habit of dividing Shakespeare's career, like the history of England, into periods, has naturally led people to presume that since *Timon of Athens* is a tragedy, then it must belong to the 'tragic period'. Moreover the thought has not proved thinkable that the play should be Shakespeare's last word. Its incompleteness therefore, and its near-exclusion from the Folio, which are the only objective information we have about the play, have been used as something to be explained away, not as a means of explanation. Explanations have ranged all the way from the author's boredom to his nervous breakdown, although the more temperate romancing of our own day is content to suggest that the play is unfinished because the material proved 'undramatic', or because the work did not 'go well'.[3] But just as there are no signs in *Timon of Athens* of a mind enfeebled by neurosis or disease, neither is there any sign of anything not going well. The most likely reason for the play's incompleteness is that, like *Edwin Drood* or *Don Juan*, it was left incomplete when its author died unexpectedly.[4] It is certainly a conceivable successor to *The Two Noble Kinsmen*.[5]

\* \* \*

Superficial formal and stylistic similarities between *Timon of Athens* and the mediaeval morality play, the Renaissance dramatic satire, whether comic or tragic, and the Jacobean pageant are misleading if they encourage the reader's low expectations of a play that very few critics have enjoyed; but if they encourage a reader to expect a play that appeals to the mind rather than to the feelings, then they are very helpful. *Timon of Athens* is a metaphysical tragedy. Like *The Tempest* and *The Two Noble Kinsmen*, it is touched by the neo-classical influence. Its tone, following upon the darker portions of its predecessors, is predominantly ironic and satirical, the satire ranging from Horatian urbanity to Juvenalian moral violence. Diction tends to be sharp and plain, less decorative than we expect in a Shakespearean play. Where style grows more convoluted, as in the speeches of the poet, the elaboration is significant of the speaker's character. The choice and placement of the play's images seems equally calculated. The plot is simple, demonstrative, even schematic, and the play as a whole has not pleased readers who like their drama warm and luxuriant. Hazlitt, who admired the play very much, sums up its general effect very well; it is written, he says, 'with as intense a feeling of his subject as any one play of Shakespeare. It is one of the few in which he seems to be in earnest throughout, never to trifle nor go out of his way. He does not relax in his efforts, nor lose sight of the unity of his design.'[6]

That unity of design grows out of the conception of a city, i.e. a society dominated not by anything so concrete as *The Two Noble Kinsmen*'s sex and aggression, but by the motive underlying all other motives, the inarticulate, formless will itself. For dealing with a subject so abstract, money, which is the play's overt theme, provides an ideal medium. The pursuit, possession and spending of money are necessary for the enjoyment of life, so that money, bright, cold, golden and metallic, is a substitute sun. To speak sentimentally, money is therefore an illusory symbol of the means of life just as the golden crown in *III Henry VI* is an illusory symbol of royalty, integrity and contentment. But just as one can sentimentally test gold by the standard of life, one can satirically test life by the standard of gold. This is because the ultimate guarantee of the gold standard is not gold itself, but the desire it satisfies whose vocabulary contains only the one word, 'More!'

Money therefore consumes reality. It converts time and thought to means of purchase, and in doing so subverts all relationships between human beings as well as those between humanity and the external world of its perceptions. When gold has finally done its work, and all of reality is converted to images of desire, then gold itself is no longer necessary because life has turned into currency. To say, however, that desire consumes life is the same as saying that life feeds upon itself, self-absorbed. The true image of the desire mediated by gold is death; the gold is just the phantom in the economic opera. This is why satire on money-worship converts gold to images of corruption, to excrement, garbage and such like, and converts the desire for money into various perversions, such as necrophily and coprophagy.

The idea that love of gold is the root of evil is very ancient, but Shakespeare's use of it in *Timon of Athens* is very modern. In the play's world the presence of gold is like a reductive argument, explaining everything, reducing everything to its own terms. Put to the gold test, all appearances are false. It is as if the dramatist, like a man using a microscope for the first time, were seeing things from a new point of view. The play imitates life solely in terms of motive and character, of stimulus and response; and in a society where there is only one kind of stimulus, there can be only one set of responses. The quality in *Timon of Athens* that so many critics have disliked, its singleness of motive and uniformity of character, is the basis of the play's action.

The action as a whole has the appearance of a behaviourist fable. The plot looks like an experiment, and Timon in his innocence is both experimenter and experimented upon. The hypothesis tested is that men are everywhere the same, that reason and perception are secondary to the strivings of the will. Such an experiment, of course, is a tautology because the method determines the result. An objective analysis of human behaviour requires some prior assumption about the basis of behaviour, so that what looks like objectivity from the standpoint of method is really grounded in subjectivity. *Les extrêmes se touchent,* and the experiment only proves that the experimenters are good mirror-makers.

*          *          *

When a Renaissance author treats a fiction set in either Athens or Rome, one can be sure that he intends the city to be an image of the secular life, moral and intellectual, of his own time. Similarly, his re-creations of classical heroes present images of contemporary humanity in idealised forms. The technique is a way of simplifying the complexities of a writer's raw material, of abstracting and isolating certain themes, ideas, values or tendencies from the mass of experience. So we find Renaissance material 'fixed' or suspended in a classical medium and displayed, like a biologist's specimen, so that all can observe it clearly.

Timon's Athens is the opposite of Theseus' Athens, a city governed by cupidity more than by reason. Though there is frequent mention of 'the gods', Athens' true gods are money and traffic (I. i. 244, v. i. 50), and it seems to be a city without institutions except banks, brothels and private houses. Its senators are usurers who exact the penalties of justice as mercilessly as they exact their interest (III. v). When they banish Alcibiades, the Athenian army turns into a band of mercenaries and camp followers. The city has a poet, a painter, a jeweller and a merchant, all of them mercenary characters, but it has no centre, no organic being, no ceremony. Timon's banquets are the nearest things to ceremony in the play, and Timon is a typical Athenian in believing that wealth and sentiment are more important than ceremony, which he regards as a form of lying:

> Ceremony was but devis'd at first
> To set a gloss on faint deeds, hollow welcomes,
> Recanting goodness, sorry ere 'tis shown;
> But where there is true friendship, there needs none.
>
> (I. ii. 15–18)

Put to the test, however, wealth will not underwrite sentiment. Financial obligations are the city's true bonds, wealth its only integument.

The Athenians, from what we see of them, only consume. They do not produce. They grow rich from usury, gifts or, as in Timon's case, simply by finding money, and the city's economic sterility is paralleled by its curious sexual atmosphere. The only women in the play are whores and courtesans and, as the play's imagery suggests, the men spend their sexual energy in ambition. The success they desire so much 'doth embrace and hug' the fortunate 'with amplest entertainment' (I. i. 44–5). The less fortunate 'labour on the bosom of this sphere to propagate their states' (ll. 66–7). The usurers stand by to help; their servants are 'bawds between gold and want' (II. ii. 61), an image that connects the banks and the brothels and suggests an element of sexual perversity in the relations of banker and client. A client 'woos' (III. iii. 15) his banker, and if his suit is successful his banker 'pleasures' (III. ii. 62) him. In his prodigal phase, therefore, Timon is like a prostitute who hasn't the sense to charge the customers who 'taste' him (III. ii. 84), and who even talk to him in lovers' language:

> 2. *Lord* [*To Timon.*] Joy had the like conception in our eyes,
>      And at that instant like a babe sprang up.   (I. ii. 115–16)

The idea of Timon and his flatterers 'looking babies' (as the seventeenth-century phrase put it) in each other's eyes is utterly grotesque.

In the first three acts such imagery provides a continual vein of ironic satire on the Athenian scene. At its mildest, the satire plays with the confusions of sex and cupidity reflected in such common innuendoes as the equivocal meaning of 'spend', e.g.:

> When men come to borrow of your masters, they approach sadly and go away merry; but they enter my mistress's house merrily, and go away sadly.   (II. ii. 105–7)

Thus the banker and the bawd both exploit the customer, who ends up 'spent' in both senses of the word. Another variety of the same kind of joke appears in the character of Lucullus, one of Timon's false friends, an outrageous old person who has exciting dreams of things like silver basins and ewers. The bulge under Flaminius' cloak sets him off:

> —And what hast thou there under thy cloak, pretty Flaminius?
> —Faith, nothing but an empty box, sir.   (III. i. 14–16)

The significance of the joke is its revelation of the old man's shamelessness which, we discover as the scene proceeds, is not altogether unconscious. In *Twelfth Night* we find the same kind of obscene *double entendre* used to expose Malvolio's sordid imaginings.[7]

At it strongest, the satire declares, and the story bears it out, that in a consumer society the thing consumed is really humanity itself. At first Apemantus is the exponent of this opinion: 'O, [ladies] eat lords; so they come by great bellies.' (I. i. 209). Alcibiades, the professional soldier, 'eats' his enemies; when they are 'bleeding-new', he says, 'there's no meat like 'em.' Timon himself is the grand exemplum of this social cannibalism. 'O you gods,' says Apemantus at the banquet in Act I, 'what a number of men eats

Timon, and he sees 'em not! It grieves me to see so many dip their
meat in one man's blood; and all the madness is, he cheers them up
too.' (ɪ. ii. 39–43)

Like the first three acts of *The Winter's Tale*, the first three acts
of *Timon of Athens* are a strategy aimed at making the audience see
and suspect the worst. To enjoy the play fully therefore, an audience
needs to be rid of any sentimental reluctance to draw conclusions;
and this applies as much to the characterisation as to the imagery.
For instance, Shakespeare evidently took great pains over the portraits of the poet and the painter. Their chatter about art and
criticism (ɪ. i. 20–38) is beautifully finished in Shakespeare's most
developed manner and it is very easy, taking the portraits satirically,
to assume that they are a pair of bad artists. Their speech has the
note of sophistication and affectation that we have already found in
the tragi-comedies, but because they are hangers-on at Timon's and
talk foolishly is no reason for deciding that they are bad artists. That
would allow us to reserve our belief in the existence of good artists
elsewhere in Athens; whereas the presumption is surely that the men
who write and paint for Timon are as good as any. Conditions in
Athens subvert all artists, not just the bad ones. In this city money
comes before everything else because it represents an ineradicable
fact of human nature, and these two artists can no more change or
advise Timon than they could remove a dye with clear water. All
they can do is sell their product by flattering their client.

Similarly the Athenian senators are efficient, practical, civically
minded. Unfortunately, like everyone else in Athens, they are consumed by self-interest.

With one exception, no one goes free of the gold blight. It seems
at first that Apemantus might represent a free man. He enjoys the
philosopher's licence to criticise, and his non-involvement looks like
a protection against Athens' falsehoods. Later, however, the long
dialogue with Timon (ɪᴠ. iii. 197–398) brings out his own version of
vanity and self-interest. His cynicism is inverted Athenianism, a role,
and he takes it for granted that Timon, in the desert, is an amateur
playing the same part. Timon's misanthropy is beyond him because
his cynicism has limits. Like the fool with whom he appears in Act ɪɪ,
he is kept by the people he mocks. He is not a real philosopher.
Thought, unlike poetry and painting, has no market value, and so
there is no philosophy in Athens. Apemantus is an intellectual brute
barking his negatives at a society he loathes but cannot transcend.
Timon's last epithets for him, 'slave', and 'rogue', are accurate; he
represents the degradation of reason in a materialist city.

Alcibiades is another promising candidate for freedom. Although
on his first appearances (ɪ. i. 256–62, ii. 74–85) he talks in the same

strain as the other Athenians, he is the nearest to a real friend that Timon has. When his revulsion at the senate's ingratitude and cruelty brings banishment upon him, his situation is somewhat similar to Timon's, and he makes war upon Athens in Timon's cause as well as his own. But the quality of Alcibiades' life is pretty sharply defined by his appearance (IV. iii. 48) as a leader of mercenaries followed by whores. His bravery and soldierliness, like Apemantus' cynicism, are contained by the hypothesis of egoistic self-interest that governs the plot. Nonetheless some readers have interpreted him as the play's *honnête homme*, the sane corrective to Timon's unbalanced rage. To such pushes does *Timon of Athens* put its critics.

There is one exception to the Athenian rule, and this is Timon's steward Flavius whose loyalty makes Timon cry, 'How fain I would have hated all mankind' (IV. iii. 506). Although some have compared Flavius to Kent in *King Lear*, his fidelity is altogether pure of any possible hint of self-interest or practicality because his relationship to Timon is solely an economic one of employer and employee, not the feudal loyalty of lord and vassal. The steward owes the master nothing, so that his fidelity is quite gratuitous, free of everything meant by 'Athens', and the pathos of his character is that he has nowhere to go. He is a servant without a master, and his situation has in it the makings of a loneliness more complete even than Timon's. Nor does his fidelity, though it mitigates a little Timon's pain, alter in any way the focus of the play's action. Far from it: Flavius is the key witness against the city. As the one honest man, he validates Timon's invective. Although his presence puts a limit to the mystery of iniquity, it also opens up the mystery of goodness. Flavius' part, which seems to be one of the least finished things in the play, looks like one of those threads by which Shakespeare traced his way from the action of one play to the next.

\*　　\*　　\*

Timon himself, inseparable from his city, the exponent and the victim of the Athenian way of life, is the great test of an audience's ability to see the object before it. Whether one likes him or not, finds him intelligent or unintelligent, good or bad, knowledgeable or ignorant, is irrelevant to the point: is he, within the realm of the play's action, an impressive and significant character?

When he first appears, Timon is a thorough Athenian, but an innocent one. He is a rich man who believes that spending wealth is the purpose of life because it relieves, employs and pleases others, and also because in the act of spending a man experiences life most keenly and shows at his most splendid. For Timon, spending is an ecstatic experience, combining relationships with others with the feeling of his own power. At the climax of his last great feast, his

joy is at its zenith. 'Lights, more lights!' he cries, rapt by the desire
to burn ever brighter in the world's eye.

By standards of common worldly prudence, as anyone can see,
Timon is a fool. His own wealth is all gone, his present glories are
financed by loans, and the bills are about to fall due. In *Timon of
Athens*, however, worldly standards are as much in question as
Timon, and for two reasons. First, Timon's spending is a form of
nobility. Whatever dirty jokes others make about it, its purpose as
far as Timon is concerned is to do good and adorn life. He commits
no sin against any moral code. He merely breaks economic custom.
Second, his spending has a metaphysical aspect. Athens is a materialist city where relationships, actions and wishes are finite, and so
expressible in monetary terms. Timon's wish to spend, however, is
unlimited and insatiable and so, by implication, are the desires it
expresses, his wish to love and be loved in return:

> We are born to do benefits; and what better or properer can we
> call our own than the riches of our friends? O, what a precious
> comfort 'tis to have so many, like brothers, commanding one
> another's fortunes!   (I. ii. 105–9)

When Timon settles men's debts and repays their gifts twenty-fold,
he acts contrary to the city's whole system. He is unaware of this
because he thinks that other Athenians, given the chance, would
behave similarly.

Thus Timon's behaviour, without his knowing it, confronts the
finite with the infinite, and the result is a moral explosion. His
naïveté, his unawareness of the motives of ordinary prudence, are
necessary to the action. When the usurers' men present their masters'
bills, Timon's reaction overleaps common explanations or rationalisations, arriving instantly at the truth:

> *Philotus.*   All our bills.
> *Timon.*     Knock me down with 'em; cleave me to the girdle!
> *Lucius.*    Alas, my lord,—
> *Timon.*     Cut my heart in sums.
> *Titus.*     Mine, fifty talents.
> *Timon.*     Tell out my blood.   (III. iv. 90–5)

In his naïveté Timon sees, as more cautious reasoners would not,
that if there is no credit for Timon, no return for his gifts, then there
is no community in Athens. The city, like its citizens' protestations,
is a fiction:

> Piety, and fear,
> Religion to the gods, peace, justice, truth,
> Domestic awe, night-rest, and neighbourhood,
> Instruction, manners, mysteries, and trades,
> Degrees, observances, customs, and laws,
> Decline to your confounding contraries,
> And let confusion live! (IV. i. 15–21)

What Timon's invective invokes as a curse is really the present truth of Athens taken to its logical conclusion.

Timon's discovery is simultaneously pathetic and comic. His enemies are so commonplace, so normal, so perfectly, so shamelessly ordinary in all their lies and evasions, that the meaning of his rage is beyond them. When he sets bowls of warm water before them and commands, 'Uncover, dogs, and lap!' (III. vi. 95), they simply do not know what he means. He tells them that he feels as though their flattery had covered him with filth; when he rinses himself, throws the water over them and chases them from his house, they still don't know his meaning:

> *3. Lord.* Push! did you see my cap?
> *4. Lord.* I have lost my gown.
> *1. Lord.* He's but a mad lord, and nought but humours sways
> him. He gave me a jewel th'other day, and now he has
> beat it out of my hat. Did you see my jewel?
> *3. Lord.* Did you see my cap?
> *2. Lord.* Here 'tis.
> *4. Lord.* Here lies my gown. (III. vi. 119–27)

The great scene of the mock-feast, the pivot upon which the action turns, has much in common with other instances of a favourite motif in post-Renaissance literature, namely the mock-apocalypse in which humanity is judged by standards it is incapable of understanding.

*Timon of Athens*, like *The Winter's Tale*, is plotted in two halves, the first part enacted in Athens, mainly in Timon's villa, the second in the woods near the sea, presumably not very far from Athens. Because the characters behave in the woods as they behave in the city, the effect is a counterpoint without a contrast, implying an equivalence between two symbols of human alternatives, the city and wild nature. Only Timon, turned from philanthrope to misanthrope, presents a contrast.

Even so, Timon's misanthropy is powered by the same quality of infinity that planned the great feasts and, in the mock-feast, confronted the Athenians. His invective follows up, with rising power, his discovery that in Athens there is no law, moral or natural, but the law that men shall consume each other. Gold is the means of their mutual destruction, and it is the 'visible god' (iv. iii. 387), the concrete sign of an unseen force, 'worshipp'd in a baser temple/ Than where swine feed' (v. i. 51–2). Gold is the fuel of human enterprise:

> 'Tis thou that rigg'st the bark and plough'st the foam,
> Settlest admired reverence in a slave.  (v. i. 53–4)

It perverts the attempt to establish human affairs on an ideal basis:

> O thou sweet king-killer, and dear divorce
> 'Twixt natural son and sire! thou bright defiler
> Of Hymen's purest bed! thou valiant Mars!
> Thou ever young, fresh, lov'd, and delicate wooer,
> Whose blush doth thaw the consecrated snow
> That lies on Dian's lap!  (iv. iii. 382–7)

It dominates life, standing for a desire stronger than sex and so private that its public display appears to Timon's imagination as an obscenity. Gold turns phallic in his mind:

>                 thou'lt go, strong thief,
> When gouty keepers of thee cannot stand.
> Nay, stay thou out for earnest.  (iv. iii. 45–7)

Timon's gifts to Alcibiades' whores are a parody of Zeus' appearance to Danae in a golden shower. 'Hold up, you sluts,/Your aprons mountant,' he says, as he puts his gold in their laps:

>             Plague all,
> That your activity may defeat and quell
> The source of all erection.  (iv. iii. 134–5, 162–4)

His gift makes internal reality concrete and visible in the girls' behaviour: 'Believ't, we'll do anything for gold.'

*Timon of Athens* has a masque of ladies whose dance represents the gratification of sensuous desire, and Cupid, the god of desire, presents them to Timon as the patron of the senses. Otherwise the play contains nothing like a theophany. Consumption is a universally ruling principle:

> The sun's a thief, and with his great attraction
> Robs the vast sea; the moon's an arrant thief,
> And her pale fire she snatches from the sun;
> The sea's a thief, whose liquid surge resolves
> The moon into salt tears; the earth's a thief,
> That feeds and breeds by a composture stol'n
> From gen'ral excrement; each thing's a thief.   (IV. iii. 439–45)

'How came the noble Timon to this change?' asks Alcibiades, and Timon answers him:

> As the moon does, by wanting light to give:
> But then renew I could not, like the moon;
> There were no suns to borrow of.   (IV. iii. 66–9)

In other words, Timon has a glimpse of the ultimate failure of credit in a consumer universe.

Through Timon's eyes we see that Athens is a solipsist city. The play's action, right up to the beginning of the end, shows how the notion of representing men's actions objectively, by analysing motive and character, stimulus and response, leads straight to subjective nihilism. The mind, looking in upon itself or out upon the world, up to 'the marbled mansion all above' (IV. iii. 191), sees nothing without or within but shadows cast by the light of its own curiosity. *Timon of Athens* takes us into a place of the kind that J. B. Priestley calls, in one of his essays, 'Skull Cinema'.[8] Reason, demoted to a frontier-guard, lets nothing through not native-born. No message from the outside challenges the regency of the will and its stooges, the belly, sex and violence. Timon's discovery of the truth about Athens and its implications kills him; like Mamillius and Queen Katherine, he dies because he loses the will to live.

In Act V, with Timon dead and Alcibiades about to carry out Timon's curses upon Athens, it looks as though the determinist logic of the action will end the play by reducing city and hero alike to nothingness; but, by a surprising turn at the play's end, Timon, dead, saves Athens from itself as well as from Alcibiades. Although the last few scenes are unfinished, there is enough of them to communicate a moving ending to the tragedy.

Even at its most violent, Timon's invective is salutary. Like a fever, his disgust is a natural reaction to a real condition, and the cogency of his indictment shows that reason is reasserting itself. His revulsion from others and from himself is a sign that something not accounted for by Athenian economics finds Athens intolerable, and the same unnamed quality in Timon shows itself finally in the 'rich conceit' of his tomb by the sea. Timon's first mention (IV. iii. 379) of a grave 'where the light foam of the sea may beat [his] grave-stone daily', may be a superfluity like the warning of the poet's and the painter's approach in the same scene; but it may also be a sign that the significance of his death is on Timon's mind. At the end, the manner of his death is his only message to Athens, his grave-stone the only oracle:

> Come not to me again; but say to Athens,
> Timon hath made his everlasting mansion
> Upon the beached verge of the salt flood,
> Who once a day with his embossed froth
> The turbulent surge shall cover; thither come,
> And let my grave-stone be your oracle.   (v. i. 217–22)

Thus Timon finally has his release from Athens, drawn in death to the sea, symbol of the infinity that is his proper element.

The news of Timon's death reaches Athens as Alcibiades is about to enter the city as a judge, and it ends the play. The First Senator has dissuaded Alcibiades from plundering the city by being as matter-of-fact as Dr Johnson kicking the stone: the city's mere existence is the basis of his case:

> These walls of ours
> Were not erected by their hands from whom
> You have receiv'd your griefs; nor are they such
> That these great towers, trophies, and schools should fall
> For private faults in them.   (v. iv. 22–6)

Men's works transcend individuals and societies by lasting longer, and so the answer to the generalising sweep of Timon's or of Alcibiades' rage is that Athens was not built yesterday. One cannot indict the whole city:

> All have not offended;
> For those that were, it is not square to take
> On those that are, revenge; crimes, like lands,
> Are not inherited.   (ll. 35–8)

These arguments succeeding, Alcibiades is on the point of marching through the gates when the soldier's account of Timon's end changes the tone of these events:

Though thou abhorr'dst in us our human griefs,
Scorn'dst our brain's flow and those our droplets which
From niggard nature fall, yet rich conceit
Taught thee to make vast Neptune weep for aye
On thy low grave, on faults forgiven. Dead
Is noble Timon, of whose memory
Hereafter more. Bring me into your city,
And I will use the olive with my sword,
Make war breed peace, make peace stint war, make each
Prescribe to other as each other's leech.    (v. iv. 75–84)

In the unfinished state of the text it is not clear whose faults are forgiven, or by whom. It is certain, however, that Alcibiades' purpose turns to a positive one of peace-making and rebuilding, and it may be that the forgiveness is to be general.

There is a fine discipline in this ending. There is no hint in it of a *deus ex machina*, nothing to be theologised. As the beginning of the tragedy is in men themselves, so is its resolution. Timon's grave by the sea and the continuing city (the 'Athenian cradle', as the First Senator calls it) together put a frame around life, limiting it, but also setting it in a context of the infinite and the ideal. The ending is aesthetically satisfying, too, in a way reminiscent of the design of *Henry VIII*. In finding grounds for mercy towards Athens, we do not cease to pity Timon; as with Katherine and Wolsey, the exercise of mercy and pity reconciles enmities, and prepares for a new start.

# Epilogue

The argument that *Timon of Athens* was Shakespeare's last play, based on its incompleteness, its last-minute inclusion in the First Folio, its style, and above all its ideas, seems to me stronger than the argument supporting an earlier date. Certainty is not possible; but even if the play really was the last, it is not necessary to attribute conscious finality to an accident of fortune. Shakespeare was only fifty-two when he died, and the idea that he retired from writing has no real evidence to support it. There is no reason to think that anything but death or debility could stop the workings of that extraordinary mind. Had he lived to an advanced age, he might have carried his work to some point of completion beyond present imaginings. *Timon of Athens* is a step towards an English classical drama of ideas, but its hero is a Byronic figure who acts out his society's absurdities in his own life. Much in the play's symbolism and ideas is also Byronic.

Like some of the other plays, *Timon of Athens* has a very prophetic look about it. This may be an illusion owing to the fact that we still live in a society in which the ideas that lead Timon to imagine a cosmic failure of credit are alive and breeding. Nonetheless in his time, and despite great popular success, Shakespeare was very much the poet of the future, a writer whose characteristic themes had barely entered the consciousness of his contemporaries. This is surely because, living in times of extraordinary intellectual, religious and political change, he is *par excellence* the poet of history, reading the signs of the times by a kind of infallible poetic augury. It is significant that Hamlet, the Shakespearean character who has become part of European mythology, is a man who has to uncover the nature and meaning of secret events, and who uses the drama to do so.

T. S. Eliot, making one of several comparisons between Dante and Shakespeare, says in the 'Preface' to *The Sacred Wood* that the older poet had 'a saner attitude towards the mystery of life.' This reflects Eliot's distaste, which he also expresses elsewhere, for the fragmentariness and pessimism of Shakespeare's thinking compared to Dante's; but the comparison is hardly fair to Shakespeare, writing in vastly different circumstances and times. Eliot is nearer the mark when, in the essay on Dante in the same collection, he comments upon Shakespeare's unusually critical and analytical turn of mind. For the whole movement of Shakespeare's work is away from himself and outwards to the world of men, events and ideas. No doubt he had a philosophy, and a religion as well, both of which he reserved to himself; but there is one Shakespearean belief, reflected in the quality of his work, about which there can be no doubt at all: he believed in his capacity to discover and express in dramatic poetry the significance of human affairs.

This belief, which is not a modest one, gives his works their scope, seriousness and, on occasion, their prophetic quality. When we find Shakespeare, especially in his later plays, anticipating qualities that appear in the writing of later poets such as Pope, Swift and Byron, this is probably the effect neither of coincidence nor of the later men's copying, but of an intellectual energy that impelled Shakespeare's imagination beyond the circumference of his own times. Such anticipations reflect upon the range and accuracy of Shakespeare's perceptions and upon the fertility of his technical invention, not upon either his personality or his beliefs, about which we know very little. To adapt his own words, his genius had its sympathy with the prophetic soul of the wide world, dreaming on things to come.

# Notes

## Introduction

1. Aristotle, *Poetics*, 1450a.
2. Peter Ure (ed.), *Richard II* (London, 1956) p. lix.
3. The phrase 'Armada idiom' is from E. A. J. Honigmann (ed.), *King John* (London, 1954) p. xlvi.
4. T. M. Raysor (ed.), *Coleridge's Shakespearean Criticism* (London, 1930) I, pp. 133, 237–42.
5. S. Schoenbaum, *Shakespeare's Lives* (Oxford, 1970) p. 496, observes that Hardin Craig's college edition of Shakespeare (1951) preserves Dowden's notion of the four periods, popularised in his *Shakspere* (1877). The four periods also appear in the chronological listing of the plays in W. A. Neilson and C. J. Hill, *The Complete Plays and Poems of William Shakespeare* (Cambridge, Mass., 1942).
6. On this subject, see E. A. J. Honigmann, *The Stability of Shakespeare's Text* (London, 1965).
7. Notable examples will be found in Peter Alexander, *Shakespeare's Henry VI and Richard III* (Cambridge, 1929); *Shakespeare's Life and Art* (London, 1939); E. A. J. Honigmann (ed.), *King John*; T. W. Baldwin, *On the Compositional Genetics of 'The Comedy of Errors'* (Urbana, Ill., 1965).
8. S. Schoenbaum, *Shakespeare: A Documentary Life* (Oxford, 1975) p. 228.

## Chapter 1

1. Geoffrey Bullough, *Narrative and Dramatic Sources of Shakespeare* (London and New York, 1960) III, pp. 16–17.
2. C. J. Sisson (ed.), *Thomas Lodge and Other Elizabethans* (Cambridge, Mass., 1933) p. 415. Through his connection with Thomas Digges, Shakespeare could have known a distinguished Saville of his own time, the scholar and antiquary Thomas (Leslie Hotson, I, *William Shakespeare* [London, 1937] p. 123).
3. Bullough, op. cit., III, p. 17.
4. For *King John*, see below, pp. 93–4. Queen Elizabeth thought *Richard II* was a personal attack on her. Falstaff was interpreted as an anti-Protestant caricature (Ure, *Richard II*, p. lix; Thomas Fuller, *Worthies* [3 vols, London, 1840] II, p. 455; *Church History* [3 vols, London, 1837] I, p. 489).
5. Arthur Sherbo (ed.), *Johnson on Shakespeare* (New Haven and London, 1968) p. 607.
6. For an example of the comic style of treatment, see *Richard II*, v. iii; for an example of negligence, see *Richard II*, v. vi.
7. Thomas Nashe, *Works*, ed. R. B. McKerrow (Oxford, 1958) I, p. 212: 'How would it have joyed brave Talbot (the terror of the French) to think that after he had lain two hundred years in his tomb, he should triumph again on

236 *Notes*

the stage, and have his bones new embalmed with the tears of ten thousand
spectators at least (at several times), who, in the Tragedian that represents
his person, imagine they behold him fresh bleeding.'

8. J. Dover Wilson (ed.), *III Henry VI* (Cambridge, 1952) p. xliv.
9. The basic account of the form of *Henry VI* is Hereward T. Price, *Construction in Shakespeare* (Ann Arbor, Michigan, 1951). A. S. Cairncross (ed.),
*The First Part of King Henry VI* (London, 1962) pp. xli *et seq.* gives an
excellent analysis of the first part.

## Chapter 2

1. However neat the emblematic staging, it is at odds with characterisation.
None of the exits between lines 146 and 214 of Act I, scene i, has a
convincing reason given for it. The characters leave because the staging
requires them to.
2. See Sherbo, *Johnson on Shakespeare*, p. 591.
3. J. P. Brockbank, 'The Frame of Disorder—"Henry VI"' in J. R. Brown
and Bernard Harris (eds.), *Early Shakespeare* (London, 1961) pp. 87–90.
4. Ibid., p. 91.

## Chapter 3

1. Like much of Shakespeare's imagery, this image is as ancient, natural and
ubiquitous as it is powerful. In the *Odyssey* we are told repeatedly that
Agamemnon was 'butchered like a stalled ox'.
2. Bullough, op. cit., III, p. 210.
3. Lydgate, *Minor Poems*, ed. H. N. McCracken (*Early English Text Society,
Ordinary Series 192* [London, 1934]) pp. 784–5.
4. In Shakespeare's will, body and soul are 'commended'.
5. Yeats, *Letters*, ed. Allan Wade (London, 1954) p. 710.

## Chapter 4

1. Paul Murray Kendall, *Richard the Third* (New York, 1955) p. 506.
2. Sherbo, *Johnson on Shakespeare*, p. 632.
3. J. Dover Wilson (ed.), *Richard III* (Cambridge, 1954) pp. xvi–xvii.
4. Lancelot Andrewes, *A Pattern of Catechisticall Doctrine* (Oxford, 1846)
pp. 79–80: '... when one law is opposite to another, ... one of them must
needs have a restraint. ... And for our direction in this restraint we must
understand that ... "no man is so straightened between two sins but that
a way of escape lies open without a third sin"; and we may obtain this
*exitus*, or deliver ourselves, on this manner;—
    ... 2. if [the conflicting precepts] cannot be agreed, *agat id ad quod est
obligatus*, "let him do that to which he is obliged." For,
    a. God hath ordained things in their order;
        His own glory, which passeth every man's
        salvation;
        our salvation;
        the salvation of others; and
    b. every one of these must be respected in his order;
        first, God's glory;
        secondly, our own salvation; and
        thirdly, the salvation of our brethren.'

## Chapter 5

1. Honigmann, *King John*, p. lxxi.
2. Cf. *King Lear*, IV. vii. 45–8, 71–2, for a similar treatment of tears. Salt is an ingredient of holy water, signifying purity.
3. Honigmann, op. cit., note *ad loc.*
4. Cf. *Psalms*, cix. 18: 'Let it be unto him as the cloke that he hath upon him: and as the girdle that he is alway girded withal.'
5. Op. cit., IV, pp. 7, 23.
6. Op. cit., lxxi–ii.
7. (London, ed. 1894) p. 443.
8. For a thorough treatment and summary of the parallels, see Honigmann, op. cit., pp. xxvii–ix.

## Chapter 6

1. Observations here and later in this essay upon the kingship are based on a comparative study of English coronation liturgies, 1400–1837. See Christopher Wordsworth (ed.), *The Manner of the Coronation of King Charles the First of England* (London, 1892); J. Wickham Legg (ed.), *Three Coronation Orders* (London, 1900); Leopold G. Wickham Legg (ed.), *English Coronation Records* (London, 1901). The liturgiological commentaries in these works are invaluable. A standard work on the mediaeval monarchy, well known to literary students, is E. Kantorowicz, *The King's Two Bodies* (Princeton, N.J., 1957); this contains an essay on *Richard II*. See also Philip Edwards, *Person and Office in Shakespeare's Plays* (Oxford, 1970).
2. On this subject, see Hermann Broch, 'Notes on the Problem of Kitsch,' rptd in Gilo Dorfles, *Kitsch: An Anthology of Bad Taste* (London, 1969) pp. 49–76.
3. For the latter, see G. H. Ford, *Dickens and his Readers* (Princeton, N. J., 1955) p. 69, and R. F. Fleissner, *Dickens and Shakespeare* (New York, 1965) pp. 258ff.
4. John Calvin, *Institutes of the Christian Religion*, trs. Henry Beveridge (4 vols, Edinburgh, 1845), I, p. 314.
5. The obvious anti-Richard, usurpationist bias of the exposition explains Elizabeth's dislike of the play. See Introduction, pp. 3–4.
6. Ure, *Richard II*, p. 67.
7. Bolingbroke, therefore, speaks of the castle as an emaciated body holding the king prisoner.
8. *Appreciations* (London, ed. 1910) p. 198.
9. *Selected Essays* (London, 1951) p. 137. Eliot speaks of 'the deep surge of Shakespeare's general cynicism and disillusionment'.

## Chapter 7

1. See below, pp. 220–1.
2. See below, p. 241, note 5.
3. *Shakespeare and 'The Two Noble Kinsmen'* (New Brunswick, N.J., 1965).
4. Philip Edwards, 'An Approach to the Problem of *Pericles*,' *Shakespeare Survey*, 5 (1952) pp. 25–46; *Pericles* (The New Penguin Shakespeare, 1976) pp. 31–41, 193–9.
5. As Professor Edwards suggests (*Pericles*, p. 41), the decasyllabic choruses may be the work of a collaborator, the octosyllabics Shakespeare's.
6. John Skelton, *Poems*, ed. R. S. Kinsman (Oxford, 1969) p. 50.

7. See Alwyn and Brinley Rees, *Celtic Heritage: Ancient Tradition in Ireland and Wales* (London, 1961), 'Introduction' (from which the present examples are taken).
8. Edwin Muir, *Essays on Literature and Society* (London, 1965) p. 11.
9. For example, 'Now could I drink hot blood,/And do such bitter business as the day/Would quake to look on' (*Hamlet*, III. ii. 408–10); 'The mailéd Mars shall on his altar sit/Up to the ears in blood' (I *Henry IV*, IV. i. 116).
10. Sir Philip Sidney, *Prose Works*, ed. A. Feuillerat (Cambridge, 1923) III, p. 20.
11. Goethe's remark, 'An old man is always a King Lear' (quoted by Kenneth Muir, *King Lear* [London, 1952] p. lii), is a Romantic overstatement. Lear is abnormal as to both his emotional and physical energy. His appetite for flattery and attention is more nearly normal, but it is not necessarily the consequence of old age.
12. J. C. Maxwell (ed.), *Pericles* (Cambridge, 1956) p. xxix.
13. *Poets on Fortune's Hill* (London, 1952) p. 101. 'It seems', says Danby, 'as if Shakespeare has broken his own wicket.'
14. F. D. Hoeniger (ed.), *Pericles* (London, 1963), note to v. i. 225.
15. Michael Hamburger (ed.), *Beethoven: Letters, Journals, and Conversations* (New York, 1960) p. 99.

*Chapter 8*

1. At the end of the play Imogen, still in disguise, berates Pisanio ('Dangerous fellow, hence! Breathe not where princes are.' [v. v. 237]), whereupon Cymbeline immediately recognises her ('The tune of Imogen!'), a charming comic touch.
2. The working of the eye divorced from the other senses is one of the subterranean themes of *Cymbeline*. Imogen imagines Posthumus' departure from Britain as a movement into the third dimension of a picture, passing into and beyond its vanishing point into unbounded space. As long as she can see him, if only in her mind's eye, he is in some sense there; the perspective sight-lines controlling the third dimension hold Posthumus in her society:

> I would have broke mine eye-strings, crack'd them, but
> To look upon him, till the diminution
> Of space had pointed him sharp as my needle;
> Nay, follow'd him till he had melted from
> The smallness of a gnat to air, and then
> Have turn'd mine eye and wept. (I. iii. 17–22)

There is an attempt to control space as Macbeth hoped to control time by holding events in a net: no matter how they swim away from him in the stream of time, the net's 'vanishing point' is a hypothetical point of security: 'If the assassination/Could trammel up the consequence, and catch/With his surcease success; that but this blow/Might be the be-all and end-all here,/But here . . .' (*Macbeth*, I. vii. 2–6).

In the bedroom scene, Iachimo sees Imogen, but since to her knowledge he is not there and since he does not touch her, they might as well be in different 'worlds', an oddity of the scene reflected in the disordering of time. Then Posthumus, imagining Imogen with Iachimo, loses her. This theme takes us back to the first histories where the imagined fall into a third dimension was the beginning of change and movement.

*Chapter 9*

1. For a similar point somewhat differently made, see M. M. Mahood, *Shakespeare's Wordplay* (London, 1957) pp. 146–7.
2. G. K. Chesterton, *George Bernard Shaw* (London, 1909, rptd 1925) p. 179.
3. Narrated paradox strikes some readers as silly, e.g., D. G. James, *Scepticism and Poetry* (London, 1937) p. 233: '... the coming to life of the "dead" obsessed [Shakespeare's] imagination to the point of making his work silly to a degree it never had before been.' The sentence indicates a dislike of drama and narrative as well as of paradox.
4. G. K. Chesterton, *The Everlasting Man* (London, 1925) pp. 191–3.
5. *Shakespeare's Imagery* (New York, 1935) p. 305.
6. 'Perdita' is not an allegorical name because she is herself the lost one. She does not represent something else that has been lost along with her, such as faith, national integrity, childish innocence etc.
7. The double sestina 'You goatherd gods' is a particularly brilliant example.
8. S. L. Bethell, *The Winter's Tale: A Study* (London, 1947) pp. 47ff.
9. J. H. P. Pafford (ed.), *The Winter's Tale* (London, 1963) p. 133, note to IV. iv. 855.
10. C. S. Lewis, *Of Other Worlds* (New York, 1966) p. 18.

*Chapter 10*

1. S. T. Coleridge, *Shakespearean Criticism*, ed. T. M. Raysor (London, 2 vols, 1930) I, pp. 131, 133.
2. George Wilson Knight, *Christ and Nietzsche* (London, 1948) p. 22.
3. On the connection between Romanticism and Fascism, see Peter Viereck, *Metapolitics: From the Romantics to Hitler* (New York, 1941) pp. 16ff.
4. 'Romanticism, then, and this is the best definition I can give of it, is spilt religion' (T. E. Hulme, *Speculations* [New York, 1924] p. 118).
5. On this aspect of the play, see Frank Kermode (ed.), *The Tempest* (London, 1954) pp. lxxiv–vi.
6. Some such dance is suggested by Gonzalo's words describing their condition (III. iii. 104–9), and by Prospero's calling their motions 'fits' (ll. 88–91).
7. A frequent technique in Shakespeare, later much used by composers of opera, and called by them *melodrama*. The proper performance of such passages requires considerable musical training.

*Chapter 11*

1. The subtitle is from Sir Henry Wotton's letter of 2 July, 1613 describing the performance of *Henry VIII* which burnt down the Globe Theatre. Quoted in Neilson and Hill, op. cit. p. 903.
2. G. E. Bentley, 'Shakespeare and the Blackfriars Theatre', *Shakespeare Survey, 1* (1948) p. 42: 'We can be perfectly sure, then, that from the day of the first proposal that the King's men take over the Blackfriars they had talked among themselves about what they would do with it and had discussed what kinds of plays they would have to have written to exploit it.'
3. Frank Kermode, 'What is Shakespeare's *Henry VIII* about?', *Durham University Journal*, N.S. 9 (1948), rptd in W. A. Armstrong (ed.), *Shakespeare's Histories* (Penguin Shakespeare Library, 1972).
4. Hardin Craig, *An Interpretation of Shakespeare* (New York, 1948) p. 357.
5. R. A. Foakes (ed.), *Henry VIII* (London, 1957) pp. lix–x. In his *Shakespeare: The Dark Comedies to the Last Plays* (Charlottesville, Va., 1971) pp. 173–83, Mr Foakes has toned down the exaggerations of his *New Arden*

introduction: 'Rule is necessary, but kings, as Henry is an example, have to operate within the limited perspectives of all men' (ibid., p. 180); but he still maintains that the 'emergence of Henry as ruler is part of the "religious truth" of the play, overriding the contradictions, injustices and suffering that recur' (p. 182). Henry's emergence, however, is part of the political, not the religious, truth of the play.

6. Foakes, *Henry VIII*, p. lx.
7. See above, pp. 17–18.
8. Shakespeare's casting of the audience as the crowd in the christening scene (v. iv) is a sign of his confidence that the theatre would be filled to capacity.
9. Holinshed, *Chronicles* (ed. 1587) iii, p. 907.

*Chapter 12*

1. The warring deities of *The Knight's Tale* appear in *A Midsummer's Night's Dream* as Oberon and Titania.
2. Theodore Spencer, 'The Two Noble Kinsmen', *Modern Philology*, xxxvi (1939) pp. 255–75. This essay illustrates a peculiarity of much writing on Shakespeare's last plays, which is to talk about Shakespeare as if he were an old man when he wrote them. Spencer talks of the 'style of old age' and 'an old man's imagery'. But whatever the differences between the expectation of life now and in the seventeenth century, no one in any century is an old man at fifty, let alone forty-four, Shakespeare's approximate age when he wrote *Pericles*.
3. Thebes was traditionally the infernal city, the antithesis of Athens and Rome. See Dante, *Inferno*, trs. John D. Sinclair (London, revised ed., 1948), Cantos 30, 33, and note 4 to Canto 33.
4. That is, they groan under the mastery of passions that Theseus has learned to conquer.
5. Philip Edwards, 'On the Design of "The Two Noble Kinsmen"', *A Review of English Literature*, v, no. 4 (Oct., 1964) pp. 89–105.
6. See above, pp. 24, 159–60.
7. Op. cit., p. 271.
8. Ibid., p. 274.
9. W. H. Auden, 'Introduction' in *Shakespeare's Sonnets* (New York and London, 1964) p. xxxvii.
10. Op. cit., p. 105.

*Conclusion*

1. *Shakespeare and 'The Two Noble Kinsmen'* (New Brunswick, N.J., 1965).
2. The subject is well reviewed by H. J. Oliver (ed.), *Timon of Athens* (London, 1963). M. C. Bradbrook, *The Tragic Pageant of 'Timon of Athens'* (Cambridge, 1966) argues that *Timon* is a pageant written for the opening of the Blackfriars Theatre. There are elements of pageantry in *Timon*, as in other plays by Shakespeare, but Miss Bradbrook's lecture substitutes the part for the whole.
3. H. J. Oliver, op. cit., p. xxviii.
4. Several readers have seen a connection between *Timon of Athens* and the tragi-comedies, among them Northrop Frye in his *A Natural Perspective: The Development of Shakespearean Comedy and Romance* (New York, 1965), and Clifford Leech, *Shakespeare's Tragedies* (London, 1950). Theodore Spencer compares Timon's Athens to Palamon's and Arcite's Thebes (op. cit.). All these writers assume that *Timon of Athens* precedes the other

late plays. The suggestion that it came last was first made, I believe, by Paul Bertram, op. cit., p. 254. Clifford Leech (ed. *The Two Noble Kinsmen* [New York and London, 1966] p. 181) comments upon a similarity in stage directions between *Timon* and *Two Noble Kinsmen*, both printed from holograph MSS. This may be evidence of proximity of composition.

5. Not to mention the lost, hypothetical *Cardenio*. A play of this name was acted at Court in the winter of 1612–13 and later on 8 June, 1613. A *History of Cardenio* was entered for publication by Humphrey Moseley, 9 September, 1653, and by him attributed to Shakespeare and Fletcher. Then in 1728 Lewis Theobald published a successful play, *The Double Falsehood*, which he claimed was his revision of an original by Shakespeare which he possessed in manuscript. It has been assumed by many that these three phenomena are the same thing, a play by Shakespeare, possibly/ probably in collaboration with Fletcher, based on Cervantes' story of Cardenio and Luscinda in *Don Quixote*, and finally mutilated by Theobald, the original MS being lost or destroyed.

Whatever the truth of the matter, the original is utterly lost. Cervantes' plot, however, might have attracted Shakespeare, since it is about a man who, betrayed by one whom he took to be a faithful friend, goes mad and takes off to a mountainous wilderness where he lives upon the kindness of goatherds. There is also a heroine disguised as a boy. But without the fortuitous intervention of Don Quixote, who also decides to go mad in the same mountains for love of his Dulcinea del Toboso, the story (to a critical, not creative eye) loses much of its quality. For information and theory about *Cardenio*, see W. W. Greg, *The Shakespeare First Folio* (Oxford, 1955) pp. 98–9; Kenneth Muir, *Shakespeare as Collaborator* (London, 1960) pp. 148–60; Paul Bertram, op. cit., pp. 180–96.

6. William Hazlitt, *Characters of Shakespeare's Plays* in *Works*, ed. A. R. Waller and Arnold Glover (13 vols., London, 1901–6), I, p. 210.

7. 'These be her very C's, her U's, and her T's; and thus she makes her great P's' (II. v. 95–7).

8. *Essays of Five Decades* (Boston, 1968) p. 301.

# Index